MAN IN MOTION: The Psychology of Travel

MAN IN MOTION:
The Psychology of Travel

James Reason

Weidenfeld and Nicolson   London

ISBN 0 297 76688 0

Printed in Great Britain by
Cox & Wyman Ltd,
London, Fakenham and Reading

For Rea, Paula and Helen

Some men a forward motion love
But I by backward steps would move,
And when this dust falls to the urn,
In that state I came, return.
HENRY VAUGHAN

Contents

Acknowledgements

I would like to thank my friends and colleagues who have made valuable comments on draft chapters. In particular, I am grateful to Roy Davies, Alan Benson, Elgin Diaz, Andrew Mayes, John Rolfe and Mary Smyth. Special thanks are also due to Dugal McArthur who prepared most of the illustrations; and to George Ottley of the University of Leicester Library whose encyclopaedic knowledge of the transport literature proved an invaluable help; also to Julia Hornak and Eileen Wood of Weidenfeld and Nicolson whose careful editing has spared the reader much confusion and some, at least, of the jargon. I must acknowledge a special debt to my wife, Rea, whose intolerance of vehicle motion put me on the track in the first place, and whose tolerance otherwise has helped me stay the course.

Acknowledgements are also due to the following for illustrations: Dr F. E. Guedry Jr for Figures 4 and 5; the Director, US Naval Aerospace Medical Research Laboratory for Figures 9 and 10; Dr J. M. Rolfe for Figure 19; the Director, Transport and Road Research Laboratory for Figures 20, 21, 22, 23 and 24.

Introduction: Travel and the Evolution Barriers

It is sometimes said by reluctant air travellers that if man had been intended to fly, he would have been provided with wings of his own. But this is only part of the truth. If man had been intended to move about by any means than under his own power, he would have been built to an altogether different set of specifications. As it is, *all* forms of vehicle motion, be it that of a car, aeroplane, train, ship or spacecraft, are alien to both his physical and psychological nature. During the first few months of life we are physically incapable of effective self-propulsion, but beyond this time any form of passive motion is an unnatural experience, and it is with the psychological consequences of this experience that this book is primarily concerned.

Most of the physical 'evolution barriers' to our locomotion – the fact that we cannot naturally fly, travel through space, live under-water, or move at great speeds over land – have largely been removed by the remarkable achievements of man-made tech-nology. And the most dramatic of these developments have occurred within the span of a single lifetime. But the psychological constraints remain. They are the legacy of countless generations of evolutionary adjustment to a particular kind of environment, and continue to hold sway even though our present life-style, in which passive has largely superseded active locomotion, may render them obsolete and even dangerous. No matter how far or fast we are capable of travelling, our position and motion senses as well as our capacity for processing information remain those of a self-propelled animal designed to travel at around three to four miles per hour through a mainly two-dimensional world under conditions of normal terrestrial gravity. In short, man was intended to walk, run and climb the occasional tree; but no more.

When he exceeds these locomotory evolution barriers, as he now does in many different kinds of vehicle, various penalties are likely to be exacted – penalties that range from the commonplace and banal, like travel sickness, to the rare and exotic, like the eery feelings of 'other-worldliness' experienced by jet pilots flying at very high altitudes. In the western world there are very few who have not encountered at least one of the many different kinds of problem engendered by the unnatural circumstances of passive motion at some time in their lives; and when these disturbances do occur their true origins quite often go unappreciated. The principal aim of this book is to describe the nature and causes of these problems as they are met with in the wide variety of transport systems now available to us, and, where possible, to suggest practical means whereby we may combat them.

The main source of all these problems lies in the enormous difference between the time scales of technological progress on the one hand, and biological adjustment on the other. The slow progress of evolutionary adaptation, stretching as it does over millions of years, has provided us with a nervous system which is eminently well suited to cope with our natural terrestrial environment; the kind of environment, in fact, that our pre-neolithic ancestors knew. But one of the most important characteristics of this nervous system is the intellectual capacity to modify the circumstances under which we live; and this we have done, almost beyond the recognition of our prehistoric forefathers, and within an extremely short space of evolutionary time. From a purely biological point of view, however, modern man is indistinguishable from neolithic man living over seven thousand years ago. Human history occupies a negligible period of time when measured along the evolutionary scale, and it is far too short for any significant changes to have occurred within man himself – despite the fact that the changes we ourselves have wrought in our environment clearly demand them. During the brief span of human history, and especially within the last half-century, we have so altered our natural circumstances that many of our slowly acquired evolutionary adaptations are ill-fitted for the activities we now engage in, to say nothing of the alien environments into which these activities now transport us. And perhaps nowhere has this biological 'capability gap' between the way we are built and the things we strive to do been made more apparent than by the incredibly rapid development of transport systems. Table 1 gives some idea of the rate at which this progress has been achieved.

TABLE 1   HISTORICAL DEVELOPMENTS IN THE SPEED OF
TRANSPORT SYSTEMS

Year	Mode of Transport	Speed (miles per hour)	
6000 BC	Camel caravan	Maximum	8
1600 BC	Chariot	Maximum	20
1784	First English mail coach	Average	10
1825	First steam locomotive	Maximum	13
1890	Later steam locomotive	Maximum	100
1931	Land speed record (*Bluebird:* Sir Malcolm Campbell)	Maximum	246
1938	Land speed record (Napier-Railton car: John Cobb)	Maximum	350
1938	Piston aircraft	Maximum	400
1952	Liner *United States* New York–Le Havre	Average	41
1958	Jet fighter aircraft	Maximum	1,300
1961	Vostok 1 (Gagarin)	Orbiting at	17,560
1967	Rocket plane (Maj. W. Knight)	Maximum	4,534
1970	Fighter-bomber (Mirage IV)	Maximum	1,450
1970	Commercial aircraft (Concorde)	Maximum	1,320

Alvin Toffler, author of the recent bestseller, *Future Shock*, argues that this great leap in vehicle speeds over the past few years is indicative of a general phenomenon that he calls 'accelerative thrust'. This is the ever-increasing tempo of change in our life-styles that stems in large measure from the enormous technological advances occurring in modern industrial societies in recent years. 'Millenia or centuries go by,' he writes, 'and then, in our own times, a sudden bursting of the limits, a fantastic spurt forward.'[1] And this, as the figures in Table 1 show, describes exactly what has happened to the speed of transport systems. Just before the turn of the century, man reached a speed of 100 mph. It took him millions of years to get there. Previously, nothing had moved faster than a galloping horse. In 1888, for example, Mr J. Selby driving the horse-drawn coach, 'Old Times', from London to Brighton achieved a record average speed of 13·79 mph, and a maximum speed of 21¼ mph for nearly one hour. But less than a century further on we have reached the point where a man can circle the earth at speeds of nearly 18,000 mph, and where commercial aircraft can fly at twice the speed of sound.*

John Maynard Smith has provided us with a graphic illustration of how man's history and technical achievements fit into the evolutionary time-scale:

About 400 million years ago the first aquatic vertebrates evolved: half a million years ago man's ancestors first chipped stones to make simple tools. Less than ten thousand years ago, in the neolithic revolution, animals and plants were first domesticated. If a film, greatly speeded up, were to be made of vertebrate evolution, to run for a total of two hours, tool-making man would appear only in the last ten seconds. If another two-hour film were made of the history of tool-making man, the domestication of animals and plants would be shown only during the last two minutes, and the period between the invention of the steam engine and the discovery of atomic energy would be only three seconds.[2]

Since this was written in 1958 man has ventured into space and cavorted on the face of the moon: developments which, in their implications, are almost as dramatic and far-reaching as those that occurred when fish first crawled on to the land and began raising families there. Yet, in our two-hour film of tool-making man, this latest development would have flashed by in the blinking of an eye. A small wonder, therefore, that we should encounter psychological problems when we attempt such a radical modification of the way of life for which we were so slowly and painfully evolved.

* With regard to the recent rate of technological progress, Donald Schon makes a further point: 'As it has gone its exponential way, technological change has become increasingly *pervasive*. Changes whose impacts might have been contained in particular industries, in particular regions or in particular aspects of life, now penetrate all industries, all regions and all of life.' To illustrate this, he cites the length of time required for technological innovations to spread throughout populations: he calls this 'diffusion time'. For example:

Invention	Diffusion time (in years)
Steam engine	150–200
Car	40–50
Vacuum tube	23–30
Transistor	about 15

Donald A. Schon, *Beyond the Stable State* (London, Temple Smith, 1971).)

As stated earlier, the aim of this book is to present an account of these psychological problems as they relate to travel in different modes of transport. However, since the term 'psychological' tends to mean different things to different people, it is necessary to spend a little time at the outset explaining how the word will be used here. The best way to do this is briefly to summarize exactly what it is that psychologists do.

Contrary to popular opinion, very few psychologists spend their working days seated beside a patient recumbent on a couch, delving into the inner needs and motives of a disturbed mind. Although these professional props are frequently ascribed to the psychologist, they more properly belong to the psychoanalyst, usually a medically qualified person who has chosen to apply the clinical methods developed by Sigmund Freud and his followers. In general, psychologists tend to leave the treatment of the mentally ill to those best qualified to tackle it, namely, doctors who specialize in that branch of medicine called psychiatry. The psychologist is primarily a scientist, not a clinician. This means that he is concerned with making general statements about mental life and with understanding and predicting the behaviour of normal people, and this, of course, includes the behaviour of the car driver, the aircraft pilot and their respective passengers.

Psychology as a science has always been oriented towards the solution of practical problems, particularly when they arise in the control and safety of vehicles. Psychologists have been employed in or on the fringes of the transport industry since the early years of this century, a fact that becomes less surprising when it is realized that the infant science of psychology and the internal combustion engine grew up together.

Since the way people behave in vehicles tends to mirror the complexity and diversity of their behaviour out of them (as one accident investigator put it: 'people drive as they live'), psychologists are called upon to tackle a wide variety of transport problems. For example, what causes travel sickness, and how can it be prevented? What factors are responsible for the dangerous illusions of position and motion experienced by pilots and astronauts? How do stresses like fatigue, monotony, confinement, vibration, noise and an excessive inflow of information affect the performance of the driver or pilot? How can we best display the bewildering array of vital information on an aircraft's instrument panel? Why does the motorist tend to underestimate his speed on a motorway? What are the psychological consequences of crossing several time zones in a few hours? Does the personality of the driver or pilot reveal itself in the characteristic way he handles his vehicle? How can we design vehicles so as to capitalize on man's natural talents and minimize the effects of his built-in limitations? These are a few of the problems dealt with by psychologists, and many of them will be discussed at some length in the chapters that follow.

The organization of any book is inevitably idiosyncratic, and so it is with this one. It makes no claim to being a definitive account of what might be termed 'the psychology of men in transport systems'. Instead it concentrates upon those problems that arise when two vital psychological processes are disturbed by the unnatural circumstances of passive motion. The first of these is the *acquisition of sensory information*, particularly by those senses which keep the brain informed about the position of the body, and how it is moving relative to its surroundings and its component parts. The second process is concerned with the way the brain *handles* the information once it has been transmitted by the senses. Thus, the book divides into two main parts. The *information-acquisition* problems of motion sickness, pilot disorientation, and erroneous judgements of vehicle speed on a motorway are dealt with in Chapters 1–4. The *information-processing* problems – having limited brain capacity, being presented with too much or too little information, being fatigued and stressed – are considered in Chapters 5–7. Chapter 8 discusses consistent individual differences in vehicle-handling style and how these relate to accident liability. The concluding chapter, as its title suggests, reviews some of the ways by which we may reconcile man and vehicle. Man is increasingly becoming the weak element in the man–vehicle partnership. To preserve not only the quality of life but life itself, we need to concentrate our efforts upon removing the rapidly growing inequalities in this relationship.

1 Motion Sickness

Motion sickness – or travel sickness – needs little introduction. Most of us are too familiar with it already, particularly in childhood. Although the condition hardly ever proves fatal, it should not be underestimated as a source of human misery. In this respect, it probably ranks close to the common cold. It may never actually kill us, but there are times when we wish it would.

Paradoxically, it is not really a sickness in the pathological sense at all, but only in so far as it makes us 'feel sick'. It is, in fact, a perfectly natural (though usually inappropriate) response to an unnatural situation, namely, one in which we are moved – or appear to be moved – passively by some means other than our own two feet. Far from being a true illness, the appearance of motion sickness is an indication of normality, for the only people who are really immune to this disorder are those who have suffered some damage to their organs of balance, or *vestibular system*, situated in the non-auditory part of the inner ear. Thus, in the face of a really disturbing stimulus it is the absence of sickness rather than its presence which suggests that something is wrong. We shall be considering the structure and function of the organs of balance and the essential part they play in the production of symptoms at a later point in this chapter.

It is also true, of course, that not everyone with a healthy vestibular system is equally susceptible. We know from bitter experience that in circumstances where some of us are rushing for the side of the ship or groping for paper bags, others remain infuriatingly nonchalant and unaffected – at least until the motion becomes rougher! In other words, people differ markedly in their proneness to the various forms of motion sickness: sea sickness, car sickness, air sickness, and so on. As a general rule, those easily disturbed by, say, the motion of a ship are also those who readily produce symptoms in other forms of transport. There are exceptions to this rule: for instance, an astronaut's general susceptibility to earthbound forms of motion sickness has not been found to be a particularly good predictor of his proneness to space sickness – the latest and perhaps most dangerous form of travel sickness (to be discussed in the next chapter). Nevertheless, apart from this rather exotic exception and the fact that some people are peculiarly susceptible to certain forms of motion, we can say with some confidence that motion sickness susceptibility is a relatively stable and enduring characteristic of the individual. However, as stated earlier, everyone can be made to meet their 'Waterloo' given the right quality and quantity of sick-making stimulus – providing, that is, they possess intact organs of balance.

I shall be examining the various factors which influence individual susceptibility at a later point. Meanwhile, let us briefly consider the main signs and symptoms of motion sickness, and outline the various ways in which it can develop in different provocative situations.

Signs and symptoms

It is convenient to divide the various motion sickness reactions into two broad categories: those we can label *head symptoms*, and those we can call *gut symptoms*.

Head symptoms range from a vague loss of well-being – which may include drowsiness, a disinclination to eat, and a general feeling of apathy – to more intense reactions such as a violent headache, a feeling of constriction in the throat, or the sensation of a tight band around the head. Gut symptoms, on the other hand, are more stereotyped and range from a faint but disconcerting awareness of the stomach region to acute nausea* and vomiting – which, if prolonged, can lead to the terrible 'dry heaves'.

It used to be thought that the apparent predominance of either the head or the gut symptoms reflected constitutional differences between people. It was believed that some people were predisposed to produce head symptoms, while others typically produced gut symptoms. But in the light of recent research,[1] it

---

* The term 'nausea' derives from the Greek word '*naus*', meaning a ship.

seems more likely that head and gut reactions represent two distinct stages in the development of a single symptom complex. In general, the kind of symptoms that a particular individual is likely to present depends upon the interaction of three factors: the strength of the sick-making stimulus; the susceptibility of the person; and the length of time for which he has been exposed to the stimulus (i.e. the vehicle motion).

As a crude approximation, we can say that when the motion stimulus is fairly weak and the exposure of long duration – as, for instance, on a ship riding a mild sea-swell – the really susceptible people will first develop head symptoms which are then superseded by gut symptoms. Under the same conditions, however, fairly resistant individuals may only show mild head symptoms, or remain unaffected. On the other hand, when people are suddenly exposed to a severe motion stimulus – as, for instance, when a ship leaves the calm water of the harbour and heads into rough seas – the relatively susceptible tend to produce gut symptoms almost immediately. Head symptoms may also be present, but they are likely to be overshadowed by the turmoil in the stomach. In more resistant travellers the gut symptoms take longer to develop, and may be preceded by a phase in which head symptoms predominate. In extremely resistant people, of course, these mild head symptoms may be the only sign of disturbance.

While the specific form of the head symptoms varies widely between people, that of the gut symptoms is more consistent and predictable. Consequently, we have a fairly clear idea of the sequence of events leading up to vomiting.

The very first reactions to a motion stimulus need have nothing to do with the subsequent sickness. They are likely to include feelings of anxiety or excitement – depending on temperament – and also sensations of dizziness or the blurring of vision which follow automatically when the organs of balance are disturbed. These initial reactions are likely to occur irrespective of whether sickness follows. They are reflex reactions to the motion in much the same way that a sneeze is a reflex response to a tickle in the nose.

The first signs of sickness proper are likely to be a faint pallor and the beginnings of a cold sweat. Along with this comes 'stomach awareness' – something which is not yet queasiness, just an unfamiliar sensation of being able to 'feel' the stomach. At this stage, there is usually only a mild loss of well-being, and if the stimulus were removed at this point, recovery would occur in a matter of seconds. It is useful to be able to recognize these early warning signs since they can prompt remedial actions – like keeping the head still – which serve to reduce if not actually avoid the coming disaster.

Compared with their subsequent rate, the development of gut symptoms up to this point is fairly slow, often taking several hours. But beyond this we encounter the 'avalanche phenomenon' in which the reactions already present rapidly get worse and take on a momentum entirely their own. Once the 'avalanche' has begun, vomiting or acute nausea are almost inevitable. Moderate queasiness quickly replaces stomach awareness, and this in its turn is rapidly superseded by acute nausea. If nausea is allowed to persist, then vomiting usually follows, although there are some people who find it very difficult to vomit and they usually suffer more than those who vomit easily.

Together with these subjective changes come an increase in salivation (or, in some people an increasing dryness of the mouth), and an increase in the intensity of the pallor and sweating already established. This is also the point at which the sufferer starts to feel really miserable; so miserable, in fact, that the feelings of depression and wretchedness can take on pathological proportions. It sounds like a bad joke, but some people would honestly welcome death at this point – or so the real sufferers claim. In any event, most people become listless, morose, and resigned to their fate.

If the disturbing motion is stopped during the early phase of the 'avalanche', recovery for some individuals can still occur in a matter of minutes. For others, the development of symptoms is not arrested by removing their initial cause: like Frankenstein's monster, once established, they take on an independent existence.

To most people, the act of vomiting brings some relief – albeit temporary, since a fresh cycle of nausea and vomiting often follows in its wake. If the vomiting and retching continue unchecked, as they can do on a lengthy voyage through rough seas, serious complications may arise as the result of the fluid loss from the body. This problem is particularly acute in downed flyers or shipwrecked sailors awaiting rescue in small, unstable liferafts.

So much, then, for the character of travel sickness. Now let us turn to a more important issue, the cause of these reactions – or, more exactly, to theories about their cause. These fall into two groups: the early theories which did not take account of the crucial role played by the organs of balance; and modern theories which all accept this essential part, but differ in the kind of role they attribute to the balance senses.

Early theories of motion sickness

Until the outbreak of the Second World War motion sickness sufferers were not served, with a few exceptions, by the best scientific and medical brains of their time. Although there have been countless unknown and unaided victims since primitive man first ventured out in a dugout canoe, it takes something like a world war, or more recently, the space programme, before motion sickness is taken seriously and sufficient financial backing is given to research directed at prevention. With the advent of modern warfare came the need to transport large numbers of unacclimatized troops by land, sea and air; the inevitable consequence was a very considerable travel sickness problem. The military were not slow to appreciate the significance of this – a sea-sick marine or an air-sick paratrooper does not make the most effective fighting man. Consequently, military-sponsored money was poured into laboratories in all the combatant countries to help find out why people got sick and how it could be prevented. But before they could get very far the investigators had to sift through a mass of folklore, old wives' tales and the writings of innumerable ship's physicians in order to sort out solid fact from the all-too-prevalent fantasy. Some of these ideas are set out below.

Until about 1880 probably the most accurate statement about motion sickness was that written by Hippocrates several centuries earlier. He wrote that 'sailing on the sea shows that motion disorders the body'.[2] Or, to put it even more simply, that motion sickness is caused by motion. It is our misfortune that so many later theorists chose to ignore this apparent truism.

During the nineteenth century, and particularly in the heyday of the British Empire, when thousands travelled by sea to the 'far-flung outposts', there were almost as many theories of sea sickness as there were so-called remedies. And there were about as many of those as there were drugs in the Pharmacopoeia. This glut of theories and 'cures' was due in no small part to Victorian physicians who, in the course of travelling for their health or acting as ship's surgeons, were brought face to face with the problem of sea sickness, perhaps for the first time in their professional careers. On their return to dry land a great many of them felt the need to communicate their observations and ideas to some journal like the *Lancet*. As might be imagined, these communications were not all of the highest quality; in fact, many of the recommended treatments were – as we shall see later – considerably more dangerous and unpleasant than the condition they were trying to cure.

While it fails to do justice to their richness and variety, it is convenient to lump the early theories of motion sickness into two groups. These we can label the 'all-in-the-mind' group, and the 'blood-and-guts' group.

Ignoring Hippocrates' sound observation, the first group looked for the causes of motion sickness in all parts of the mind except those concerned with perceiving motion. At one time or another they blamed the smell and sight of food, or other people being sick, fear, anxiety, suggestion, and a neurotic or nervous disposition. Underlying it all was a strong hint of patrician disapproval, and the implicit suggestion that susceptibility to travel sickness could be equated with 'lack of moral fibre'.

There is some justification for these 'psychological' explanations. When people find themselves becoming queasy without really understanding the cause they are just as likely to attribute it to, say, the smell of cooking, the sight or taste of a fried egg, and their state of mind, as they are to blame the motion of the vehicle. For instance, when wartime aircrew were asked what they thought was the main cause of air sickness, some 90 per cent said it was due to fear.[3] Nowadays, we do not deny that psychological factors can influence both the speed with which you get sick and the way you feel once you are sick, but it is clear that, by themselves, psychological factors of the kind mentioned above are not the primary cause of travel sickness. I shall advance more arguments to support this statement later on in the chapter.

The 'blood-and-guts' theorists had a more sensible idea, albeit a wrong one. They began, logically enough, with the obvious cause of the disturbance – passive motion – and asked themselves what, inside the body, was sufficiently mobile to be upset by being pitched and tossed around? Equally logically, at least in their state of knowledge, they came up with the answer that it must be either the various bodily organs suspended within the abdominal cavity, or else the blood, particularly within the blood vessels of the brain. Thus, sickness was thought to be due, in the first case, to a mechanical irritation of either the liver or stomach lining as the result of being churned around inside the body; and, in the second case, to the movement of the blood within the vessels of the brain. The latter was thought to produce nausea and vomiting either through an excess of blood in the brain or because of too little. Both notions had an approximately equal number of supporters.

There were basically two things wrong with these ideas. First, animals can still be made motion sick even when the nerves between the brainstem and the gut are cut.[4] This clearly rules out mechanical irritation of the gut as the primary source of the disorder. Second, and most important, these theorists did not appreciate the function of the organs of balance in detecting and signalling the movements imposed upon the head and body by the vehicle. Today there is no arguing with the fact that the organs of balance play an essential part in the production of symptoms. If they are damaged by illness or, as in the case of experimental animals, the nerves connecting them to the brain are cut surgically, susceptibility to motion sickness is completely eliminated. Any acceptable theory of motion sickness must take account of this fact. For this reason, it is necessary to spend some time examining the structure and function of the organs of balance before we go on to consider the latest theories of motion sickness. Unavoidably, this following section on the vestibular system is a little technical; but the reader is asked to persevere with it because an understanding of how these balance senses work will make the subsequent parts of this chapter as well as some of the following chapters much easier to follow.

The organs of balance (the vestibular system)

As sense organs go, the vestibular system is comparatively simple – although we still have a lot to learn about how it works. This simplicity stems from the fact that the organs of balance are the most ancient and primitive of all our senses. Their basic design has remained virtually unchanged throughout the millions of years of evolution that intervened between the fish and man. And this accounts for many of the problems we shall be discussing in this book. A sense organ designed for a self-propelled animal becomes outdated when that animal contrives to have itself moved passively. Under normal, active conditions, the system functions extremely well; so well, in fact, that it would be hard to better its design if we were forced to start from scratch. But this reliability and accuracy is no longer guaranteed when we adopt a totally alien – from a biological point of view – mode of locomotion. A system that worked for the fish can hardly be expected to function adequately for the jet pilot or the astronaut.

How does the system operate? Let us begin with its structure. The organs of balance are situated in the non-auditory part of each inner ear. A simplified diagram of these sense organs within one ear is shown in Figure 1. They are made up of two distinct receptor systems: the *semicircular canals* and the *otoliths*.

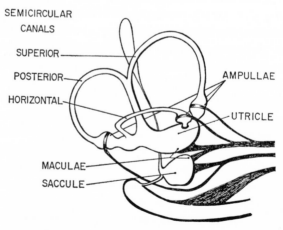

Figure 1   Principal features of the vestibular system.

The semicircular canals are three fluid-filled tubes lying at right angles to one another (they are labelled 'superior', 'posterior' and 'horizontal' in Figure 1). They open into a sac-like structure called the *utricle*, which is also filled with the same fluid, termed *endolymph*. These canals are concerned with detecting turning movements of the head. More specifically, they are capable of sensing the rate of turn in any direction as the head is rotated. However, they only react to *changes* in head-turning velocity. They remain unaffected by a constant rate of turn of the kind we might experience on a roundabout turning at a steady speed.

The otoliths are flat blobs of jelly covered with dense crystals or stones (the term 'otolith' comes from the Greek word for 'stone'). One of these blobs lies roughly in the horizontal plane and is attached to the walls of the utricle by springy hairs. The other blob lies in the vertical plane and is attached (also by springy hairs) to the wall of the *saccule*, another sac-like structure lying beneath the utricle (see Figure 1: the otoliths are not visible because they lie inside these sacs). The most important function of the otoliths is as head-tilt indicators. On earth we are constantly exposed to the force of gravity which, since it always acts in a vertical direction, constitutes our primary indication of the 'upright'. When the head is held at an angle, signals from the otoliths tell the brain how far the head is deflected from the upright. Another job of the otoliths is to detect changes in velocity when the head moves in a straight line, as for instance during take-off in a jet aircraft, or during a sharp braking manoeuvre in a car. Whereas the canals respond to angular accelerations, the otoliths are designed to register *linear* accelerations. They too remain unaffected by a constant velocity, this time when the body (and head) moves in a straight line.

Under natural conditions of self-propelled motion, the canals and otoliths work together in close harmony to register the movements of the head and to maintain an upright position. They also initiate reflex eye-movements – termed 'nystagmus' – which help to stabilize the visual field when the head is moved relative to stationary objects in the environment. Without these compensatory eye-movements, stationary objects in the visual field would tend to lose their clarity as we moved in relation to them. It is known that individuals who have lost this stabilizing reflex as the result of damage to the vestibular system find that shop signs and other stationary objects in the outside world tend to jog around in concert with their movements as they walk along.

When we are moving under our own power as Nature intended, the organs of balance operate in a rather secretive fashion. They yield little or no conscious sensations equivalent to those of sight, hearing, touch, taste and smell. So long as they are performing the task for which they were designed, we hardly notice their existence at all. The vestibular system only intrudes upon consciousness when it is overstressed by the unusual forces associated with passive motion, or when it is attacked by disease or physical damage. In either case, however, the acute distress which can result is a good indication of the important part the system plays in maintaining our stability under normal circumstances.

Now let us look in a little more detail at the structure and function of these receptor systems, beginning with the semicircular canals. Even though they share part of their length with other canals inside the utricle, each functions mechanically as a complete unbroken ring of fluid. In Figure 1 it can be seen that on each canal, close to its point of origin with the utricle, there is a swelling of the wall. This swelling is called the *ampulla* (the Latin word for 'swelling') and it contains that part of the sense organ which is responsible for detecting head turns and for signalling this information to the brain. A transverse section through this swelling, in diagrammatic form, is shown in Figure 2.

From Figure 2 it can be seen that the ampulla is sealed off by a flap called the *cupula*. This is a flap of jelly held rigid by springy hairs that project up from a ridge at the floor of the ampulla. It is in fact hinged about this ridge like a door, and the job of the cupula is to detect the movement of the fluid within the canal. When the fluid shifts, the cupula is deflected, and the amount by which it is pushed away from its neutral or resting position is communicated to the brain by sensory cells lying at the base of the springy, supporting hairs. The pattern of nerve-firing which is triggered off by these cells also tells the brain in which direction the cupula has been deflected – and this, of course, depends upon the direction in which the head has been turned.

When the head is turned, the canals (being embedded in the bone of the skull) move at the same angular rate as the rest of the

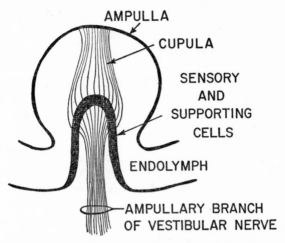

Figure 2 Simplified diagram showing the cupula–endolymph system. A transverse section has been made through the ampulla (see Figure 1) to reveal the cupula sealing off the canal, and also the sensory and supporting cells (in black) lying beneath it.

head. But the fluid inside those canals lying in the plane of the motion tends to lag behind the head movement because of its natural inertia (the tendency of an object to stay in the same place). The effect of this lag is to push the cupula away from its resting position in a direction opposite to that of the head movement, and by an amount proportional to the rate of turn at any one moment. The sense receptors at the base of the cupula signal both the amount and the direction of this deflection back to the brain, and, on the basis of these messages received from complementary canals on either side of the head, the brain is able to determine the speed and direction of the head movement.[5]

From an evolutionary standpoint, the otoliths are far older than the semicircular canals. Animals needed to orientate themselves to the gravitational vertical long before they required anything as sophisticated as head-turn indicators like the canals. Nevertheless, in man, the function of the otoliths is less clearly understood than that of the canals. For instance, it was only very recently that the saccular otoliths were accepted as playing any part in maintaining bodily orientation, and even now it is not entirely certain just how their function is integrated with the utricular otoliths.

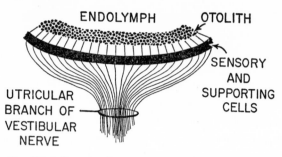

Figure 3   Simplified diagram of a vertical section through the wall of the utricle, showing the dense mass of the otolith. The black dots represent the calcium carbonate crystals embedded in a jelly-like substance.

Figure 3 shows a cross-section through the utricle wall (a similar arrangement is found in the saccule except that the otolith lies in the vertical plane). The wall of the sac constitutes the base and receptor portion of the sense organ. It provides a bed for the sensory cells and the branches of the nerves which carry the information to the brain. The otolith is held out from the wall by hairs projecting from the sensory and supporting cells. Like the cupula, the otolith is immersed in the fluid, endolymph; but unlike the cupula which has the same specific gravity as the surrounding fluid, the specific gravity of the otolith is greater than that of the endolymph. This discrepancy in specific gravity makes the otolithic receptors highly sensitive to linear accelerations. A tilt of the head with respect to the vertical, or a linear acceleration applied to the head (as when we travel in a vehicle that speeds up or slows down), causes the otolith to shift its position relative to the wall of the sac.

This movement of the otolith on its springy hairs is communicated to the brain by the sensory cells. Consider, for example, what happens when we sit in a jet aircraft that is accelerating down the runway just before take-off. Because of its inertia the otolith will always shift *against* the motion of the head. As the plane accelerates, the otolith will lag behind the motion of the supporting wall which is fixed relative to the skull. Thus, the same force that pushes the passenger back into his seat also stimulates his otolithic receptors. The movement of the otolith is communicated to the brain by the sensory cells which signal the direction and amount of deflection in the supporting hairs. However, in this particular example of an accelerating jet aircraft, the orientation information so communicated is not always accurate, as we shall see when we come to Chapter 3. But under natural circumstances the otoliths function very adequately. As a test of this, you can try out the following simple observation on yourself. Stand in front of a mirror and pick out some salient feature in the iris or a blood vessel in the white of the eye. Now tilt your head slowly towards one shoulder. As you do so, you will notice that the whole eyeball is counter-rolling in the opposite direction to compensate for the head-tilt. The rolling of the eye is driven reflexly by signals from the otoliths, and, up to a certain angle of tilt, is just enough to compensate for the movement of the head – and so preserve the stability of the visual world. Incidentally, this is one way of establishing the normal function of the otoliths.

Now let us return to the causes of motion sickness and see how modern theorists have applied their knowledge of vestibular function to explaining the occurrence of nausea and vomiting during passive motion in a vehicle.

Modern theories of motion sickness

At the present time, there are two main contenders in the theoretical stakes: the vestibular overstimulation theory, and the sensory conflict theory. We shall examine each of these in turn.

The vestibular overstimulation theorists claim that motion sickness is caused by an excessive stimulation of the organs of balance, and, in particular, of the otoliths (the linear accelerometers).[6] They argue that the movements of a vehicle, especially its vertical oscillations (i.e. linear accelerations acting in an up–down direction), cause an unnaturally large influx of neural messages from the otolith organs to the brain, some of which may 'spill over' into those areas of the brainstem responsible for triggering-off the characteristic motion sickness reactions.

The first problem with this theory lies in its assumption that linear accelerations (detected by the otoliths) rather than angular accelerations (detected by the canals) are the prime cause of sickness. This assumption, as we shall see, rests on a number of rather dubious pieces of evidence.

First, there were the physical measurements of ship motion in a seaway which suggested that the angular accelerations involved in its rolling action were too slight to be detected by the semicircular canals; whereas the linear accelerations created by its up and down motions (pitching and scending) were more than adequate to be picked up by the otoliths.[7] Apart from the fact that recent measurements of the sensitivity of the canals have shown them to be far more sensitive than previously thought (sensitive enough to detect the rolling motion of a ship),[8] and that the accuracy of these shipboard measurements has, in any case, been seriously questioned, there is also the problem that these measurements of ship movements do not take account of the independent angular motions of the head that are superimposed upon those of the body when it is pitched and tossed around. The neck is not a rigid structure, and there is a great deal of evidence to show that when these independent head wobbles are restrained by some mechanical device (like a head clamp), a person's susceptibility to motion sickness is dramatically reduced. This suggests that these *angular* movements of the head – which deliver a stimulus to the canal system – play a very important part in the production of symptoms. So this is one factor which weakens the case for the overstimulation of the otoliths.

Another piece of evidence which the overstimulation advocates claim supports their view is that lying down on one's back confers considerable protection against sickness,[9] particularly on board ship where such a position is feasible. I have no quarrel with this fact, only with the limited interpretation the overstimulation theorists have put upon it. They argue that adopting the supine position reduces susceptibility because it places the otolith organs in a 'dead spot'; that is, a position in which they are at their least sensitive. This may indeed be true. But there is an equally acceptable explanation which ties in with the head movements mentioned above. Lying on one's back is also a very effective way of preventing the independent head wobbles that we know play an important part in the production of sickness.

There are additional pieces of evidence, supposedly supporting the overstimulation view, which can be accounted for equally well by other kinds of explanation. We do not need to go into these in any further detail; instead, let us examine the various facts about motion sickness which the overstimulation theory cannot possibly explain.

Perhaps the most potent single stimulus for motion sickness is the situation where a person is seated on a platform rotating at constant velocity (like, say, a merry-go-round at the fair) and then tilts his head about an axis which is different from the axis of platform rotation. The sickness which is readily produced by this manoeuvre has nothing to do with overstimulation of the otoliths. It arises because this type of head motion produces a bizarre stimulus to the semicircular canals. The response to this strange stimulus is called the *Coriolis vestibular reaction*,[10] and although the detailed mechanics involved are rather complex, we can explain its essential features fairly simply.

Consider a person seated upright on a rotating chair. So long as the platform is rotating at constant speed, and he keeps his head perfectly still, there is no stimulus to the semicircular canals because, as we said earlier, they only respond to angular accelerations. But what happens when he now tilts his head towards one shoulder? Very simply, this movement produces a response from the canals which is normally associated with pitching forward or backward (depending on the direction of rotation). This occurs because the vertical canals, which normally signal nodding or pitching motions of the head, are brought into the plane of the chair rotation, and are hence stimulated. Thus, the canals incorrectly signal a pitching motion about an axis running through the person's ears. But the otoliths have not been affected by the rotation and so signal the correct fact that the head is tilted to one shoulder. The net result is that the poor brain is informed by two normally reliable and harmonious receptors that the head is moving in two directions at once! This situation is summarized in Figure 4.

The brain is unable to resolve these two conflicting sources of information from the canals and the otoliths, and registers its protest by triggering off the symptoms of motion sickness. The intervening nervous mechanisms are not fully understood; but the connection between this type of stimulus and motion sickness is well-established. In fact, it would probably be true to say that nausea follows this kind of stimulation as surely as pain follows the continuing pressure of a blunt needle: it may not appear so

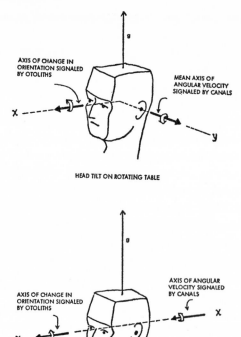

Figure 4   Effects of a lateral head-tilt on a rotating table, as compared with the same head-tilt made in a stationary environment. (By courtesy of Dr F. E. Guedry Jr.)

rapidly as the pain, but it is just as inevitable. It is this kind of bizarre stimulus that constitutes a major hazard in future space-craft which rotate to produce artificial gravity – but more of that in Chapter 2. In the meantime, we can return to the criticisms of the overstimulation theory and state, quite definitely, that this theory is inadequate to explain the sickness produced by the Coriolis reaction.

Another well-established fact that the overstimulation theory cannot explain is that motion sickness can be evoked by certain kinds of *seen* motion *in the absence of any bodily movements*.[11] In other words, as many people have discovered, we can be made to feel queasy simply by watching something like a Cinerama film shot from, say, the front of a rollercoaster car while we are sitting still in our cinema seats. That is, in the complete absence of any motion stimulus to the vestibular system, otoliths or canals.

The important thing about this type of seen motion, however, is that it must be of the sort which, under real-life conditions, would be accompanied by some vestibular input. In other words, it must be the kind of visual stimulus which leads the brain to expect – on the basis of past experience – that it will be coupled with signals from the vestibular senses. Consequently, not every type of motion picture will produce sickness: only those that would normally be associated with accelerations acting on the head and body, supposing that one was actually 'on the spot', can achieve this. This also implies that the film must be one in which the camera is viewing the external scene as the observer's eyes would see it if he were being transported under the same conditions in reality. Thus, only a film taken from *inside* the rollercoaster car would have this effect. A film shot from the ground, say, of the car moving relative to the observer would have no effect – as indeed would standing on the ground and watching the motion of the car in reality have no effect.

This type of visually-induced sickness often occurs in fixed-base or static vehicle simulators which create the sensation of motion by a moving visual scene which is observed through the windscreen by the driver or pilot. When this visual display is a fairly faithful representation of what the world looks like from the seat of a moving car or aircraft, there is a very high incidence of nausea and loss of well-being among the 'drivers' and 'passengers' of the simulator. Interestingly enough, it is the *experienced* drivers and pilots who are more readily disturbed by simulators.[12] This is presumably because the experienced vehicle operators have had more opportunity of matching up the various sensory inputs, particularly the visual and vestibular signals, that are characteristic of real vehicle motion. Consequently, when they come into a simulator and observe a familiar visual stimulus in the *absence* of the normally correlated vestibular signals, it conflicts more drastically with the expectations built up in their brains as the result of previous experience in the actual vehicle, and so they are more easily upset than those people who have not had so much opportunity to establish these expectations. We will talk more about these 'unfulfilled expectations' when we come to consider the sensory conflict theory of motion sickness. The point at issue here, however, is that motion sickness can occur in the complete absence of any vestibular stimulation at all. So, clearly, this phenomenon cannot be explained by the vestibular overstimulation theory.

Finally, the overstimulation theory has no way of accounting for the phenomenon of *land sickness*, or *mal de débarquement*, that occurs when people return to dry land after a lengthy sea voyage; or, in fact, immediately after any prolonged exposure to a potentially sick-making stimulus (like a session in a rotating room, for instance). Here, we have sickness in the complete absence of real motion, and hence, of vestibular stimulation. Once again, we cannot hope to explain this fact by saying that it is due to overstimulation of the vestibular system when no such stimulation is present.

The clue to understanding the origin of land sickness lies in the fact that it only occurs after a person has adapted to the motion which preceded it. Adaptation means that a person has become so accustomed to the sick-making stimulus that it no longer disturbs him; and this process of adjustment is common to all circumstances that provoke sickness. The reason why people become ill on disembarking is that they have become so used to the motion of, say, the ship that its absence, once they have left it, conflicts with the expectations built up in their brains during the voyage. The reverse of this process occurs when they first embark upon the ship. In this case, the expectations are those of a land-based animal. But when they get off at the other end – providing they have adapted in the meantime – their expectations are now those of a pitching and rolling, sea-based animal. As a result, living on *terra firma* has to be relearned in much the same way that the unusual conditions aboard ship have to be learned before the traveller is granted a respite from sea sickness. And it is during this period of maladaptation that motion sickness occurs. I shall return to this point later on.

Only a theory which places the origins of motion sickness in the conflict existing between information coming in through the various senses and that expected on the basis of prior experience can satisfactorily explain the potency of the Coriolis vestibular reaction, visually-induced sickness, and land sickness; and, at the same time, make sense of the process of adaptation. Although there can be no doubt that the vestibular system plays an essential part in producing sickness, we need to extend our thinking beyond this fact in two ways. First, we must consider that the function of the vestibular system overlaps with that of our eyes and the other position senses in maintaining our orientation so that, under natural conditions, the information conveyed by one of these spatial senses is corroborated by all the others. Second, we must take into account the type of information communicated by these spatial senses in the immediate past, as well as that which is available in the present. In other words, we need to know a person's 'exposure history' to understand his susceptibility to motion sickness at any one point in time. This will become clearer as we consider the arguments of the 'sensory conflict' theory, set out below.

From the point of view of making sense of the many different kinds of motion sickness, the sensory conflict theory is clearly the most acceptable. Its basis is the assumption that all situations which provoke motion sickness are characterized by a condition of *sensory rearrangement*. That is, a situation in which the signals from our various spatial senses, the organs of balance, the eyes, and the nonvestibular position senses (in the joints, muscles, and tendons), are incompatible with one another and, in consequence, are at variance with what we have come to expect on the basis of past experience – or exposure history.

Its second basic premise is that regardless of what other senses are party to these 'rearrangements', the vestibular system *must* be implicated – either directly or indirectly – for motion sickness to be the outcome. This also tells us something about the nature of the effective motion stimulus: namely, that it will involve a changing rather than a constant velocity component, since the vestibular system only responds to angular or linear *accelerations*.

One of the more difficult problems with understanding motion sickness is the need to identify common causative factors in the vast array of different motion circumstances that can provoke this disorder. Some idea of the variety of these situations can be gained from the different ways we label the same condition: sea sickness, car sickness, train sickness, swing sickness, simulator sickness, even camel sickness (but not, curiously enough, horse sickness), and most recently, space sickness.

The sensory conflict theory states that all of these situations involve either one or both of the following types of sensory rearrangement: (a) *visual-inertial rearrangement* (where the term 'inertial' includes both the vestibular and nonvestibular position senses); and (b) *canal-otolith rearrangement*. The former involves a conflict *between* the various spatial senses, while the latter involves a conflict *within* one spatial sense, the vestibular system.

As stated earlier, both pairs of receptors (visual-inertial and canal-otolith) work together in close harmony in 'natural', self-propelled locomotion. But when the body is moved passively – or is confused into 'thinking' that it is being moved passively as in the Cinerama and simulator examples – this harmony can be disrupted to produce three basic types of sensory conflict. If A and B represent portions of normally correlated receptor systems (i.e. visual-inertial or canal-otolith system), then these three conflict situations can be summarized as follows:

Type 1 when A and B simultaneously signal contradictory or uncorrelated information.

Type 2 when A signals in the absence of an expected B signal.

Type 3 when B signals in the absence of an expected A signal.

Each of these three types of conflict can be identified for both visual-inertial and canal-otolith rearrangements. Thus, we can specify six basic conflict situations that are known to provoke motion sickness. Real-life and laboratory examples of each of these conflicts are given below. For convenience, these examples are also summarized in Table 2.

An example of the *type 1, visual-inertial conflict* is that of a man standing at the side of a ship looking down at the waves. In this situation his organs of balance and other inertial receptors are registering the motion of the ship which, inevitably, is going to be quite different from the motion of the waves seen by his eyes. Thus, the brain is receiving two unrelated sets of motion information when it is only accustomed to receiving the same message from both sensory systems. In fact, the only way the two sets of messages can be made to correspond aboard ship is by fixating a point on the horizon, or some visible landfall, which provides a

TABLE 2   SOME EVERYDAY AND LABORATORY EXAMPLES OF THE SIX KINDS OF SENSORY REARRANGEMENT THAT CAN PROVOKE MOTION SICKNESS

	Visual (A) – Inertial (B)	*Canal (A) – Otolith (B)*
Type 1 (A and B)	1 Watching waves over the side of a ship. 2 Looking out of the side or rear windows of a moving vehicle. 3 Making head motions while wearing some optical device that distorts vision.	1 Head movements made about some axis other than that of bodily rotation – Coriolis vestibular reaction (see text). 2 Low frequency oscillations – less than one cycle per second (i.e. less than 1 Hz). Otoliths signal head motion out of phase with canal signals.
Type 2 (A not B)	1 Watching Cinerama (see text). 2 Operating a fixed-base vehicle simulator equipped with a moving visual display. 3 'Haunted-Swing' type of fairground device.	1 Weightless space flight. 2 Caloric stimulation of the outer ear (see text). 3 Lying down after drinking alcohol – positional alcoholic nystagmus.
Type 3 (B not A)	1 Reading a map in a moving vehicle. 2 Riding in a vehicle without a view of the outside world. 3 Being swung in an enclosed cabin.	1 'Barbecue-spit' rotation (see Figure 5). 2 Any rotation about an off-vertical axis.

fixed datum against which the motion of the body through space can be accurately and synchronously registered.

The visual and inertial inputs do not have to be wholly uncorrelated to produce sickness. It is sometimes enough that they should be related in an unfamiliar way, as when we ride with our back to the engine and look at the landscape streaming by outside the window. In this situation the seen motion of the landscape and the bodily motion perceived by the inertial receptors are not uncorrelated in the sense that one message has no relationship to the other; the two messages are simply matched in an unusual way as compared to normal self-propelled locomotion. A similar 'rearrangement' occurs when we look out of the side window of any moving vehicle, irrespective of whether we are facing front or back. When we move under our own power, the visual scene does not 'stream' from one side of the visual field to the other; it expands outwards from a central point dead ahead of us. I shall be discussing these visual motion cues further in Chapter 4.

A type 1, visual-inertial conflict can also be created in the laboratory under more controlled conditions. The most effective technique is to wear an optical device that turns the world upside-down and side-to-side by inverting and reversing the retinal image.[13] When people first wear these distorting lenses, they can become sick when they walk around, or simply when they stand still and move their heads. Here, the familiar visual cues are present but completely reversed, while the inertial receptors are unaffected. Once people have become accustomed – adapted – to this strange combination of the spatial senses, simply removing the optical device can reinstate the sickness because what was once the familiar (before wearing the device) has now become the unexpected.

The *type 2, visual-inertial conflict* occurs when we see motion in the absence of the expected back-up or corroboration from the organs of balance and the other position senses. The most common instances occur in the Cinerama and simulator situations mentioned earlier. But we can also create this type of conflict in the laboratory by seating a person in a stationary chair – which, although still, looks as though it could rotate – and then spinning the walls of the room around him.[14] People find this most disturbing at times when the seen motion of the walls is changing direction: that is at the points where – if the person were actually moving – he would be receiving vestibular stimulation.

This kind of situation is also popular in the fairground – with the showmen rather than the customers. For example, there was a device called the 'Haunted Swing' that caused much discomfort to those visiting the San Francisco Midwinter Fair of 1894. Customers were led into a large fully-furnished room capable of holding forty people. They sat on a huge swing which was hung from the centre of the room. The circumstances caused them to expect that the swing would move while the room stayed still. In fact, of course, it worked the other way round. The swing proper remained stationary – merely being joggled around a little to heighten the illustration – while the room itself was put into motion, the furniture being screwed to the floor. The sick-making powers of this device are testified to by a visitor who wrote: 'I have met a number of gentlemen who said they could scarcely walk out of the building from dizziness and nausea.'[15]

The *type 3, visual-inertial conflict* is the opposite of that described above. In this case, we have an inertial input without the expected visual confirmation that the body is being moved. A notorious example is that of the car passenger who tries to read a map while being driven along a winding, bumpy road. His vestibular senses, as well as the 'seat of his pants', tell him that he is being shaken by the movement of the car. But his eyes, which are fixed on a map that is stationary with respect to his body, fail to corroborate the inertial messages. Many sufferers from car sickness will confirm that to read a book or a map while travelling is to invite sickness.

The same type of conflict is present in all types of transport where the passenger does not have a clear view of the way ahead. Thus, it contributes to the sea sickness experienced by the ship's passenger in his cabin, as well as to the air sickness suffered by the air passenger who lacks an adequate view of the outside world. That external reference is important in preventing sickness is revealed by the fact that the highest incidence of air sickness in aircrew is among navigators, radar-operators and the like, who are generally shut off from a view of the horizon and whose condition is further aggravated by the need to read a map or watch a radar screen.

Canal-otolith conflicts occur when the two vestibular receptors signal incompatible information about the position of the head in space. Logically, it is difficult to separate these conflicts from visual-inertial conflicts since, unless the eyes are closed or covered, there is going to be some incongruous visual information present as well. For simplicity's sake, we will describe the various canal-otolith conflicts as if they were uncomplicated by vision. In practice, though, they are usually part of a much wider visual-inertial conflict.

The clearest example of a *type 1, canal-otolith conflict* is the Coriolis vestibular reaction discussed earlier. It will be recalled that during a head-tilt made out of the plane of bodily rotation, the canals signal illusory head rotation about one axis while the otoliths signal head-tilt about a second axis at right angles to the first (see Figure 4). As a result, the brain receives information from the vestibular system which would be compatible with having the skull split in two, and the halves travel in different directions. Small wonder that the consequences turn out to be so unpleasant!

While the type 1 conflict is likely to be a problem in rotating spacecraft of the future, the *type 2, canal-otolith conflict* is a cause of much discomfort in the present generation of weightless spacecraft. In space, of course, there is no gravitational force. Consequently, there is no input to the otoliths. But even in zero gravity, the semicircular canals still respond to turning motions of the head. Thus, when an astronaut moves his head in weightless flight, his canals signal the movement much as they would on earth, but in the absence of the usual corroborating signal from the otoliths. This, as I shall show in the next chapter, is highly provocative of sickness and disorientation.

On earth we can produce a similar kind of conflict by irrigating the outer ear with water which is either hotter or colder than blood temperature. This *caloric* stimulus creates illusory sensations of apparent rotation by setting up convection currents within the endolymph – the fluid which fills the semicircular canals. These, in turn, cause a deflection of the cupula which causes an erroneous message to be sent to the brain. Since this procedure is usually carried out while the subject is lying on his back, there is no accompanying otolith message, and nausea is readily provoked.

A more familiar example of this conflict, however, is the wretched situation that some of us find ourselves in after we have had too much to drink, and then go to bed. As soon as you lie down, the world begins to spin. Faster and faster it goes, defying all your efforts to halt it, and with the dizziness comes a steadily increasing nausea and an overwhelming urge to be sick. If you are lucky, blessed sleep intervenes; but more often this only comes after you have retched and strained yourself into a state of near collapse.

As we know from the staggering gait of the drunk, alcohol affects the body's balance mechanism, and one of these effects is to induce a condition called *positional alcoholic nystagmus*, or PAN for short. I mentioned earlier that one of the functions of the vestibular system was to stabilize the visual world by causing the eyes to move in such a way that an image of a stationary object remains fixed for as long as possible on the retina as the head turns. These reflex eye-movements are called nystagmus, and they can be seen most clearly when a strong stimulus, like spinning round and round on the spot, has been delivered to the semicircular canals. If you look at someone's eyes after they have been spun rapidly, you will notice that they beat regularly from side to side. While this is happening, the person will also tell you that he sees the world spinning round, and often he finds it very difficult to stand upright. In a way that is not yet fully understood, these nystagmus eye-movements induce an illusion of apparent motion (termed the *oculogyral illusion*) in which stationary objects appear to spin around you – without, curiously enough, actually going anywhere; that is, they possess velocity but not displacement.

This is what you experience when you lie down with a lot of alcohol in your bloodstream. But in this case, the eye-movements are not caused by a direct stimulus to the vestibular system; they are due to a combination of alcohol and head position – hence the term *positional* alcoholic nystagmus. PAN only occurs when the head is held in certain positions – like, for example, in the supine position, particularly with the head turned to one side. It is probably not much of a consolation to learn that the nausea and vomiting which so frequently follow these post-spree whirls are a kind of motion sickness; but that is exactly what they are. The PAN situation closely fits the prescription for a type 2 canal-otolith conflict. The alcohol and head position combination produces a spinning sensation which is normally associated with a canal stimulus (even though, in this case, the canals are not directly stimulated); but the otoliths continue to signal correctly the head's stationary orientation with respect to gravity. So we have canal sensations in the absence of corroborating signals from the otoliths, just as in the caloric stimulation discussed earlier. This is one form of 'motion' sickness where the vomiting serves a useful purpose: it removes whatever alcohol is still swilling around inside your stomach (which, unfortunately, is usually very little since the stomach lining absorbs alcohol very rapidly).

The next time you have too much to drink – and it happens to the best of us – remember that the big mistake is to lie down in bed. A compromise solution which I hit upon by accident, but which also fits the physiological facts, is to sleep in a sitting position, propped up with pillows, and with the head lolling on the chest. It is by no means a certain remedy, but it gives sleep a much better chance of getting there first. The hangover, however, is just as bad.

As before, the *type 3, canal-otolith conflict* is the reverse of the type 2 conflict. In this case, there is otolithic information without the customary canal signals to confirm them. This kind of conflict does not generally occur in conventional modes of transport; it has to be created artificially in the laboratory. One way of doing this is by rotating a person about an earth-horizontal axis like a chicken on a barbecue spit. This situation is illustrated in Figure 5.

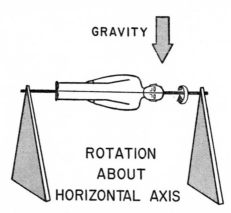

GRAVITY

ROTATION
ABOUT
HORIZONTAL AXIS

Figure 5   What happens when a person is rotated around an earth-horizontal or 'barbecue-spit' axis.

When a person is spun at constant velocity in this fashion, there is no input to the canals (they only respond to changes in angular velocity), but the otoliths are continually signalling the change of body position with respect to the gravitational vertical. This pattern of stimulation has no counterpart in everyday life – except perhaps in the fairground – and it makes the victim feel sick very rapidly.

We have argued that one or many of these six types of conflict are present in all situations that cause motion sickness. What, then,

are the events which intervene between the detection of the conflict and the appearance of symptoms?

There is no easy answer to this question, but we can get some
idea of what is happening from the characteristic pattern of events
which occur (a) when a person is first exposed to the sick-making
stimulus (i.e. the sensory conflict), (b) when he has been exposed
for a considerable time, and (c) when he returns to natural surroundings. We can label these three phases: *initial effects, adaptation* and *after-effects*, and summarize their essential features below:

(*a*) *Initial effects.* Motion sickness and its associated disturbances
appear soon after the rearranged sensory input is first encountered.
They may take some time before they reach their peak of severity,
but the events leading up to nausea and vomiting are set in train
almost immediately providing the exposure is sufficiently intense.
As experienced sea travellers will know, it is the first few hours
of rough weather that cause the most discomfort.

(*b*) *Adaptation.* With continued exposure to the sick-making
motion, the symptoms usually begin to subside and eventually
disappear leaving the sufferer immune from further upset – at
least while conditions remain the same. On a ship it usually takes
something like three days before the average passenger acquires
his 'sea legs' and ceases to be troubled by sea sickness. But he will
not acquire this protective adaptation unless he meets the sick-
making stimulus more than halfway. In other words, adaptation
is rather like vaccination: to get protection it is necessary to be
exposed to the thing that makes one ill. Simply taking to one's
bed aboard ship may delay the onset of sickness, but it will not
help the passenger to acquire any immunity for the future. That
only comes from a direct interaction with the provocative
stimulus.

Adaptation occurs in something like 95 per cent of all normal
individuals, although the rate at which it develops varies enor-
mously between people. The remaining 5 per cent are individuals
who – like Lord Nelson – never seem to acquire immunity to
sickness no matter how frequently they are exposed to the motion
stimulus. These individuals make up the bulk of the chronic
motion sickness sufferers.

Another feature of adaptation is that its protection is highly specific to the type of motion for which it was acquired. Sailors who have grown accustomed to the relatively violent motion of, say, a destroyer can become seasick on transferring to the comparatively sedate motion of an aircraft carrier. It is this specificity of adaptation which gives us a clue to the mechanisms underlying it, as we shall see later.

(c) *After-effects*. Providing that a person has acquired adaptation to a particular motion, its cessation can cause the reappearance of the motion sickness symptoms typical of the initial exposure. This is the phenomenon of land sickness, or *mal de débarquement*, that was mentioned earlier. These after-effects may last for hours, and sometimes days after disembarkation. And, following a lengthy sea voyage, these reactions are frequently accompanied by the sensation that the land is pitching and rolling, and there is quite often a swaying motion to the gait – the traditional 'sailor's rolling walk'.

All of these after-effects are the consequence of having adapted to the motion which initially caused sickness. Adaptation is a two-edged business. While it gives us protection – eventually – against the rigours of an alien motion environment, it also renders the familiar unfamiliar, at least as far as the co-ordinating centres of the brain are concerned. Motion sickness is essentially a maladaptation phenomenon, occurring at the two phases when the disparity between the sensory reality and expectation is at its greatest: that is, during the initial period of exposure to the sensory conflict, and during the period immediately following the return to normal.

The fact that this pattern of effect and after-effect remains fairly uniform over a wide range of sick-making situations suggests that both the pattern, and the sensory rearrangement from which it stems, hold the key to our understanding of the essential nature of motion sickness. One way of explaining this sequence of events is to suggest that the brain possesses two specialized units. The first is a *storage unit*, or spatial memory store, that retains the important characteristics of the previous sensory inputs from the visual and inertial receptors; namely quality, intensity, duration, and so on. The second is a *comparator unit* that compares the contents of the storage unit with the information currently reaching

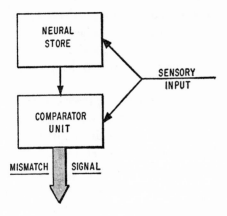

Figure 6   Basic neural components of the mismatch theory of motion sickness.

the brain from the various spatial senses. The interrelationship between these two brain units is shown diagrammatically in Figure 6. How do these two units function to produce sickness?

It is suggested that during the initial phase of the exposure to one of the six basic conflict situations, the contents of the storage unit are markedly different from the information being signalled by the spatial senses – as, for example, when a person first encounters the motion of a car or ship. The contents of the store relate to the individual's preceding experience of typical self-propelled locomotion and so have little in common with the kind of signals that stem from passive, vehicle motion. This discrepancy is picked up by the comparator unit which, as a result, generates a *mismatch signal* reflecting the size and direction of the deviation between stored and incoming spatial signals. The mismatch signal is then directed along reflex nerve pathways to the various brain mechanisms responsible for the production of signs and symptoms. It is also assumed that the strength of this mismatch signal determines, to some extent, the severity of the motion sickness reactions.

With continued exposure to the sensory conflict, the contents of the storage unit are gradually updated by incorporating elements of information about the rearranged sensory inputs, so that eventually there is no discrepancy between them and the information at the 'top' of the store. When this occurs, the mismatch signal is no longer transmitted, and the symptoms disappear. At this point, the person is said to be adapted to the atypical conditions.

On returning to the previously typical or familiar environment, the contents of the neural store – having previously adjusted to the atypical conditions – are again at variance with the incoming signals from the spatial senses. This causes the reinstatement of the mismatch signal and, with it, the reappearance of the symptoms. On remaining in the familiar environment, however, the contents of the storage unit are rapidly readjusted to be compatible with the typical arrangement of the sensory inputs. Because these inputs are so familiar, this part of the adaptation cycle (the re-adaptation part) is likely to occur quite rapidly as compared to the initial adjustment to the atypical, sick-making conditions. In other words, land sickness is likely to last for a shorter time, and be less severe, than the sea sickness which preceded it. By the same token, however, subsequent encounters with the same sick-making stimulus are likely to be less unpleasant than the first because the relevant information, once stored, is never entirely lost, so that later adaptations will occur more quickly with less chance of sickness during the process.

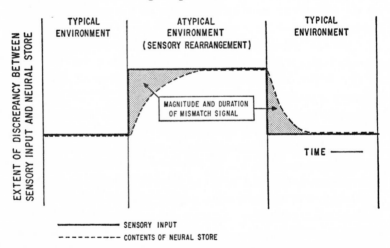

Figure 7   Effects and after-effects of sensory rearrangement as predicted by the mismatch theory of motion sickness.

The sequence of events described above is shown in Figure 7. These ideas do not explain why sickness as such should be the response to sensory conflict – it is, after all, an absurd response for the circumstances – nor do they tell us why the symptoms take the particular form that they do. The best we can offer in this regard is to suggest that motion sickness is the result of a basic design defect. It is hard to see what useful purpose it could serve, either in expelling some noxious substance (which is the defensive function of vomiting), or in furthering our survival as a species. The biological role of motion sickness remains an imponderable question, but the ideas put forward earlier serve to provide a rational basis for (*a*) understanding the factors which contribute to motion sickness susceptibility, and (*b*) for explaining how certain preventive measures achieve their results. We shall be considering these two issues in the final part of this chapter.

Motion sickness susceptibility

It was mentioned at the beginning of the chapter that people vary considerably in their proneness to travel sickness, and that the degree of susceptibility appears to be a relatively consistent feature of any one individual – at least for conventional modes of transport. Here we are concerned with identifying those factors which appear to influence or contribute to this degree of susceptibility.

We can dismiss at the outset the old-fashioned notion (which still holds sway in some quarters) that a 'nervous disposition' predisposes a person to motion sickness. There are too many contrary pieces of evidence for this idea to be allowed to persist. The counter-arguments are enumerated below:[16]

1. A large-scale wartime survey found no relationship between fears of drowning, explosion, and fire aboard ship, and susceptibility to sea sickness.

2. A person's susceptibility to air sickness – in which the role of anxiety has been particularly emphasized – correlates highly with his proneness to car sickness, train sickness and swing sickness, in which there seems little likelihood that fear would play a part. However, while on the subject of air sickness, it must be

acknowledged that people can be made sick as the result of fear and anxiety about flying. But this condition would not be motion sickness as we have described it, rather it would be 'fear sickness'.

3. Naval heroes of noted fearlessness have been lifetime sufferers from sea sickness. Many of Nelson's contemporaries, equally courageous in battle, found it necessary to keep to their cabins until they had passed beyond the rough waters of the Bay of Biscay on their passage south from England. Nelson himself remained a victim all his life, even on the final voyage to Trafalgar. This, it must be admitted, is a rather naïve counter-argument, but it should help to shake the equally naïve belief, held by some military men, that susceptibility to motion sickness can be equated with 'lack of moral fibre'.

4. In certain individuals, susceptibility may continue after long experience of a particular kind of vehicle when whatever anxiety might have been present at the beginning could reasonably be expected to have disappeared.

5. Many people who say they are nervous of travelling on ships or aircraft do not become sick; while others, who claim to be unafraid, succumb.

The only other purely psychological factor which is known to influence susceptibility is that of mental activity. It has been established by many experiments, and is borne out by our everyday experience, that people are less inclined to become ill when their minds are occupied with some demanding task. The brain has a limited capacity for processing information, and it is not unreasonable to suppose that a demanding mental activity will preempt the nervous pathways involved in producing symptoms.

Age and sex are two factors which clearly have a considerable influence in determining a person's susceptibility. Children start to become susceptible at around the age of two, and this susceptibility then increases to a maximum at around the ages of ten to twelve. Thereafter it diminishes so that motion sickness is a fairly rare occurrence among the middle-aged and elderly. At all ages, however, women are considerably more prone than men. Why this should be is not certain, but it is likely to have something to do with a woman's hormonal make-up which makes her generally more prone to nausea and vomiting (morning sickness, for example).

One explanation as to why resistance should increase with age is that advancing years bring with them a greater experience of the various forms of sensory conflict that make us sick. Consequently, the storage unit in the brain, referred to earlier, is likely to contain traces of information left over from previous exposures, so that the updating (adapting) process can occur more rapidly. To put it another way, older people have had more opportunity to 'learn' the characteristics of sensory rearrangement, and this allows them to form and retrieve the appropriate stored traces more rapidly than the younger person with less experience of vehicle motion. After a certain amount of exposure (which we can equate with vehicle experience), it is probable that adaptation will be almost instantaneous, so that no symptoms will appear. Whatever the reason, however, it is a comfort to know that, in this case at least, time is a great healer.

But even if we were to take a group of people of the same age and sex, whose minds were equally occupied, we should still find wide individual differences in susceptibility. The two factors which appear to account for most of this residual variation are *receptivity* and *adaptability*.

Receptivity[17] is a term used to describe the way a person characteristically experiences the intensity of environmental stimulation. Recent studies have shown that people vary consistently in their subjective response to a given level of physical energy, whether it be sound, light, pressure, smell or whatever. To some people the world is a brighter, louder, smellier, heavier, faster and more painful place than it is for others. The people whose sensory experiences are typically more vivid, we can label *receptives*; while those whose sensations – evoked by the same level of physical energy – are more subdued by comparison, we can label *nonreceptives*.

These characteristic differences in the strength of 'feeling' do not come from differences in the keenness of sight or hearing, nor from variation in the sensitivity of any other particular sense organ. What we are considering here is something like a volume control within the brain which adjusts the strength of the sensory message once it has been picked up by the sense receptor. The fact that variation in the way individuals 'augment' or 'reduce' their sensory experiences remains much the same regardless of the type of sensation involved suggests that these volume control adjustments are a property of the brain rather than the specific sense organs concerned. And it is those people who habitually amplify or boost up the strength of their sensations that show the greatest susceptibility to motion sickness. In other words, receptives tend to be more prone than nonreceptives.

Why should the way a person processes stimulus energy affect his susceptibility to motion sickness? We can start to answer this question by considering a group of passengers on board ship. It is well known that the number of cases of sea sickness tends to increase as the sea gets rougher – at least up to a certain degree. Taking the group as a whole therefore, we see that the incidence of sickness increases with the strength of the motion stimulus. If this is the case, it is reasonable to assume that a given level of ship motion will be more likely to produce sea sickness in those receptive individuals who are more attuned to the intensity of the motion. Thus, receptives can receive sufficient stimulation, and hence sufficient sensory conflict, to trigger the symptoms at relatively mild levels of motion intensity. But nonreceptives will require increasingly greater levels of intensity to provoke the same degree of disturbance. Going back to the events summarized in Figure 7, we can suggest that the initial discrepancy between the current sensory input (solid line) and the stored information (dotted line) will be greater for receptives than nonreceptives by virtue of the fact that the former will characteristically 'augment' the motion signals from the atypical environment. On the basis of this argument, we can make two predictions: first, in conditions where the strength of the motion stimulus is gradually increasing, receptives will become sick sooner than nonreceptives; second, where both receptives and nonreceptives encounter a severe motion stimulus – as when a squall blows up suddenly – the former will suffer more severe reactions than the latter.

The importance of the second factor, *adaptability*, is more immediately obvious in the light of our earlier discussion of protective adaptation. As with receptivity, people vary widely and consistently in the rates at which they adapt to sensory rearrangement. And it is to be expected that those who adapt slowly will suffer their symptoms for longer than those who adapt rapidly – all other things being equal. In Figure 7 differences in adaptability will show up as inter-individual variation in the time taken for the contents of the neural store to become compatible with the rearranged sensory input. In other words, these differences will be reflected in the time taken by the dotted line in Figure 7 to catch up with the solid line.

Finally, we can speculate about the way these two factors – receptivity and adaptability – interact with one another to determine a person's response to a sick-making stimulus. Assuming that receptivity and adaptability are independent of one another, we can suggest that there are basically four types of individual:

(a) *High receptivity – low adaptability*: the kind of person who suffers most from motion sickness. The high receptivity will ensure that his reactions will be initially severe, while the low adaptability guarantees that they will persist for a long time.

(b) *High receptivity – high adaptability*: this person will suffer initially severe reactions, but they will diminish rapidly because of the high rate of adaptation.

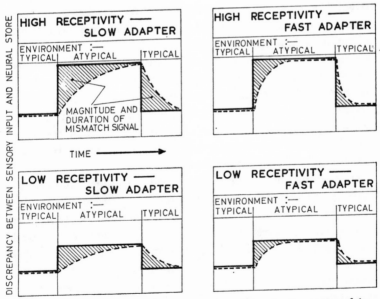

Figure 8   The four possible susceptibility types shown in the context of the effects and after-effects of adaptation depicted in Figure 7.

(c) *Low receptivity – low adaptability*: this person will suffer mild symptoms for a relatively long time.

(d) *Low receptivity – high adaptability*: this person is the most fortunate as far as motion sickness is concerned. He will suffer only mild symptoms, if any, for a relatively short time.[18]

These differences between the four susceptibility types are summarized diagrammatically in Figure 8. This shows how these variations are related to the theoretical ideas depicted in Figure 7.

So far in this chapter we have considered the signs and symptoms of motion sickness, various theories about its cause, and the factors which determine an individual's susceptibility. Now, in this final section, we turn to what must for many readers be the most relevant topic: namely, methods of prevention.

Methods of prevention

Motion sickness, once established, is not something which is easily cured if the sufferer remains exposed to the provocative motion; aside, that is, from the working of Nature's own cure, adaptation. In the pre-adapted state, the only certain remedy is to arrive! However, there are various techniques that have been employed with varying success to prevent the condition from arising in the first place.

Some of the oldest preventive measures have been concerned with specifying what the intending traveller should eat or drink before embarkation, and on the voyage. Most of these dietary measures are predicated on the notion that motion sickness originates in the stomach and intestines – which, of course, it doesn't; consequently, they are of very dubious value. But some of them do have a certain bizarre charm.

Two of the many suggestions made by nineteenth-century ship's physicians are worth recalling: one because it evokes nostalgia for more splendid days, and the other for its inspired lunacy. The first prescription was for 'soup made of horse-radish and rice, seasoned with red herrings and sardines' to be washed down with liberal quantities of champagne or a 'light sparkling wine' – definitely for first-class passengers only. (No matter how they differed with regard to the right food, all of these recommendations were agreed on the benefits of alcohol.)

The second recommendation was based on the idea that sickness was due to a vacuum in the abdominal cavity caused by the fact that when the ship pitched downwards, the bodily organs slid upwards against the diaphragm, thus acting like a vacuum pump. To combat this, the intending voyager was advised to eat a large number of pickled onions before embarkation so that the resulting gas might distend the stomach and so maintain a positive pressure within the abdominal cavity!

In actual fact, whatever is eaten before travelling – so long as it would not disturb the digestion anyway – makes very little difference to susceptibility. There is, however, one sound piece of dietary advice, which is that the would-be traveller should eat, if not a hearty breakfast, at least an adequate one. My experience of research on motion sickness is that experimental subjects who have missed their breakfast tend to suffer far more than those who have taken care of the inner man. I have no idea why this should be; but there is little doubt that motion sickness thrives on an empty stomach.

Another form of prevention depends upon control of posture. For instance, in vehicles where it is possible to lie down, adopting the supine position gives marked protection against sickness. The incidence of sickness in the supine position has been found to be as low as one-fifth that found in the sitting or standing positions. Where possible, therefore, the traveller should lie flat on his back, or as near this position as he can manage. Lying face-down does not, for some reason, give the same degree of protection.

Another extremely effective form of postural control involves restraining the independent wobbles of the head. In some experiments using a large swing to induce motion sickness, the incidence of symptoms when the head was clamped in a special holder was only 5 per cent as compared to 37 per cent when the head was free to move. Similar findings have been obtained in ships and aircraft. It is not necessary to have a special device to restrain the head. Simply holding it against a high-backed seat or just using the neck muscles voluntarily can be a great help. Of all the preventive measures that the traveller can adopt without outside help, keeping the head still is probably the most effective.

By far the commonest kind of prevention has involved the administration of some drug. In early times alcohol was the universal cure-all for seasickness. In general, the French favoured absinthe. But the English, if this 1607 prescription is typical, had more fanciful ideas:

> If in your drinke you mingle Rew with Sage
> All poyson is expel'd by power of those,
> Who would not be sea-sick when seas do rage
> Sage-water drinke with wine before he goes.

In the nineteenth century, as we mentioned earlier, physicians tried every preparation in the book including creosote (creosote!), strychnine, morphine and cocaine – which probably ensured a good 'trip' at least. So dangerous were these remedies that an editorial in the *Lancet* of 1891 strongly advised that 'as a rule, medicine of all kinds should be eschewed by those who do not wish to aggravate what is already hard to bear'.

Nowadays effective motion sickness preventives fall into two main pharmacological classes: the belladonna drugs and the antihistamines.[19] In both cases, the discovery of their preventive function was quite accidental – considering the state of the art, how could it have been otherwise? Certain belladonnas, in particular hyoscine hydrobromide, have an effect on the ciliary muscles which control the focus adjustment of the eyes; they cause blurring of vision. They were originally prescribed for sea sickness to eliminate some of the supposed aggravation to the eyes caused by seeing the motion of the ship or waves. It has since been discovered that l-hyoscine hydrobromide is the single most effective preventive among the drugs in use. Very recently, it has been found that when hyoscine is mixed with amphetamine (a stimulant drug) the unpleasant side-effects of hyoscine alone – drowsiness, dry mouth, blurring of vision – are removed; while, in addition, the protection conferred by the combination of drugs is far greater than that found with just hyoscine. This combination of drugs is now available to the American astronauts aboard the Apollo flights. However, in view of the dangerous nature of amphetamine, it is unlikely to find its way on to the market as a travel sickness preventive.

The antihistamines, on the other hand, are commonly used in the treatment of allergies. In the case of one particular lady being treated for 'hives', it was noticed that giving her antihistamines also eliminated her excessive proneness to travel sickness. A great deal of research, mostly done just after the Second World War, has confirmed that certain kinds of antihistaminic preparations (but not all) are reasonably effective in preventing sickness, and these together with the hyoscine-type drugs form the basis of most of the 'travel pills' we can buy in the chemist's shop.

No one knows exactly why these antihistamines and belladonna alkaloids give the protection they do. It has nothing to do with their typical pharmacological action, since not all belladonnas or antihistamines are effective. Those drugs that work probably do so through their depressant action on the central nervous system. In view of what was said earlier, we could speculate – and only speculate – that they achieve their effect either by bringing about a temporary decrease in the person's level of receptivity, or by causing an increase in his rate of adaptation, or through a combination of both. A lot more research is needed before we fully understand the effects of these preventives.

Finally, we must mention the most recent preventive technique, developed largely by NASA to combat present and anticipated space sickness, which involves pre-exposing crew members to the kind of sick-making stimulation they are liable to encounter in space. These are called *adaptation schedules*, and their purpose is to build up adaptation at graded stimulus levels that are not severe enough to make the individual sick. The rationale is derived in part from the theoretical ideas discussed earlier. If we can build up traces of a particular nauseogenic stimulus within the storage unit *before* a person encounters the real thing under operational conditions, we will probably save a good deal of in-flight time that might otherwise have been lost through sickness. However, I shall be discussing these adaptation schedules further in the next chapter, which is devoted to the problem of space sickness. Those readers who feel they have had enough of this topic can skip Chapter 2, and go straight on to Chapter 3.

2 Space Sickness

It is somewhat ironical that motion sickness should remain as one of the more pressing problems of manned space flight, particularly when the very same disorder probably made its first appearance along with the prototype dugout canoe. If human ingenuity can put man on the moon, it is not unreasonable to expect that the same ingenuity would have put paid to this wretched and undignified condition a long time ago. But not so: in fact, the size of the problem grows apace with our rapidly expanding transport technology. Indeed, our failure to overcome this disorder serves to underline the basic theme of this book: that while man's technical genius is now capable literally of taking him out of this world, his own physical and psychological make-up remains that of an animal whose feet – in biological terms – are still very firmly planted on the ground. Viewed in this light, it makes some sense that the further we depart from our customary habitat and natural modes of locomotion, the more evident our built-in design limitations become.

Nausea and vomiting provoked by earthbound vehicles can be extremely unpleasant, but rarely dangerous. But in space this normally rather banal disorder takes on a much graver significance. Aside from its debilitating effects which are likely to reduce efficiency in an environment highly intolerant of error, there is the very real danger that vomitus, expelled within a spacesuit, could cause a serious malfunction of the astronaut's life-support system. It is hard to design a gas exchange unit that is entirely vomit-proof.

After something close to 14,000 man-hours in space,* it is quite obvious that symptoms, akin to those of sea sickness and air sickness, are readily provoked by the weightless or zero-gravity state. This is the problem of space sickness as we know it today;

* Exact cumulative man-hours in space up to and including Apollo 16 and Soyuz 11: US = 8,593 hrs 54 mins; USSR = 4,397 hrs 41 mins.

but, as we shall see later, it is likely to recur, perhaps in a more serious form, in projected spacecraft that rotate to produce artificial gravity. We shall be considering these rotating craft towards the end of this chapter, but in the meantime let us briefly review the known episodes of space sickness among the crews of the present generation of weightless space vehicles.

Incidence of space sickness in weightless flight

During the early years of manned space flight, it seemed as though space sickness was going to be a Russian monopoly. The first reported episode occurred in August 1961, during the fourth orbit of the cosmonaut Gherman Titov's flight in Vostok 2. Describing his experiences after the flight, Major Titov said: 'I felt changes of mood during abrupt movements of my head which produced unpleasant sensations resembling sea sickness.' His main symptoms were dizziness, loss of appetite and nausea. In addition, he also felt that he was upside-down immediately on reaching the weightless state. This is called the *inversion illusion*, and has been reported by a number of Russian cosmonauts, but rarely by American astronauts, at least during the Mercury and Gemini programmes. In Titov's case, both the sickness and the inversion illusion were lessened after a brief period of sleep, and disappeared completely with the onset of the re-entry forces. Although Titov's problems resulted in little or no loss of efficiency, their occurrence produced a flurry of concern among Soviet space scientists, who set about redesigning their already rigorous training and selection procedures. I shall come on to these later.

Despite these additional efforts, two further episodes occurred during the twenty-four-hour, multi-orbital flight of Voskhod 1 in October 1964. Aboard were the late Colonel Komarov, flight commander and pilot; Konstantin Feoktistov, a thirty-eight-year-old scientist and chess-playing intellectual; and Dr Boris Yegorov, a twenty-seven-year-old space physician. During the second hour of the flight Yegorov noted the first signs of space sickness, which took the form of a decrease in appetite and nausea. Feoktistov observed similar reactions, but they were less severe. In both cases the symptoms – like those of Titov – were contingent upon sharp movements of the head which also caused unpleasant sensations of dizziness. Both men also reported the inversion illusion, which persisted regardless of whether the eyes were open or shut. But, as in Titov's case, all these symptoms were eliminated during the re-entry phase.

Colonel Komarov, a highly experienced pilot, suffered no ill effects whatsoever. At the time his immunity was attributed to his extensive experience of the unusual accelerations encountered in high-speed jet flight, and to the fact that his organs of balance were relatively insensitive compared with those of his fellow crew members. An alternative explanation, and one that is more acceptable to contemporary thinking, is that Colonel Komarov was one of those fortunate individuals who are, by nature, relatively immune to motion sickness.

In the rival American camp the story was quite different, at least during the early years of manned space flight. Aside from a slight episode reported aboard Gemini VII, American astronauts in the Mercury and Gemini programmes seemed immune to space sickness and the associated inversion illusion. At a time when their Russian counterparts were receiving extensive training specifically to prevent sickness (and still getting sick), the Americans seemed to bear a charmed life. Except, that is, for occasional bouts of sea sickness when their flimsy capsules splashed down into a rough sea. Captain Schirra, who flew soon after the Titov mission, complained that all the publicity given to the Russians' symptoms had caused him to feel queasy during the pre-launch period, but he felt no ill effects during the flight itself.

It cannot be said that the apparent immunity of the early astronauts to space sickness was due to any great preventive efforts on the part of American space physicians. They, like the astronauts themselves, were generally sceptical about the likelihood of space sickness affecting individuals with as much flying experience as the Mercury and Gemini crews. The only specific countermeasure used on these early flights was the inclusion of some anti-motion sickness drugs in the medical kits carried on board during each mission. Despite this indifference to the problem – on the very good grounds that as far as the Americans were concerned there was no problem at that time – the Russian episodes did have considerable influence on the allocation of NASA research funds. From the early 1960s onwards, a great deal of financial support was given to research directed at finding the causes and the means of preventing motion sickness in rotating environments. This work was largely carried out under the direction of Dr Ashton Graybiel at the Naval Aerospace Medical Institute at Pensacola, Florida, and I shall discuss this research later when I come to consider artificial gravity.

Thus, by the end of the Gemini flights, the problem of space sickness – anticipated in the 1950s as one of the big bogeys of manned space flight – had receded in American thinking to a position of secondary importance: something to be anticipated in the future rotating craft, but of no great significance in weightless vehicles. While they recognized that it was still theoretically possible, even in weightlessness, they felt that the considerable conventional flying experience demanded of the early astronauts effectively immunized them against the likelihood of sickness in space. This was a reasonable assumption, since most of the Russian cosmonauts who had fallen prey to sickness had had little or no flying experience as compared to the Mercury and Gemini astronauts. Unfortunately, this happy state of affairs was rudely shattered with the coming of the manned Apollo flights which began in the latter part of 1968. With Apollo, the tables were turned. Now it was the turn of the Americans to experience frequent episodes of space sickness, while the Russians, at least up to Soyuz 10, remained – as far as can be judged – immune.

According to Dr Charles Berry, the astronauts' chief physician, ten of the twenty-one astronauts who have so far flown in the Apollo programme have suffered some symptoms of space sickness.[1] These have ranged from mild sensations of tumbling to serious cases of prolonged nausea and vomiting. In the few months between Apollo 7 in October 1968, and Apollo 13 in the spring of 1970, there were more recorded episodes of sickness than in all the preceding seven years of manned flight. These are summarized in Table 3.

Of these instances of space sickness, perhaps the most dramatic and the most operationally disruptive was that suffered by Astronaut Russell Schweickart, the Lunar Module pilot aboard Apollo 9. From the moment he became weightless,[2] Schweickart felt a definite queasiness and loss of well-being. Although he dosed himself with the anti-motion sickness drugs available in the

Apollo medical kit, these unpleasant sensations persisted without relief until they finally erupted into acute nausea and vomiting when he attempted to climb through the hatch from the Command Capsule to the Lunar Module. Just before this, as he was donning his spacesuit, he felt a violent spinning sensation when he ducked his head down to enter the suit via a zipped opening in the back. This illusory spinning stopped as soon as he raised his head, but it seems likely that these feelings of dizziness precipitated the bout of vomiting which occurred shortly afterwards. So severe and debilitating was this episode that the scheduled Lunar Module docking exercise was postponed for several hours until he recovered. Although he was later able to carry out his assigned tasks, and with considerable skill, Schweickart continued to feel queasy for the remainder of the flight. He only fully recovered when he was aboard the carrier at the end of the mission.

TABLE 3   EPISODES OF SPACE SICKNESS AMONG APOLLO ASTRONAUTS* (Figures in parentheses indicate the number of crew members reporting the particular symptoms.)

Mission	Nature of symptoms
Apollo 7	Mild sensations of tumbling (1).
Apollo 8	Stomach awareness, nausea and vomiting (3).
Apollo 9	Strong sensation of tumbling, loss of appetite, queasiness (2); persistent nausea and vomiting (1).
Apollo 10	Stomach awareness, loss of appetite, nausea (1).
Apollo 11	Mild loss of appetite (1).
Apollo 12	No reported symptoms.
Apollo 13	Stomach awareness (2); nausea and vomiting (1).
Apollo 14	No reported symptoms.

Subsequent investigations showed that Schweickart was by no means unusually susceptible to the conventional, earthbound forms of motion sickness. In fact, compared with the population as a whole he was fairly resistant. The same was found to be true in the case of the cosmonaut, Titov, and together the two cases fit in with the general research finding that it is extremely difficult

* The most recent episodes of space sickness were those reported by the second Skylab crew during the early stages of their fifty-six day sojourn in weightless conditions (July-September 1973).

to estimate an individual's susceptibility to space sickness before he actually gets into the weightless state. Certainly, there appears to be very little relationship between proneness to earthbound forms of motion sickness – air sickness, sea sickness, car sickness, and the like – and proneness to sickness in zero-gravity conditions.

The most recent Russian episode of space sickness apparently occurred during the flight of Soyuz 10 in March 1967, when an attempt was made to transfer one of the crew to the orbiting space station, Salyut. The Russian press reports suggest that the flight was ended prematurely owing to the 'unpleasant feelings' experienced by the engineer-cosmonaut, Nikolai Rukavishnikov. There is as yet no direct confirmation that this loss of well-being was due to motion sickness, but, if it was, this episode would seem to be even more disastrous in terms of lost flight time than Schweickart's in Apollo 9. This would also be the first time that a mission was actually abandoned as the result of space sickness.

The origins of space sickness in weightless flight

From the reports of both Russian and American space travellers, there seems little doubt that the initial appearance of sickness and its subsequent intensification are associated with rapid or extensive turning movements of the head. To understand the causal significance of these head movements, we need to appreciate how their vestibular consequences differ in normal terrestrial gravity and in space.

The otoliths, as I pointed out in the previous chapter, function as head-tilt indicators by virtue of the fact that they signal the head's position with respect to the force of gravity, which on earth is our primary datum for the vertical. The canals, on the other hand, signal the rate and direction of a head turn about any of three possible axes. Thus, when the head is tilted to, say, the left shoulder under normal gravity, its altered position is signalled both by the otoliths and – during the movement itself – by those canals lying in the plane of the head tilt. Under these circumstances, therefore, the two vestibular receptors work in perfect harmony, each telling the brain essentially the same information: namely, that the head has moved towards the left shoulder.

Now, in weightless space flight, there is no gravitational force, and hence no datum from which the otoliths can signal the position of the head. In other words, they can no longer function as head-tilt indicators. But the canals are not affected by the absence of a gravitational force; their design allows them to function independently of gravity, so that they are capable of working normally, even in weightless flight. Consider what happens, then, when the head is tilted to the left shoulder in zero gravity: the appropriate canals signal the turning motion of the head as usual, but the otoliths register no change. Thus, we have all the ingredients for a type 2, canal-otolith conflict (see Chapter 1): an uncoupling of the normally harmonious relationship between the two vestibular receptors such that the canals signal the head movement in the absence of the *expected* corroboration from the otoliths. This, as we argued in the previous chapter, is a sufficient stimulus for motion sickness.

But this canal-otolith conflict is only part of the story. When the eyes are open, the shift in the visual scene produced by the head movement will agree with the canal information but not that from the otoliths. Having been rendered inoperative by the absence of gravity, these will be signalling 'no motion' irrespective of how far or how fast the head is turned. Thus, when the head is tilted in space with the eyes open, there is a tripartite conflict between the eyes, canals and otoliths which, as the previous section shows, is extremely conducive to sickness. If we can extrapolate from earth-based laboratory findings, it is probable that closing the eyes in weightlessness will eliminate some, but not all, of the conditions that promote symptoms. The canal-otolith conflict will still be present during any angular movement of the head.

Of particular interest to those concerned with the causes of space sickness is the fact that it appears to be the unusual *combination* of canal, otolith and visual signals that produces sickness. Even when the head is still in weightlessness, the 'resting' neural activity (the neural discharge from a sense receptor when it is not responding to a stimulus) will be different from that obtained under similar conditions on earth. The otolith blob will have no weight in space, so that it is bound to produce a different alignment of the supporting hairs, and this in turn must result in a different pattern of nervous discharge. To some extent, therefore, the difference between the resting neural discharge on earth and that which is likely to occur in space meets our theoretical requirements for producing sickness: namely, that the sensory inputs in space should differ from those we expect as the result of our earth-based experiences. But evidently these differences in resting otolith discharges are not, by themselves, enough to cause sickness (no one has ever reported that the head-stationary position produces symptoms). For sickness to occur, it seems that we need the presence of an *active* canal signal (that is, one produced by a head motion) in the absence of the expected otolithic back-up information. This suggests that it is the positive combination of two or more incongruous signals that creates the necessary stimulus for motion sickness, and this theoretical point has some important practical implications. For one thing, it tells us that the head-still position will not, by itself, produce sickness and hence it is one that the astronaut can adopt with impunity whenever he begins to feel the onset of symptoms. To some extent, therefore, the factors which cause space sickness are under the astronaut's direct control, and this is an important piece of information for those who seek to prevent its occurrence.

Prevention

Preventive measures fall into two broad categories: pre-flight and in-flight techniques. The former include specific selection and training methods whose aim is to ensure that the space traveller enjoys a reduced susceptibility to motion sickness. In-flight measures to combat space sickness have not, as yet, been widely used, but to date they include the administration of anti-motion sickness drugs, head restraint and the execution of controlled head movements designed to accelerate the development of protective adaptation. I shall consider the pre-flight measures first.

With regard to the selection of space crews, both the Russian and American space authorities have initially recruited from among military jet pilots – a selection criterion that guaranteed a certain amount of pre-exposure to unusual force environments. The Americans have always been more concerned with this aspect of selection than the Russians. Until recently, candidates for the astronaut programme had to satisfy the following minimum selection requirements: a Bachelor's degree, graduation from the test pilot's school, at least 1,500 hours flying time in conventional aircraft, and qualifications as a jet pilot. Nowadays, these flying requirements are less stringent. The current pool of American astronauts includes scientists, physicians, and engineers without previous pilot experience. Nevertheless, some 250 hours of the training programme are still given over to acquiring basic jet pilot qualifications.

The Russians relaxed these previous flying requirements quite early in their space programme. In the early 1960s their cosmonauts included a scientist (Feoktistov), a physician (Yegorov), and the first woman to orbit the earth, Valentina Tereshkova, who before selection was a textile worker with a sporting interest in parachute jumping. By contrast, however, the Soviet selection procedure has always placed much greater emphasis on various measures of vestibular function, balance, and bodily co-ordination than the American procedure. The only test of this nature that has so far been given regularly to American astronaut-candidates is a simple caloric assessment of canal function. Occasionally, astronauts have received more extensive vestibular testing, but not as a regular part of either selection or training.

The Russian cosmonauts are not only given the usual clinical battery of vestibular tests, they are also put through a very challenging series of laboratory procedures designed to assess motion sickness susceptibility and what the Russian scientists call 'statokinetic stability'.[3] This concept of 'stability' is central to the Russian philosophy of training and selection. Basically, it reflects a person's ability to regain his balance after he has been subjected to something like rapid rotation which artificially disturbs his sense of balance. After the candidate has been spun for a while in a rotating chair, the Russian scientists measure how long it takes him to recover his normal orientation, and also how long the feelings of dizziness, caused by the rapid spinning, take to subside. People vary a great deal in these respects, both as a result of previous experience and through built-in factors. The Russian aim is to screen out those individuals who take an abnormally long time to recover from – or adapt to – an unusual force environment.

It is to improve this basic 'stability' that Russian trainee astronauts are regularly exposed to a wide variety of exercises designed to condition the sense of balance. These consist of three types of activity, termed 'active', 'passive' and 'combined' exercises. 'Active' procedures include gymnastics and callisthenics, trampolining, complex aerobatic springboard exercises, figure skating, and free-fall parachuting. 'Passive' procedures consist of being exposed to motions produced by rotating chairs, four-pole swings, elevators, complex centrifuges and various multi-axis devices capable of spinning the cosmonaut about a number of different axes at the same time. The 'combined' procedures are a mixture of both active and passive exercises in which the cosmonaut exerts voluntary control over part of his total movement pattern while being moved passively.

The Americans, by comparison, devote very little of their astronaut training time to the elimination of space sickness. This, of course, is a reflection of their freedom from sickness episodes during the Mercury and Gemini missions. However, there are three kinds of routine training carried out by American astronauts which have some relevance to prevention: the maintenance of current flying practice in high-speed aerobatic manoeuvres; regular exposure to acceleration stresses in centrifuges and disorientation devices; and experience with short periods of weightlessness in specially modified aircraft (see Figure 9). The only way of achieving weightless conditions within the earth's atmosphere is by flying the ballistic trajectory illustrated in Figure 9. Depending on the aircraft type, the period of zero gravity may last up to thirty seconds. In addition to examining reactions to free-floating or self-paced activities in weightlessness, both Russian and American studies have looked at how individuals respond to passive rotation during the zero-gravity period of the manoeuvre. Some recent Russian studies have attempted to use this technique as a basis for selecting cosmonauts. They recommend that selection should depend on a comparison of the time for which the post-rotatory dizziness persists after three sessions of rapid spinning: one before the flight in normal gravity, one during the brief period of weightlessness, and one after the flight. The Russian scientists argue that the most suitable candidates are those in whom the post-spin experiences become progressively shorter with each successive rotation test. Those who show a progressive increase in the severity and duration of these after-effects, and who also show concomitant large

a

variations in pulse and respiration rates, are likely to make unsuitable cosmonauts. Similar techniques are also presently being explored in the United States.

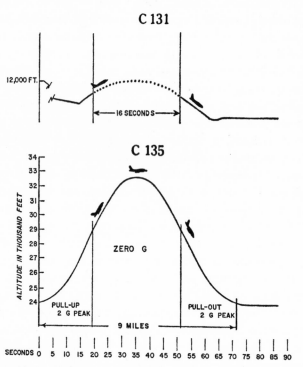

Figure 9   Flight profiles of zero-gravity manoeuvres for two types of aircraft, the C 131 (Convair) and the C 135 (Boeing 707). (By courtesy of the US Naval Aerospace Medical Institute, Pensacola, Florida.)

An alternative method of simulating the conditions of weightlessness is being evaluated in the United States. This involves installing a full-scale mockup of a space cabin on the floor of a glass-walled watertank. The researchers, termed *aquanauts*, are submerged in a condition of neutral buoyancy; that is, they neither sink nor rise, due to the carefully measured weights attached to their 'wet' suits. Such a situation achieves much of the 'feel' of weightlessness and is useful for training astronauts to manoeuvre themselves physically; but of course it does not create the sensory conflict necessary to produce motion sickness, since the otolith is still able to respond to the gravitational force. However, something quite like zero-gravity conditions – as far as the otolith is concerned – can be simulated by rotating the subjects in a pitching or head-over-heels mode while under water.

With regard to in-flight preventive measures, there is little or no information concerning the use of anti-motion sickness drugs by the Russian cosmonauts, but it is reasonable to assume that they, like the American astronauts, carry some kind of preventive preparation aboard their spacecraft. In their earlier missions the Americans relied heavily on conventional antihistamines like Cyclizine, Marezine and Tygan. But, as we mentioned in the previous chapter, these have been very largely replaced by a combination of hyoscine and amphetamine which has been shown to exceed any other known drug or drug combination in its protective power. Not only that, it also appears to be relatively free from the unpleasant side-effects associated with the traditional preventives.

But despite their proven effectiveness, anti-motion sickness drugs should not really constitute the main line of attack against space sickness. In the first place, most astronauts are reluctant to use them since they feel that such drugs might impair their concentration. A second disadvantage is that these preparations have a preventive rather than a therapeutic action. To produce the maximum benefit, they have to be taken before the symptoms occur; once established, they can do little to alleviate them. Since most astronauts do not regard themselves as susceptible, they are unlikely to take these drugs before a mission or during its early stages, particularly in view of their apprehension about side-effects. A third factor which argues against their use as the prime preventive is that we have little understanding of how these drugs achieve their action, so that we can say very little about what additional problems might be created if they are taken regularly over long periods of space flight. At best, therefore, they are little more than a stopgap measure; and at worst, they could be dangerous if their effects were modified by some little-understood condition of space flight.

By far the most effective long-term protection against space sickness is the natural phenomenon of adaptation that I discussed in the previous chapter. Sooner or later, the astronaut will adapt to the alien conditions of space and become immune to its ill effects. The human brain is capable of achieving this adaptation without any outside help, but there are certain things we can do to speed up this adjustment process. These procedures have been labelled *adaptation schedules*, and work on a principle analogous to vaccination, although quite different mechanisms are involved. When the body receives a small dose of something potentially nasty, as in vaccination, its defence mechanisms are mobilized so that they are 'standing to' when a larger and more dangerous dose comes along. The same kind of thing occurs in the brain when a person is exposed to a mild level of a potentially sick-making stimulus. By giving the astronaut a moderate exposure to the stressful stimulus at a level insufficient to cause sickness, a record of this stimulus is laid down in the spatial memory store (see Chapter 1). The presence of this stored information then accelerates the process of adaptation when a more stressful level of the same sick-making stimulus is subsequently encountered. It does this by modifying the brain's expectations regarding the sensory inputs from the various spatial senses – the eyes, the vestibular receptors, and so on. After sufficient exposure, the unfamiliar rearranged inputs have become the norm – so much so, in fact, that when the previously 'natural' conditions are reinstated the person has to re-adapt all over again. We see the consequences of this in the phenomenon of land sickness, discussed in the previous chapter.

Adaptation schedules were used for the first time aboard Apollo 10, immediately following Schweickart's bad bout of sickness on the Apollo 9 mission. In many respects, Schweickart's disruptive episode had the same effect as that of Titov seven years earlier: it caused the appropriate medical authorities to sit up and take notice. Previous cases of sickness in the Apollo programme had been attributed to other causes such as residual gastro-intestinal infections. But in Schweickart's case there was no escaping the obvious conclusion that he had suffered from motion sickness. Consequently something had to be done, and done quickly, to prevent a recurrence on the Apollo 10 mission which was scheduled to orbit the moon as a dress rehearsal for the Apollo 11 moon-landing.

In the event the Apollo 10 astronauts were briefed to carry out a series of small head movements, paced at about two-second intervals, during the early stages of the outbound trip when there was relatively little to be done apart from maintaining course. The rationale was that by executing these small-excursion head motions, and thus exposing themselves to a mild and easily controlled level of the sick-making stimulus, they would gradually build up a residual store of protection which, hopefully, would see them through the more strenuous and extensive head movements demanded during the lunar phase of the flight without problems. As it turned out, only one of the crew members actually carried out the head movement exercises; the other two were too busy with their operational duties. Unfortunately, the schedule did not have the desired effect, as can be judged from this report made after the flight by Dr Charles Berry:

One of the crew noted stomach awareness on movement about the spacecraft for two days. The head movements prescribed for hastening adaptation to the weightless environment were attempted on the first and second days and in both instances produced more marked stomach awareness within approximately one minute. Adaptation continued to occur through careful movements for short periods of time within the spacecraft and no further difficulty was encountered. On the seventh day, while returning from the Moon, head movements were again attempted and produced stomach awareness after approximately four minutes of movement.[4]

Although unsuccessful in preventing sickness on this occasion, these exercises did yield two important pieces of information. First, apart from confirming the causal significance of head movements, they also suggest that the sick-making properties of these motions are dependent not only on their speed and extent, but also on the time interval which separates them: the shorter the interval between the movements the more likely it is to cause sickness. Thus, it seems probable that the prescribed interval of two seconds between each head movement executed by the Apollo 10 astronaut was far too short to achieve protective adaptation without sickness. The rapid succession of unusual combinations of signals from the canals and the otoliths evidently created a greater stress than we could have guessed from earth-based researches. In other words, to achieve their purpose of creating a mild level of sick-making stress, the head movements should have been spaced at something like ten seconds apart. If this inference is correct, it tells us a great deal more about the nature of the nauseogenic stimulus in weightless flight. More importantly perhaps, it gives us a basis for advising astronauts how to make necessary head motions in the unadapted state: namely, very slowly and allowing a lengthy inter-movement interval.

The second piece of information yielded by the Apollo 10 flight was the absence of sickness during the crucial orbital phase of the mission, and the delayed onset of symptoms during head movements on the return leg. The fact that the last session of head motions provoked sickness in about four minutes, while the first session took only one minute, clearly indicates the establishment of some protective adaptation, albeit not enough, but sufficient to show that adaptation in weightlessness follows the same pattern as that acquired in other sick-making situations.

Obviously a great deal more research will have to be done before we fully understand the mechanics of protective adaptation and produce an effective adaptation schedule. But from the evidence we have accumulated so far, there seems to be little doubt that this built-in adjustment process constitutes our most effective weapon against space sickness and its related disturbances.

Rotating spacecraft

The principal need for artificial gravity arises from the fact that man is essentially a gravity-dependent animal. While space travellers have so far not been permanently affected by comparatively short spells of weightlessness lasting up to eighteen days or so, there are strong medical and physiological grounds for believing that prolonged periods in zero gravity – of the durations envisaged for the crews of manned orbiting stations and those involved in future Mars flights – could bring about irreversible changes in the circulatory and skeletal systems of the body. Even in the recent Soyuz missions, there were press reports that Soviet cosmonauts were experiencing in-flight problems – for example, the strange loss of colour vision reported by one cosmonaut during the latter stages of the mission – and also circulatory difficulties on their return to earth.

The problem is not that man may be *unable* to adapt to prolonged weightlessness: it is that the adaptation will render him
unsuited for normal terrestrial living on his return. These medical
problems, constituting as they do a permanent health hazard for
space travellers, represent the strongest argument for the provision of artificial gravity in long-term flights. But there are other
benefits to be gained from artificial gravity, as can be seen from
the following statement by Dr Gilruth, Director of the NASA
Manned Spacecraft Center at Houston:

By providing artificial gravity, fluid processes such as those associated with personal hygiene, cleaning, food preparation, and chemistry,
all can be performed in the same way as here on Earth. With the
establishment of normal gravity, the ability to walk with hands free
will provide an environment which needs little or no training for
adaptation. Artificial gravity will also provide normal man/machine
interfaces with all types of equipment – both operational and scientific.
Again, this would eliminate the need for special zero-g training and
maximize the effectiveness of Earth training, especially for the more
complex repair, refurbishment, and modification tasks we might expect
in the future.[5]

Despite these very strong arguments for the provision of
artificial gravity, there are still factions – particularly within NASA
itself – who would prefer to see a continuation of the present
zero-gravity spacecraft. Some believe that the increased costs and
fuel requirements necessary to keep the craft spinning about a
stable axis are not warranted by the health hazards and habitability benefits. The former, they argue, can be taken care of by
rotating chairs and special conditioning equipment carried within
the weightless spacecraft; and the habitability benefits, they claim,
are dubious in view of the increased likelihood of motion sickness
and disorientation associated with head and body movements in a
rotating environment. Opinions are also mixed among the
scientists who are likely to man the orbiting space laboratories.
The chemists and other physical scientists are happy with artificial
gravity because it will keep their concoctions at the bottom of a
test-tube; but the astronomers are not so pleased with the idea
because they want a stable base upon which to site their telescopes.
The debate – to rotate or not to rotate – will continue for some
time to come, but in my view there is little doubt that spacecraft

of the future will need to provide some form of artificial gravity. The Russians are certainly thinking along these lines, and in America there are vehicles, presently on the drawing board, that will possess a rotating component. The most likely outcome is a compromise: a vehicle that will have a rotating portion in which the crew quarters and some laboratories are situated, as well as a stationary or zero-gravity hub from which the astronomers can make their observations.

The basic principles of artificial gravity are fairly simple. When we ride on a roundabout we are subjected to a force, created by the rotation, that pushes us away from the centre of rotation. It is this same force that will act to pin the astronaut and his possessions to the deck in a rotating spacecraft. Ideally, the astronaut will be positioned so that his head is towards the centre of rotation, and his body aligned with the radius. In this way the centrifugal forces produced by the rotation will act vertically through his body in the same way that the force of gravity acts on earth. The degree of artificial gravity experienced by the astronaut – that is, the amount of g, where $1\,g = 32 \cdot 2\,\text{ft}/\text{sec}^2$ or $9 \cdot 81\,\text{m}/\text{sec}^2$ – depends upon two factors: the rate at which the space vehicle is spun, and the radial distance of the man from the centre of rotation. The relationship between these two variables is given by the following equation:

$$g = 0 \cdot 341 \times 10^{-3} \times \text{RADIUS}\,(\text{ft}) \times \text{RPM}^2$$

This trade-off relationship between radius and rotational speed means that the same level of, say, $0 \cdot 6\,g$ can be achieved with different combinations of radius and spin-rate: for example, by a radius of 40 ft and a rotational speed of 7 rpm, or by a radius of 120 ft and a rotational rate of 4 rpm. The implications of this trade-off are very critical. The greater the radius, the greater are the engineering problems such as weight, fuel and stabilization; yet if we reduce the radius and achieve the same g-level by an increased rpm, we also increase the likelihood of motion sickness and other human factor problems. Thus, the decision is a difficult one, but it is eased to some extent by the knowledge gained from earth-based experiments that many of the physiological problems of weightless flight can be overcome by a g-force that is less than $1\,g$. Probably forces in the region of $0 \cdot 4$ to $0 \cdot 6\,g$ would be adequate for most purposes. These 'sub-gravity' levels would also have a number of practical advantages over earth-gravity: cargo would weigh less, and men would expend less energy in moving it; the radius and spin rates would be less than those required to maintain 1 g, and hence vehicles would be cheaper and easier to design. The present consensus of opinion favours a radius of around 50 ft, which to maintain about 0·5 g would require a rotational speed between 5 and 6 rpm – a spin-rate at which most human problems can be readily overcome by adaptation.

So long as the astronaut remains absolutely still, the centrifugal acceleration created by the rotating vehicle provides a force environment comparable in most qualitative respects to that found on earth. The only slight difference so far as the stationary man is concerned is that the force acting on his head will be somewhat less than the force acting on his feet, but this should not bother him too much. What will disturb him, however, is that the force environment – unlike that on earth – will change as the result of his own movements. For convenience, we can divide these movement effects into two categories: those produced by whole-body movements, and those produced by turning movements of the head.

Whenever an object situated on a rotating platform is moved in a straight line it is subjected to Coriolis forces,[6] which act to deflect the object from its path: the same is true for an astronaut walking round within a rotating spacecraft. The direction and magnitude of these Coriolis forces will depend on where he walks in relation to the axis of rotation. Only when he moves parallel to the axis of spin will he be unaffected by them. If he moves to or from the central hub of the craft in a radial direction, these additional forces will act at right-angles to his path, and their direction will depend upon whether he is moving towards or away from the centre of rotation. On walking with the spin of the spacecraft, the Coriolis force adds itself to the centrifugal force, causing the man to feel heavier; on walking against the direction of the spin, the force will be reversed in direction, causing him to feel lighter. Whether or not these bizarre changes in the force environment will produce motion sickness is not yet established; but it is certain that turning movements of the man's head about axes that differ from the axis of rotation will evoke symptoms.

These are the angular head motions that produce the Coriolis vestibular reactions discussed in the previous chapter.

Head movements in a rotating spacecraft produce motion sickness for essentially the same reasons as they did in weightless spacecraft: that is, they cause the canals and otoliths to signal conflicting messages regarding the position of the head. However, the nature of this canal-otolith conflict in a rotating craft is different from that created in weightlessness. In artificial gravity, we are likely to have a type 1, canal-otolith conflict where the canals and otoliths simultaneously signal contradictory motion information, as opposed to weightlessness, where the canals signal in the absence of corroboration from the otoliths (i.e., a type 2 conflict). In the rotating craft, the canals will signal a head turn about one axis, while the otoliths concurrently signal head movement about an axis at right-angles to the first. And, as in weightlessness, this confusion is exacerbated by the simultaneous presence of incompatible visual information. Once again, therefore, it is the unusual *combination* of canal, otolith and visual signals that is the principal cause of sickness. As long as the head remains perfectly still, the space traveller will not be at risk.

Figure 10   The Pensacola Slow Rotation Room.

Although artificial gravity is just as likely to cause sickness as zero gravity, it does possess the enormous advantage – as far as prevention is concerned – of being far easier to simulate on earth than weightlessness. This means that in the artificial-gravity flights of the future, it will be feasible to *pre-adapt* crews to their operational space environment before they ever leave the ground. In other words, at some time before their departure astronauts can be put through an adaptation schedule in a device like the Pensacola Slow Rotation Room (see Figure 10) where they are exposed to gradually increasing levels of the Coriolis stimulus. Although these pre-flight adaptive procedures are still a thing of the future, there is considerable research evidence to indicate that they will constitute the most effective form of protection against space sickness – primarily because they rely upon the body's own adjustment mechanisms rather than upon the action of any external agency like drugs. I shall consider these procedures further in the final chapter.

3 Deceptions in the Air: Pilot Disorientation

In this chapter we shall be considering another outcome of the gap between what man was designed for and what he actually does: this time it is the problem that scientists call *spatial disorientation*, and that aviators refer to as *pilot's vertigo*. These terms encompass the many different ways in which our position and motion senses and their associated perceptual mechanisms contrive to deceive us when we take to the air. Although mental confusion about the body's orientation is not the exclusive product of air travel, it is in these circumstances where we have the unaccustomed freedom of movement in three dimensions that it occurs most frequently and with the most dangerous consequences.

Several careful surveys made over the past two decades have established that practically all aviators have experienced some form of disorientation at least once in their flying careers, and many have known several incidents. What this means is that nearly all pilots, at some time or another, formulate an incorrect mental picture of where they and their aircraft are in relation to the ground. Just how dangerous this can be is shown by the accident statistics.

Approximately half the world's aircraft accidents are attributed to pilot error. How many of these are directly due to pilot disorientation is not easy to determine, since the principal witnesses are often beyond the reach of questions. Considering only those accidents in which some positive evidence of disorientation existed, American investigators concluded that 14 per cent of all flying accidents in the US Air Force could be attributed to this cause.[1] It was also found that almost 100 per cent of the pilots interviewed had experienced at least one episode, and some had had up to twenty experiences of disorientation. Analysis of aircraft accidents in the Royal Air Force over a three-year period also revealed that disorientation or vertigo was the major cause of 14 per cent of all fatal crashes.[2] However, a more recent review of accidents in the USAF showed that disorientation was involved in more than 25 per cent of all accidents classified as being due to pilot error.[3]

These figures are now over ten years old, and there is a scarcity of more up-to-date information, but since the intervening years have seen an enormous growth of aircraft types, particularly helicopters, there is no reason to suppose that these statistics are anything but a very conservative estimate of the present situation. Certainly current investigations in the US Navy suggest that disorientation vies with enemy action as a killer of helicopter pilots and their passengers during combat operations in South-East Asia.[4] Taken overall, therefore, these investigations make it quite clear that pilot disorientation can and does have fatal consequences.

What are the basic causes of disorientation? In very general terms, we can classify most kinds of spatial confusion under two broad headings: those due to *false sensation*, and those due to *misperception*. Since these two categories depend on the distinction between sensation and perception, it will be helpful to illustrate their different functions by using an analogy. Imagine a general and his staff officers conducting a military campaign. Their head-quarters are situated several miles from the action, and their only contact with the fighting troops is through messengers who bring up-to-date intelligence from the front line. On the basis of this incoming information, the general and his staff modify their plans and issue new battle orders accordingly. In this situation – leaving aside the possible incompetence of the general – inappropriate orders could be issued for one of two reasons: either because the intelligence brought by the messengers was faulty, or because the general and his staff made an incorrect assessment of what was in fact accurate information. In a similar way, our mental picture of the outside world can be in error either because our senses – equivalent to the messengers – transmit information that does not correspond to the true state of affairs, or that the brain – analogous to the general and his staff – receives accurate information but places the wrong interpretation on it. In the former situation, therefore, our senses are at fault, while in the latter, it is a case of the brain coming to the wrong conclusions from the right information.

Thus, the category of *false sensation* embraces all those episodes of disorientation in which mental confusion or misjudgement on the part of the pilot results from inaccurate or inappropriate sensory information. The principal offenders in this type of disorientation are, as ever, the vestibular receptors – the semicircular canals and otoliths. As I mentioned in the introductory section, our organs of balance are specifically designed for a self-propelled terrestrial animal, and they were not intended to cope with the unusual and prolonged forces encountered in three-dimensional flight which stress them beyond their capabilities to function accurately, and so cause them to signal erroneous information concerning the position and motion of the body. Since, in our natural environment, these receptors are perfectly reliable within their design limits, the brain understandably accepts this false information at its face value as reflecting reality. In other words, the brain processes this information in a manner which under normal circumstances would be perfectly adequate. Here, then, we have false sensation, but unimpaired perception; that is, the mental 'staffwork' is functioning normally but on inaccurate intelligence.

In the second category, *misperception*, the situation is reversed: the sensory messages are faithful to reality, but the brain misinterprets or ignores them. This type of disorientation is mostly of visual origin, and includes such things as misjudging height or depth cues, confusing ground lights with stars at night, using a sloping cloudbank as a datum for the horizontal, and so on. These constitute true cases of 'pilot error' – unlike the false sensation type of disorientation where the source of error lies outside the pilot's control; namely, in the earthbound design of his spatial senses.

In the remainder of this chapter, we shall be considering selected instances of these two basic forms of disorientation. Examples of the false sensation type of disorientation will be separated into two groups: those stemming from inadequate functioning of the semicircular canals, and those arising from the otoliths.

Disorientation arising from false semicircular canal sensations

It will be remembered that the canals function as angular speedometers: they tell the brain how fast and in what direction the head is being turned. Consequently, all the various kind of disorientation that stem from the canals are concerned with mental confusion about rolling or turning movements of the aircraft. Perhaps the simplest, and certainly the most common kinds of disorientation is the condition that pilots have labelled the 'leans'. Subjectively, this is the erroneous sensation that the body (and hence the aircraft to which it is attached) is tilted away from the vertical. It gets its name from the fact that pilots tend to compensate for this illusory feeling of tilt by leaning in the opposite direction.

The semicircular canals, like all other sense organs, have a lower limit to their sensitivity. That is, below a certain degree of angular acceleration, the cupula is not deflected and so fails to record the turning movement. This particular level is termed the *threshold of perception* (to be really precise, the threshold is that level of stimulus magnitude at which a turning movement is detected on 50 per cent of the occasions it is presented). The basic cause of the leans is that the canals fail to register certain rolling movements of the aircraft in flight because they are below this threshold value. A typical situation in which the leans might appear is as follows: during the course of straight and level flight the aircraft is allowed to roll very slowly, say to the left, at a rate of angular acceleration which is below threshold. Subsequently it is rolled in the opposite direction at a rate which can be detected by the canals. If the second of these two rolls (to the right) had been sufficient to return the aircraft to straight and level flight, the pilot, because he failed to notice the first roll to the left, is likely to feel that he is tilted to the right (in the direction of the second, perceptible roll). In actual fact, of course, he will be upright; but the illusory feeling of tilt is so compelling that to compensate for it he leans his body to the left. The sensation of tilt associated with the leans is often extremely difficult to shake off, even when the flight instruments – in which the pilot has been taught to believe implicitly – inform him quite clearly that he is really flying straight and level.

The same tilting illusion can, of course, be created by a reversal of these conditions. In turbulence, for instance, the aircraft may roll rapidly to the right and then recover slowly to the left. But the pilot only perceives the initial displacement, not the recovery which occurs at a rate below the canal threshold. As a result, he feels that he is tilted to the right (this time in the direction of the first roll), and leans to the left to compensate. In this condition, he feels that he himself is upright, but that the aircraft is flying along with its right wing down – even though his instruments will tell him otherwise. This disturbing sensation may either die away slowly of its own accord, or it can be dispelled suddenly by an improvement in visual conditions that allows him a clear view of the horizon.

Another positional illusion related to the leans occurs when the rolling acceleration produced by banking an aircraft into a turn is below the threshold of perception of the canals. In this case, the pilot is not aware of the full extent of the roll, and so underestimates the angle of bank. This causes him to overcorrect when he attempts to reestablish straight and level flight. Because the amount of roll he applies to return the aircraft to straight flight is then too much, the aircraft ends up in a banked turn in the opposite direction.

It must be stressed that the leans, like other forms of pilot disorientation, will occur most readily in circumstances where the external visual cues, of which the most important is the horizon, are obscured by cloud, haze, or darkness. Compared with other types of disorientation, the leans, by itself, is not especially dangerous. But the nagging feeling that something is not quite right can impose an additional mental strain on the pilot and so indirectly could impair both his alertness and his flying performance.

Another form of disorientation, this time resulting from the failure of the canals to signal both the presence and the direction of aircraft turning motions correctly, is called the 'graveyard spin'. As the name implies, it often has far more serious consequences than the 'leans'.

The spin is a very dangerous manoeuvre that can be initiated, deliberately or otherwise, by flying the aircraft below its stalling speed – the speed below which there is insufficient airflow over the wings to maintain lift. If the pilot fails to take appropriate recovery action (put the nose down to increase speed), the aircraft is liable to enter a spin in which it falls out of the sky like a sycamore leaf. During the spin, which begins slowly and then speeds up to a constant rate, there is an extremely rapid rate of descent but no forward flying speed. Recovery, which is repeatedly practised by all trainee pilots, is achieved by applying full opposite rudder to check the rate of spin, and then pushing the nose hard down to gain flying speed. Once the spin ceases, the rudder is neutralized and the aircraft is flown out of the ensuing dive.

We can describe the sensations associated with the 'graveyard spin' as follows: the pilot has either unwittingly, or as a routine training exercise, allowed his aircraft to get into a spin, say to the left. As the spin continues, getting smoother and 'tighter' all the time, the pilot's sensation of turning probably diminishes – although not to the extent that he is unaware of the spin. Now he decides to recover from the spin; that is, he applies full right rudder and pushes the control column forward. Quite suddenly, the spin ceases and the aircraft is actually in a steep dive. But at this moment, the pilot has the very strong sensation that he has entered a spin in the opposite direction, namely to the right. In other words, when the real spin to the left stops, the pilot has the illusion that he is spinning to the right. So what does he do? He takes the appropriate recovery action for a spin to the right which, unfortunately, is often all that is required to reinstate the original spin to the left. In the meantime, since the aircraft is now dropping like a stone, the pilot has run out of sky and no longer has time to take corrective action. Even if he does not actually reinstate the original spin, the time lost in mental confusion could, by itself, prove fatal owing to the very fast rate of descent.

To understand how this very dangerous illusion occurs we need to re-examine the mechanics of the semicircular canals first described in Chapter 1. The cupula – the flap whose deflection signals the movement of the fluid inside the canal – behaves mechanically rather like one of the swing doors at the entrance to a 'Western' saloon. On being pushed, the saloon door tends to resist the deflecting force because of its sprung hinge; and, on being released, it returns *by itself* to the closed position. Although the cupula does not open and shut like the saloon door, because the curvature of the canal wall in its vicinity prevents any leakage of fluid from one side to the other, it obeys the same mechanical principles. Instead of the push of the cowboy's hand, the cupula responds to the push of the fluid within the canal, and this push is initiated by an angular acceleration or deceleration of the head. Now, we said earlier that the saloon door returns to its closed position under its own power once the push has been removed, and this is exactly what happens to the cupula once the 'push' of the angular acceleration (or deceleration) ceases: it moves back to its resting position, quickly at first and then more and more slowly.

This self-returning action of the cupula creates no problems during natural, active movements when the initial acceleration of the head is followed almost immediately by an equal and opposite deceleration – after all, the head can turn only so far about the neck. All that happens in these voluntary head movements is that the initial acceleration deflects the cupula by a given amount, and the subsequent deceleration, being equal and opposite to the first, merely brings it back to its resting position where it correctly signals 'no motion'. But the problems arise when the body is turned *passively* in such a way that a period of constant (or near constant) angular velocity intervenes between the initial acceleration and the final deceleration. During the period of constant rotation, there is no push on the cupula and it begins to move back to its neutral or resting position; as it does so, the sensation of rotation declines accordingly. This restoring action of the cupula means that the deceleration which terminates the rotation does not simply cancel out the initial deflection, instead – because the cupula has already returned part of the way to its resting position – it is pushed *beyond* the resting position in the opposite direction to the first deflection. As far as the brain is concerned, this is a state of affairs which is normally associated with turning in the opposite direction, and that is what we feel – an apparent rotation opposite to the initial spin while the body is actually not turning at all. We have probably all experienced this illusion when we played the childhood game of 'spinning on the spot': when we stop we feel dizzy and may fall over.

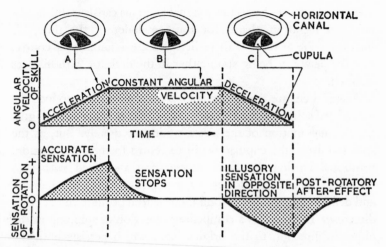

Figure 11   What happens within the cupula-endolymph system during 'graveyard spin'.

Figure 11 shows what happens within the cupula-endolymph system when a period of constant angular velocity intervenes between the initial acceleration and final deceleration. The situation described here is one where an individual is seated upright on a rotating chair, and is being spun around his vertical axis – thus stimulating the horizontal canals. However, the same general principles would apply irrespective of the axis of head rotation. There are three phases, A, B and C. What occurs within the horizontal canal during the initial acceleration is depicted in A: the endolymph lags behind the rotation of the canal walls, causing the cupula to deflect. Associated with this at a subjective level is an accurate sensation of the rate of turning of the head. But during the period of constant velocity that follows, the cupula returns to its neutral upright position (see B), and as it does so, the sensation of rotation declines until the individual feels himself to be stopped – even though he is still actually turning. During the deceleration phase, the inertia of the endolymph deflects the cupula in the opposite direction (see C), creating a sensation of turning in a direction opposite to that in which the person is actually rotating. After the person has ceased turning, there is a declining after-effect of apparent rotation while the cupula again returns to its upright position. Thus, the only time that the individual receives an accurate signal from his canals is during the initial acceleration phase; for the remainder of the time, his sensations are at odds with reality. We are assuming, of course, that the person is being spun either in the dark, or with his eyes covered.

These, then, are the events within the canals that produce the 'graveyard spin'. During the early part of the spin the canals signal the turning motion of the aircraft fairly accurately. But, as the spin stabilizes, the cupulae begin to return to their 'no motion' positions. During the rapid deceleration associated with spin recovery, the canal fluid keeps on going (by virtue of its inertia), and deflects the cupulae beyond their neutral position in the other direction. The result is a compelling sensation of spinning in the opposite direction to the original spin which persists until the cupulae return again to their resting positions. The situation is also made worse by the fact that reflex eye-movements, automatically triggered by the deflection of the cupulae, produce an apparent rotation of objects in the visual world. These can combine with the non-visual sensations of spinning to produce pilot disorientation of such severity that the aircraft may crash even in clear daylight conditions. As with most of these instances of disorientation, novices are more likely to be deceived than experienced pilots; but even the latter are not immune.

Another type of disorientation, also related to the failure of the canals to sense constant angular velocity, is the *Coriolis illusion*. The mechanics of the Coriolis vestibular reaction have already been discussed in the two previous chapters, so we need not elaborate on them further except to remind the reader that these illusory sensations occur whenever turning motions of the head are superimposed upon passive rotation of the body. Only when these turning motions are executed in the plane of body rotation do these reactions *not* occur.

The Coriolis illusion commonly arises when the pilot moves his head sharply during a long-established turning or circling manoeuvre. He may move his head to check for other aircraft in the vicinity, to scan his instrument panel, or to change a radio frequency; but whatever the purpose of the movement, it will result in an illusory sensation of aircraft roll so long as the head turn is not executed within the plane of the aircraft turn. The exact nature of this illusory roll will depend on the direction of the head movement and the aircraft turn; but the false sensation will always be in a different plane to that in which the aircraft is turning. The extreme danger of this form of mental confusion is partly due to its overwhelming quality, and partly to the fact that it often occurs quite close to the ground: for example, while the aircraft is 'letting down', or being held in a constant-rate turn over a crowded airfield prior to landing. In trying to correct for an imagined danger, the pilot may place his aircraft in real danger from which recovery is impossible. The following accounts from American navy pilots who survived their experiences of the Coriolis illusion should serve to underline its dangers, and also help dispel any feelings of clinical detachment created by the rather matter-of-fact description above. Although these personal statements abound with technical terms and flyers' jargon, no attempt has been made to edit them because to do so would be to lose some of the terrifying immediacy of these experiences.

While in the procedure turn (at 2,500 ft), the rubber band holding my let-down chart to the knee board broke, and down went the chart to the cockpit deck. I reached down to pick it up and my next look at the instruments brought a chill of horror. The needle was against the left peg, the gyro horizon was showing an eight ball, and the altimeter was plummeting downward. I felt as though I was in a right bank and pulling g.

The flight was normal until I ran into the vertigo problem. I had been airborne about three-quarters of an hour. I attempted to dial in a frequency on my radio while I was in a turn. As I did my bank steepened and my gyro horizon tumbled. When I looked up from the radio, I was disoriented. I was at 35,000 ft at the time. I tried to orient myself by visual means and by instruments. There were several thin layers of cloud in the area at the time and I was zooming in and out of them. One moment I'd be descending rapidly and the next I'd be climbing. I was losing altitude as a result, and I made up my mind that I'd eject if I went below 20,000 ft. As I passed through this altitude and still was not oriented, I ejected. I had a normal ejection and a safe landing.

If that incident failed to raise empathic goose-pimples, consider the following episode, recounted by two American investigators, involving the severe disorientation of an experienced naval aviator:

... a senior flight instructor in the torpedo squadron took his flight on a night tactics hop in TBF/M type planes. Weather was contact [i.e. good visibility]. Take-off and rendezvous were normal. Captain M made frequent rapid turning movements of his head from side-to-side to see that his flight was intact. Vertigo suddenly developed. He had a feeling that his plane was peeling off in a steep left-hand dive, and had a strong desire to use right rudder and right aileron, but saw by his instruments that he was flying straight and level. 'It took all the guts I had to believe those instruments,' he said, 'but I knew they were right and my sensations were wrong.'

Captain M led his students on the one-hour flight, which included banks, turns and dives, entirely on instruments. Throughout the flight he had the sensation that his plane was falling off in a left-hand dive. He approached the landing field and came into the groove still on instruments. Just before landing he shifted to contact (he looked out ahead) and found himself to be at a 45° angle, inclined upward to starboard, and appeared to oscillate. He landed port wing and port wheel down, started to ground loop, but corrected it. Vertigo continued for about fifteen minutes after he was on the ground.

Captain M stated that no combat experience had frightened him as had this attack of vertigo. He felt helpless and had a cold fear of impending doom. He had a strong tendency to tighten up and freeze at the controls.[5]

Two things are remarkable about this episode: first, it happened to a very experienced pilot; second, it persisted for so long after the initiating circumstances (the head motions made at the beginning of the flight) had passed. Also of great interest is the way Captain M described his struggle to believe his instruments, a source of information which his long training and experience told him must be true. If this credibility problem was so acute for Captain M, imagine what it must be like for someone with far less flying experience. All our instincts tell us to accept our sensations as being correct. To combat this often overwhelming urge, there is only the knowledge that these sensory impressions can sometimes play us false – a flimsy thing to be pitted against a lifetime of belief. Small wonder, therefore, that misleading sensations can dominate consciousness in the face of training, flying experience, and even the near certain knowledge to be gained from the cockpit instruments that the information conveyed by our senses does not correspond with reality.

Disorientation arising from false otolith sensations

Like the canals, the otoliths also give rise to false sensations of position and motion in flight. In this case, however, the disorientation occurs because the otoliths – the body's *linear* accelerometers – cannot distinguish between the gravitational force and other forces created by the aircraft motion. These superimposed aircraft forces can interact with the gravitational force in at least three different ways: they can alter the *apparent direction* of the gravitational force so that it no longer appears to be acting vertically; or they can act in the same direction to either increase or decrease the *apparent strength* of the gravitational force.

Perhaps the most dangerous of these otolith-induced forms of disorientation is the so-called *oculogravic illusion*. It occurs most commonly in the following situation: a pilot flying a high-performance jet aircraft is making a landing approach in poor weather conditions. As he nears the touchdown point, he decides (or is ordered) to abort the landing and 'go round again' – that is, to go round the airfield circuit and make another approach and landing. So, he puts on power preparatory to climbing to circuit height. The increased thrust of the jets causes the aircraft to accelerate, and, at the same time, produces an inertial force which pushes the pilot back against his seat. Almost immediately after he feels this inertial force, he has a very strong sensation that the aircraft has adopted a nose-up attitude. Not only does he 'feel' this lifting of the nose, he also sees it. His instinctive reaction is to push the nose down to avoid a stall. But that way disaster lies because in fact he is still flying level with the ground – the nose-up attitude was an illusion. Any attempt to correct for these false sensations is likely to drive the aircraft straight into the ground, and this, indeed, does happen on all too many occasions. Since this illusion can happen whenever the aircraft's forward speed is suddenly increased, it can also occur on take-off, especially at night or over unlighted terrain when there is inadequate external visual reference.

We can explain what causes this illusion with the help of the diagram in Figure 12. When the aircraft accelerates, the inertial force so created (the one that pushes the pilot back into his seat) combines with vertically-acting gravitational force to produce a *resultant force* running obliquely through the pilot's head from front to back. Now the problem is this: on earth, when we walk or stand with our feet planted firmly on the ground, the directions of 'up' and 'down' are parallel to the gravitational force, and the brain, quite rightly in these natural circumstances, has come to rely upon the otoliths as reliable indicators of the vertical. But, in flight, our primitive otoliths are unable to distinguish between the normal gravitational force and the resultant force produced by the vehicle. So when the brain receives the otolith signals stimulated by the non-vertical resultant force, it wrongly assumes that this force is, in fact, vertical, and that the body is tilted backwards. This is quite a reasonable assumption, since the otolith signal to the pilot's brain in the accelerating aircraft is very nearly the same as the one that would be produced on earth by sitting in a chair that is tilted backwards. The net result is that the pilot actually perceives himself to be tilted backwards, and since he is firmly attached to the aircraft, this must mean that the aircraft has adopted a nose-up attitude. This illusion is further enhanced by the fact that reflex nervous connections between the otoliths and the muscles which move the eyes cause the eyeballs to rotate in such a way that the visual scene moves upward by an extent which

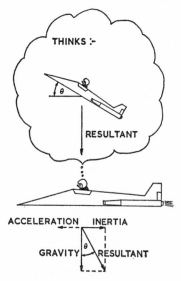

Figure 12   The oculogravic illusion in flight.

is matched to the feeling of backward tilt: it is this additional, visual effect which gives it the name of oculogravic illusion. The same illusion does not occur during the course of natural, self-propelled movements because when we walk, run or jump, the linear accelerations produced by our movements are never of sufficient magnitude or duration to disturb our perception of the vertical.

The oculogravic illusion is an example of what happens when the forces involved in passive, vehicular motion alter the apparent *direction* of the gravitational force (we say 'apparent direction' because the g-force does not actually alter direction, it only appears so the human gravity senses). Now we turn to instances of disorientation in which the apparent strength of the gravitational force is altered, but its direction remains the same. On earth we are accustomed to a gravitational force of 1 g (see Chapter 2), but in flight this value may apparently be increased or decreased as the result of vertical movements of the aircraft. In space, of course, this force is entirely absent; while on the moon's surface the pull of gravity is approximately one-sixth the value we experience on earth.

One such form of disorientation, termed the *elevator illusion*, can occur during sudden upward movements of the aircraft – like those experienced when the aircraft hits an 'updraught' in cloud or over certain kinds of terrain. The rapid rise of the aircraft causes the otoliths to drive the eyes in a downward direction (through the action of the so-called *vestibulo-ocular reflexes*) to compensate for the upward motion of the body. The effective stimulus is the increase of the downward force acting on the otolith blob, and the result is that the pilot experiences a visual illusion in which objects that are fixed relative to him – like the instrument panel and the nose of the aircraft – appear to lurch upwards. He may then interpret this upward motion as signifying a change in the aircraft's attitude from straight and level to a nose-up, climbing position. If this illusion occurs near the ground it could have the same serious consequences as the oculogravic illusion, although the evidence suggests that it is rarely the cause of aircraft accidents.

A complementary illusion, sometimes called the *oculoagravic illusion*, can occur when the aircraft makes a sudden downward movement. In this case the gravitational force acting on the otolith blobs is temporarily reduced, and this activates the vestibulo-ocular reflex driving the eyes upwards. The effect, opposite to that of the elevator illusion, is to produce an apparent sinking motion of the fixed objects in the visual field. As a result the pilot may feel that his aircraft has adopted a nose-down, diving attitude. Both the elevator and the oculoagravic illusions are effectively suppressed in good weather when there is a clear horizon, but they can prove troublesome in poor visibility. At the very least they contribute to the pilot's mental stress.

It was mentioned in the previous chapter that when the g-force is completely absent, as in space flight, cosmonauts and astronauts have experienced strong feelings of being upside-down. This *inversion illusion* can, in some cases, persist until the space traveller encounters the forces associated with re-entry into the earth's atmosphere. Some cosmonauts have also reported that they can suppress, and sometimes even eliminate, this sensation of being upside-down by flexing their leg muscles, or by pressing with their feet against a solid surface. This suggests that position senses in the muscles, tendons and joints, as well as the vestibular receptors, are involved in producing this illusion. The really puzzling thing about this phenomenon is why the absence of gravity should make space travellers feel inverted – a positive orientation – rather than simply being unaware of the direction of the vertical.

The inversion illusion has been studied fairly systematically within the earth's atmosphere using the thirty-second periods of weightlessness created by parabolic flight manoeuvres in conventional aircraft like a specially modified Boeing 707. In one experiment, carried out by investigators from the Naval Aerospace Medical Institute, two normal subjects and three with non-functioning organs of balance were exposed to a series of parabolic flight manoeuvres, twenty in all over a period of two days. All the subjects were physically restrained in an upright position. Both normal individuals reported a sudden reversal of head-up to head-down on entering the zero-gravity phase of the manoeuvre, and equally sudden restoration of the upright during the pull-out phase. However, none of the labyrinthine-defective subjects experienced the illusion on any occasion. This clearly implicates the vestibular system as the essential factor in creating the upside-down illusion, but aside from this and the knowledge that other bodily position senses can influence it, the origins of the inversion illusion remain a mystery.

Another mystery, although one that scientists are more happy to accept, is the apparent lack of disorientation or locomotion problems in the Apollo astronauts who have walked on the lunar surface. Once they acquired a gait suitable for the reduced-gravity conditions, they moved about the moon's surface with ease and evident enjoyment. Yet prior to the first moon-landing, a number of scientists had advised the NASA Manned Spacecraft Center that astronauts might experience a number of very disturbing effects in one-sixth gravity. In one case it was predicted – on valid theoretical grounds – that the astronauts would feel some or all of the following disturbances: they would feel upside-down due to the reduced gravity, but at the same time they would also feel that they were falling in the direction of their feet – in other words, it would be rather like walking on the ceiling and falling upwards at the same time. Furthermore, because of the unusual feedback signals from the otoliths when the head is tilted in reduced gravity, they would be likely to fall over whenever their heads deviated from the upright position. In the event, of course, none of these things happened. But from what was known beforehand of the effects of reduced gravity, each one of these predictions was not entirely unreasonable, although other scientists were far from unanimous in supporting them. Clearly the experts still have a lot to learn about the way our spatial senses respond to conditions of altered gravity, and since it is extremely difficult to reproduce these conditions on earth, we shall have to rely on further manned space flights to provide the facts for us.

Disorientation arising from misperception

These are the instances of pilot disorientation that result from a failure of perception rather than of sensory function. As we said earlier, they arise because the brain misinterprets or misclassifies perfectly accurate information, usually provided by the visual sense. Although the error occurs in the human brain, its origin lies in the alien nature of the aerial environment where earth-based expectations of what a particular stimulus signifies are often incorrect.

A very common kind of visual disorientation occurs during night-flying when a pilot confuses lights on the ground for those of another aircraft. A fairly typical example is the case of the American naval pilot who saw a green and a red light on a bridge while flying at 1,500 ft. He mistook them for the lights of another aircraft and dived in order to avoid them. He failed to realize their true identity until it was too late to recover from the dive. Fortunately, he hit the ground in a level attitude and slid to a stop unhurt, but his aircraft was a write-off.

The illusion is especially prevalent in formation flying at night. Quite frequently a pilot will attempt to 'join up' or 'formate on' a star or a light he sees on the ground. Here is an example: 'After take-off on a night formation hop, I followed a distant light on the ground thinking it was the plane ahead of me. My feelings were normal, and I flew the plane normally. I finally realized it was not another plane and looked about for the actual plane which I found just ahead of me.'[6]

There are numerous stories of pilots who confuse geometric patterns of lights on the ground – such as the lights on a train, or a seaside pier – with runway and approach lights. Most of these episodes get reported, but some go unrecorded because the pilots fail to notice their mistake in time. This is one reason why the statistics concerning the incidence of disorientation almost always underestimate the true situation.

Visual misperception is not confined to the hours of darkness. A very common error in pilots flying under conditions of limited visibility is to accept a sloping cloudbank as an indication of the horizontal. As a result, they align their wings with the cloud deck and thus fly in an unbalanced attitude, a situation that easily leads to a more serious case of disorientation. Here is an example of how using a false horizon can lead to near-disaster:

After leaving the British coast and flying in good visibility towards the lighthouse of Cap Gris-Nez, the pilot reduced the engine power setting to keep below the clouds. The aircraft gradually lost altitude until the trailing [radio] antenna struck the water. The crew did not realize that the angle of incidence was greater than before throttling back and, therefore, viewed the lighthouse below its fictitious horizon. The light [also] gave the pilots a wrong sensation of their height . . .[7]

This illustrates how different visual cues – the lighthouse and the combination of a grey cloud ceiling gradually merging into the grey of the true horizon – can interact to create a very compelling yet false perception of the aircraft's position with respect to the ground. Faced with indistinct or ambiguous visual cues, pilots respond like people staring at a Rorschach inkblot test: they project into the hazy outlines of the stimulus the things they want to see. The more they need to see something – like runway lights, or a certain geographical feature – the more likely they are to see it. We will be discussing this mental process further in Chapter 6 in relation to certain motorway accidents.

Illusions of relative motion are another common form of daylight disorientation. These often occur during formation flying where each aircraft (apart from the formation leader's) keeps station by remaining at a fixed distance from his neighbour. As in the incident described below, the likelihood of confusion can be aggravated by difficult visual conditions; in this case, bright sunlight in the pilot's eyes:

On a join-up with another plane from a lower altitude I could not see the details of his plane since the sun was partly blinding me and all I could see was his silhouette in a three-quarter view. He seemed to be going away from me and his plane seemed to be getting smaller. All of a sudden I saw that he was coming towards me very fast in another attitude altogether different and I slid under him at the last moment, missing him by inches.[8]

Finally, there is a form of flight disturbance which cannot easily be classified as either false sensation or misperception. This is the condition known generally as *fascination*, and more specifically as *target hypnosis*. Here there is both accurate sensory functioning and accurate perception, but the pilot simply fails to act upon what he perceives. In other words, the fault lies not so much on the input side, but on the output or response side of the system. A first-hand example will serve to illustrate the nature of this experience:

On a gunnery hop, I became fascinated with the tow [target] on one of my overhead runs. I concentrated hard on trying to hit the target and soon lost all sense of anything else. I noticed the sleeve getting bigger and bigger but it didn't soak in for a long time. It was sort of like a semi-coma. My flying of the plane was completely automatic, so much so that I don't remember what I did on the run. Finally it dawned on me I was getting too close to the tow and I ceased firing.[9]

Two American investigators, Dr Clark and Dr Graybiel,[10] have defined 'fascination' as follows: 'a condition in which the pilot fails to respond adequately to a clearly defined stimulus-situation in spite of the fact that all the necessary cues are present for a proper response, and the correct procedure is well known to him'. They distinguish two types of fascination. Type A is perceptual in nature; the pilot concentrates so hard on one aspect of the task that he fails to notice other, equally important aspects which he later recalls were present at the time. Type B fascination includes the target hypnosis example, given above, where the pilot perceives all the significant aspects of the situation but fails to respond properly, or quickly enough.

What can be done to cut down these various episodes of pilot disorientation? Built as we are, we cannot hope to prevent them: all we can do is minimize their chances of occurring. To date, the most powerful countermeasure at our disposal is training and experience. The trainee pilot must be taught that his senses are not to be trusted in flight. He must experience at first hand the situations in which disorientation is likely to occur, and he must learn that he is especially vulnerable to sensory deception when the visibility is poor, and when he is anxious, tired or under pressure. But, above all, he must know instinctively that the only true indicator of the aircraft's attitude is the information displayed on the cockpit instrument panel.

4 Deceptions on the Ground: The 'Mental Speedometer'

A motorist has access to two kinds of speed information. He can obtain an objective and reasonably reliable indication of the vehicle's speed by consulting the speedometer on the dashboard in front of him, or he can attempt to judge the vehicle's speed on the basis of his sensory impressions. These subjective impressions will be of many different kinds: the 'seat of the pants' sensations associated with changes in speed and direction, the note of the engine, the gear in use, the pressure of the foot upon the accelerator pedal, but most of all he will judge his speed from what he *sees* of the outside world. Since seen motion is the primary source of information upon which the 'mental speedometer' operates, it would be helpful to begin this chapter by considering just what it is the driver sees and how these visual impressions form the basis of his speed judgements.

As we look ahead from the front seat of a moving vehicle, fixed objects in the field of view move relative to us. If this pattern of moving images is examined carefully, it can be seen that the direction of flow radiates outwards from a stationary focal point – called the 'expansion point' – whose location is determined by the direction of the vehicle. If the vehicle is proceeding in a straight line, then the expansion point will lie straight ahead. If we should now turn round and look out of the rear window, we can see an equivalent pattern of motion but in reverse. Instead of the different visual elements appearing to radiate outwards from an 'expansion point', as they do in the forward direction, the elements in the rear field of view move inwards toward a central 'contraction point'. The expansion and contraction points are like two opposing poles on the surface of an imaginary sphere with the observer's head at its centre. As the observer travels forward looking towards the direction in which he is moving, elements in the visual field appear to stream around the surface of this sphere. Since our forward vision only extends through an arc of approximately 180°, objects disappear out of the 'corner of the eye'; but if we possessed all-round vision we could, of course, see these elements stream inwards towards the contraction point in the rear.

The important thing about this 'streaming' of the visual world as we move is that the apparent velocity of the various objects in the field of view obeys the rules of perspective. The more distant the object, the slower it appears to move relative to the total flow pattern. In other words, there is a gradient of velocity ranging from zero at the front expansion point, increasing to a maximum on either side of the observer, and decreasing again to zero at the rear contraction point. In short, this velocity gradient is determined by the gradient of linear perspective. Both the direction and the velocity of elements in this flow pattern have been shown

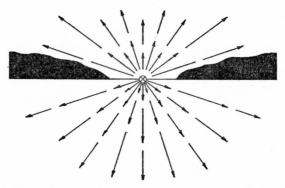

Figure 13 The 'motion perspective' of elements in the visual field as seen by an observer in a vehicle which is moving forward in a straight line. The 'expansion point' is marked with an X on the horizon.

diagrammatically in Figure 13. Here, the length of each arrow represents the relative velocity of the element in the visual field, and its direction of flow is shown by where the arrow is pointing. It has also been assumed that there is a low cloudbase so that we can observe the flow upwards and sideways from the expansion point, as well as the flow downwards and outwards over the ground.

These velocity and direction gradients – the phenomenon is

termed *motion perspective*[1] – are invariably present whenever we travel over the ground with our eyes open, and taken as a whole they represent the single most important source of information concerning our own movement. When driving a car, the expansion point is a precise indication of where we are going and gives us a point of aim; but, in the present context, our main interest in motion perspective is that it provides the driver with velocity information. Although he may not be consciously aware of motion perspective his brain employs it in building internal models of where the body is in relation to the outside world, and also where it will be a few seconds hence.

Now let us briefly consider how the eyes communicate this velocity information to the brain. Imagine for a moment that you are driving along a straight road through a flat, featureless terrain, and up ahead to one side of the road there is a single tree – the one distinct element in the visual field. As we move towards this tree, its image on the retina (the photosensitive surface at the back of the eye) will grow larger, and will also shift its position according to the principles of motion perspective, finally disappearing at its maximum velocity over the edge of the receptive surface as you pass it. As the images of the tree and its component elements move over the retina, they excite a number of the individual receptor units dotted over its surface like the marble chips in a mosaic.

From physiological studies in which electrical recordings have been made from single cells in the eyes of rabbits and the brain of cats, we know that the receptor units on the retina are direction-specific.[2] That is, they only respond when images pass over them in a particular direction, and this preferred direction is different for different units. Thus, the direction of moving objects in the visual field is signalled by the brain registering *which* of the retinal receptor units are active. Velocity information, on the other hand, is communicated by the *rate* at which these receptors fire off nerve impulses. In general, the faster the target motion, the greater will be the rate of firing of the receptors responding to that particular direction of image-motion. This, very simply, is how the eye translates or encodes the motion of images falling on it from the outside world into neural impulses which ultimately form the basis for our subjective impressions of seen motion. Exactly how the brain decodes these nerve messages and converts them into conscious sensations remains a mystery, but at least we know a little about the encoding process, and I shall return to it later in the chapter.

As I stated at the beginning, the driver can use two kinds of velocity information – the display on the vehicle's speedometer or subjective impressions from the 'mental speedometer' – but which of these two kinds of speed information does he use most often? Research carried out at the British Road Research Laboratory indicates that when drivers speed up or slow down, they tend more often than not to rely upon their subjective impressions of vehicle speed rather than upon the objective information provided on the dashboard.[3] In other words, when a driver enters or leaves a motorway, or a restricted speed zone, he is more likely to use his 'mental' speedometer than the one fitted by the vehicle manufacturer. That being the case, we are left with the important question: just how accurate is this mental speedometer?

Well, as the title of this chapter suggests, the short answer is 'not very'. Our concern here will be with the conditions that promote inaccurate estimates of speed, and with the underlying mechanisms responsible for these dangerous errors. Although there have been many studies dealing with this problem of speed estimation, I have chosen to report two pieces of research involving car driving which illustrate both the magnitude of the errors and how they arise under everyday circumstances.

The first study is concerned with the way slowing down or speeding up systematically distorts our subjective impressions of the vehicle's altered speed, and was carried out by Dr G. Denton of the Road Research Laboratory.[4] Eight members of the general public, four men and four women all with more than five years' driving experience, were used as the experimental subjects. The tests were carried out on a mile-long straight track which was flat and featureless. The car's speedometer was only visible to the investigator sitting on the back seat. In the first part of the experiment, the subjects accelerated until they reached one of five initial test speeds – they were given auditory signals to help them find this speed without a speedometer. As soon as they were settled at the correct speed, the investigator told them to reduce their speed until it felt like half as fast as the speed they were going. At no point in the experiment were the subjects given any indication of how well or how badly they were doing. Each initial speed was presented six times to each subject on the first occasion, and six weeks later the same subjects made a further three attempts at each speed. The mean results for the first part of the experiment are shown below.

TABLE 4   MEAN RESULTS FOR HALVING INITIAL SPEEDS
         IN MILES PER HOUR

Initial test speeds	20	30	40	50	60
Required speed	(10)	(15)	(20)	(25)	(30)
Speed after change	13·8	21·1	27·3	32·9	38·3
Percentage error	38%	40%	37%	32%	28%

From these results, it can be seen that on all the five initial speeds the driver-subjects slowed to a rate that was faster than the required half-speed. In other words, they consistently under-estimated their true speed, thinking that they were going slower than they really were. What do these findings mean in practical terms?

Consider the case of a driver cruising at around 60 mph on a motorway. Suppose he wishes to leave the motorway at a speed of around 30 mph along the exit road. If he judges this speed reduction on the basis of subjective impressions (and research indicates that he probably will), then he is likely to leave the motorway at around 40 mph, believing it to be 30 mph. In other words, if the present results are typical, he is liable to underestimate his exit speed by about one-third of its actual value! And, as we shall see later, when this reduction in speed has been preceded by a prolonged period driving at steady high speed, as is usually the case on a motorway, this tendency to underestimate the true exit speed becomes even more pronounced as the result of speed adaptation.

The second part of the experiment employed the same basic procedure as the first, except in this case different initial test speeds were used, and, instead of halving their speed, the subjects were instructed to double it. The results for doubling initial speeds are shown in Table 5.

Here the picture is quite different from the halving situation. In the first place, there was a general tendency for drivers to accelerate up to a rate which was less than the required doubled speed.

In other words, the direction of error was opposite to that found in slowing down. In speeding up, the tendency is to think that you are going faster than you really are; an overestimate of true speed. The second point of interest is that the size of this overestimate is systematically related to the initial speed. The smallest error occurred at an initial speed of 10 mph when the required increase was only 10 mph, and the largest error, 27 per cent, occurred at 30 mph when the required increase was three times as great.

TABLE 5   MEAN RESULTS FOR DOUBLING INITIAL SPEEDS
          IN MILES PER HOUR

Initial test speeds	10	15	20	25	30
Required speed	(20)	(30)	(40)	(50)	(60)
Speed after change	19·6	27·0	33·4	38·0	43·7
Percentage error	2%	10%	16%	24%	27%

Another experiment confirmed this finding.[5] In speeding up, the amount by which the driver overestimates his true speed is determined both by the speed held prior to the change and by the size of the change itself; that is, whether he was asked to double or quadruple his original speed. But in slowing down, the amount by which the driver underestimates his reduced speed is almost entirely a function of the size of the change demanded. It was three times greater on slowing down to a quarter of the initial speed than on slowing to a half. And these errors remained fairly consistent irrespective of the initial starting speed.

These findings suggest that drivers accelerating from access roads on to motorways will think that they are travelling faster than they really are; but when they decelerate to leave the motorway, they will judge their speed to be slower than it really is. Although the speed-up effects are potentially less dangerous than the slowing-down effects, both kinds of mental speedometer error have important practical implications for the design of access and exit roads leading to and from motorways.

At the present time we have no real understanding of why these errors of judgement occur. One possibility, although it does not constitute a real explanation, is that they reveal the influence of a general perceptual process known as *contrast*. This is the tendency for perceived differences between stimuli to appear greater than their real physical differences would warrant. A piece of grey paper surrounded by black paper seems lighter than the same grey surrounded by white paper. This is an example of *simultaneous contrast*. After the eye has been exposed to a bright stimulus, a darker stimulus will look unusually dark, and vice versa. Similarly an orange tastes sour after sugar, but sweet after lemon. These are instances of *successive contrast*, and a similar process may help us to understand the findings of the Denton studies.

We are all familiar with the fact that after travelling at a relatively high speed, a slower speed seems to be a snail's pace by contrast. Consequently, when we are instructed to halve our speed on the basis of subjective impression only, we are likely to choose a value which is faster than the true halved speed, since the latter would seem far too slow in comparison with our initial speed. Conversely, when we are told to double our speed, we are likely to end up at a rate which is less than twice our speed because the true doubled speed would seem far too fast in contrast to the original speed.

It is quite obvious that invoking the notion of contrast provides no real explanation of these judgement errors; all it does is to indicate that this is a general perceptual phenomenon common to other kinds of judgement as well. But whatever the explanation, one thing is fairly clear: unlike the car's speedometer, which once calibrated tends to give consistent readings, the calibration of the brain's speedometer is unstable, having quite a different 'scale' after slowing down than after speeding up. In both cases, however, it shifts in such a way as to magnify the difference between the old and the new speed. As a result, drivers aiming to achieve a specific fraction or multiple of their original speed end up by selecting a speed somewhere *between* the initial and the desired speed.

Another difference between the objective and the subjective speedometer is in the nature of the scale itself. In the car's speedometer, the scale is likely to be linear: that is, the extent of the pointer movement between, say, 10 and 20 mph will be the same as that between 40 and 50 mph, or any equal interval between two speeds. But whatever the nature of the subjective scale, it is not linear. Equal increments in physical speed will not necessarily result in equal increments in subjective speed. Sensory or 'psychological' scales of stimulus magnitude do not generally work like that: their sensitivity varies according to what part of the scale is operating, and what kind of stimulus preceded the present experience – to name but two of the many factors which influence these judgements. Although relatively little research has been devoted to discovering the nature of the scale on the mental speedometer, there is enough evidence available to show that it is extremely complex; probably more so, in fact, than most other sensory scales.

While these aberrations of the mental speedometer would probably cause an engineer to despair, they nevertheless make good biological sense in regard to the activities we were designed for. But these, unfortunately, did not include handling vehicles capable of travelling at great speeds along straight roads. The human nervous system is essentially a change-detector. It is programmed to take notice of differences in our surroundings and to ignore the *status quo*. For all its enormous complexity, the human brain has only a limited capacity for handling information, and one way it conserves these finite resources is by assigning different levels of priority to different kinds of stimulation. Those sensory inputs which reflect changes in the environment, and hence convey important information, tend to receive a high priority, while those inputs that maintain a steady state for lengthy periods receive the lowest priority. This means that reactions to unchanging sources of stimulation become attenuated, so that our awareness of them diminishes. Think of the clothes you are wearing at this moment. Unless they are too tight or in some other way unusually demanding of attention, it takes a conscious effort to feel them. Yet they are in contact with the skin and so excite the various pressure receptors embedded there. We are not generally conscious of the pressure of our clothes because the receptors in the skin responsible for signalling this information respond to relatively unchanging conditions by reducing the rate at which messages are transmitted to the brain.

This built-in principle of reducing the 'gain' on constant inputs leaves brain capacity free for processing more changeable inputs that tell us something new about the outside world. It serves us well in our natural self-propelled state, but in a car, cruising at

70 mph down a motorway, this same principle of the nervous system works against rather than for our survival. Because, in these circumstances, our visual impressions of speed gradually become less, so that after a period of constant-speed travel 70 mph feels like something much slower. This is the phenomenon of *speed adaptation*. It is a particularly good example of how certain characteristics of the nervous system, normally extremely useful and highly adaptive, work against us when we adopt an alien mode of locomotion. It is one thing to attenuate the pressure sensations from our clothes, it is quite another to do the same for visual impressions of speed as we hurtle through space at a steady 70 mph. But that is exactly what happens, as we shall see from the study discussed below.

In the first experiment I described, the influence of speed adaptation was deliberately kept to a minimum. This was done by maintaining the initial test speed for only a few seconds prior to the speed change. But in the study carried out by Dr F. Schmidt and Dr J. Tiffin of Purdue University,[6] Indiana, the length of time for which subjects drove at a steady speed was varied systematically, and other factors like the initial speed and the extent of the speed change were held constant.

Ten volunteers with at least two years' driving experience acted as the driver-subjects. They drove a car over a fifty-mile stretch of four-lane, limited-access highway which had a speed limit of 70 mph. The car's regular speedometer was removed from the dashboard, and a special one was mounted in a small box and was held by the investigator who sat alongside the driver. It could be positioned so that only the experimenter could read it, or, when required, it could be placed so that the driver could read it as well. But this was only done so that the subject could maintain the initial speed accurately; it was not visible to him while he was making his speed estimates. After some practice, each subject made three speed estimates under three different conditions. In the first, he accelerated to 70 mph, held that speed for five seconds, and then slowed to what he judged to be 40 mph. In the second condition, he accelerated to 70 mph and held that speed for twenty miles (as measured by an odometer), after which he was instructed to slow down to what he judged to be 40 mph. The third condition was the same except that he travelled forty miles before slowing to an estimated 40 mph. The mean results are shown in Table 6.

TABLE 6 SUMMARY OF MEAN RESULTS IN THE SPEED
ADAPTATION STUDY

	Experimental condition	Actual speed estimated as 40 mph
1	After 5 seconds at 70 mph	44·5 mph
2	After 20 miles at 70 mph	50·5 mph
3	After 40 miles at 70 mph	53·4 mph

What do these results tell us? After only five seconds at 70 mph, the drivers slowed down, on average, to 44·5 mph and called it 40 mph. In other words, they thought they were going slower than they really were, underestimating their true speed by 11 per cent. Whether adaptation played much part in this error or whether it was simply a 'slow-down' effect like that demonstrated in the previous study is hard to tell. But there can be little doubt that adaptation was a major factor in the findings for the next two conditions.

After twenty miles at 70 mph, subjects judged a real speed of 50·5 mph to feel like 40 mph – an underestimate of 26 per cent. But after forty miles at 70 mph, this error of judgement had increased to 32 per cent, so that 53·4 mph felt like 40 mph. Just as in the previous experiment, the subjects, on reducing speed, judged that they were going slower than they really were; but the extent of the error in this case was largely determined by the length of time they had previously spent travelling at a steady 70 mph. Since speed adaptation is a time-dependent effect, it was evidently the prime determinant of the underestimates.

These findings pose an interesting question: if travelling at a steady 70 mph for forty miles causes us to scale down our sensations of speed so that a true 53 mph feels like 40 mph, what would happen if instead of slowing to 40 mph, we came to an immediate halt? Put in another way, how does speed adaptation affect the zero point on the mental speedometer? If confusing 53 mph for 40 mph is indicative of a systematic shift all the way down the subjective speed scale, then zero mph should feel like motion in the opposite direction. Does this really happen? The answer is 'yes, under certain circumstances'. It happens if one is relying solely on speed information from the image-retina system; that is, on the 'streaming' of images from stationary objects on either side of the road. If you want to experience this illusion for yourself the best way to do so is as follows: the next time you stop at a set of traffic lights after travelling at a fairly steady speed, keep looking forward in the same way that you were while moving and concentrate (without looking directly at them) on the stationary objects around you – the trees or houses on either side of the road and, if your car has a short bonnet like a Mini, on the road surface in front. On many occasions you will be able to notice that these stationary elements in the visual field, particularly at its periphery, appear to be 'streaming' in the opposite direction to that which is seen when you are moving. In other words, they appear to have motion in the forward direction. They do not actually appear to go anywhere, that is, they have no real displacement, but they are imbued with a clear forward velocity which slows down rapidly as you observe it. Sometimes I have found the effect of this illusion so strong that I have checked the handbrake to ensure that I was not slipping backwards – even when I was consciously aware of what was really happening!

This illusion (much beloved by experimental psychologists) is called the *visual after-effect of motion*, or VAM for short.[7] It is not restricted to the driving situation just described; it is part of a general family of illusions which occur after a structured surface has been in constant motion relative to the retina for a sufficient period of time. The after-effect of reversed motion is seen within the previously stimulated part of the visual field whenever the gaze is subsequently directed at a stationary surface. The apparent motion appears to be quite rapid at first and then decays, first quickly and then more slowly, until the illusory motion comes to a rather indeterminate stop.

One of the earliest reports of the VAM was made by a nineteenth-century scientist, who observed it accidentally while watching a lengthy cavalry parade pass by his window. He noticed that when he looked across to the houses on the opposite side of the street, they appeared to possess motion in the opposite direction to the cavalry parade. But it was a curious kind of 'ghostly' movement in which the houses possessed apparent velocity but did not actually move. The same effect has also been termed the 'waterfall illusion'

because, after watching a point on a waterfall, something stationary like the bank of the river or the bushes surrounding it seems
to be floating upwards in the opposite direction to the motion of
the waterfall. Within the psychological laboratory it also goes
under the name of the 'spiral after-effect', since a very powerful
after-effect of apparent motion can be induced by staring at the
centre of a rotating spiral, like that shown in Figure 14. If after
watching the spiral rotate for about thirty seconds or so, the
observer were to look at some stationary object – like somebody's
nose, for example – it would appear to expand or contract in a
dramatic fashion depending on whether the arms of the spiral
radiated outwards or inwards during actual rotation, the illusion
always being in the opposite direction to the inducing motion.

Figure 14   A logarithmic spiral of the kind used to induce the spiral
after-effect.

For many years the origins of this illusion remained a mystery.
Recently, however, we have begun to have a better understanding
of its underlying mechanisms, thanks largely to physiological
studies that have revealed the function of the various receptors
involved in the visual perception of motion. But from our present
point of interest we now appreciate that the processes involved in
the VAM operate on very similar principles to those underlying a
wide range of sensory phenomena, including speed adaptation in
motorway driving. In the remainder of this chapter I would like
to show how explanations derived largely from the laboratory can
help us to understand the inaccurate functioning of the mental
speedometer, particularly with regard to the effects of speed
adaptation.

In psychology, as in other sciences, there are many different levels of explanation. At a relatively simple level, we can say that such and such a phenomenon has properties in common with a wide range of different phenomena, and so is likely to be governed by the same principles. This is one level of explanation that has been applied to speed adaptation and its sequel, the reversed motion after-effect. In 1937 the eminent American psychologist, Dr J. J. Gibson, wrote a paper which he entitled 'Adaptation with Negative After-Effect'.[8] In it he formulated the principle which is quoted in full below:

If a sensory process which has an opposite is made to persist by a constant application of its appropriate stimulus conditions, the quality will diminish in the direction of becoming neutral, and therewith the quality evoked by any stimulus for the dimension in question will be shifted temporarily towards the opposite or complementary quality.

This statement is really in three parts. In the first, Gibson states what kind of sensory processes are governed by the principle: namely, those which have an opposite, for example, the complementary colours yellow and blue, or motion in one direction and motion in the opposite direction. All of these *oppositional* processes have a number of common properties. They run from a maximum of one quality, through a neutral point (which possesses the attributes of neither quality, but which is a point of departure for both of them), to a maximum of the opposite quality. In the case of motion, the dimension runs from the fastest we can perceive in one direction, through a stationary neutral point, to the fastest we can perceive in the opposite direction; for blue and yellow, on the other hand, it runs from the most intense (least saturated) blue, through grey (the neutral point) to the most intense (least saturated) yellow; and so on for the other oppositional dimensions.

The second part of Gibson's statement defines the process of *sensory adaptation*. He states that if we are exposed to a steady stimulus from some point along the dimension, we become increasingly less aware of it. Thus, continuous exposure to travel at 70 mph makes it feel a good deal slower than it really is; similarly, if we stare at a patch of blue for a long time it appears more and more saturated (i.e. like grey). The third part deals with the consequences of this adaptive shift, namely, the *negative after-effect.* This is perceived as an alteration in the balance of sensitivity which existed between the opposing qualities in the dimension. Before exposure to the steady-state stimulus we are equally sensitive to either end; but after it we are less sensitive to the stimulated end and more sensitive to the unstimulated end. A corollary to this is that if we are now presented with the neutral point of the dimension it takes on the characteristics of the opposing end; that is the end to which we are now sensitized. Thus, after continuous exposure to, say, a stimulus moving to the right, a stationary object appears to have illusory motion to the left; likewise, after staring at a blue patch, a grey patch appears yellow; and so on.

Now Gibson's principle does not really constitute much of an *explanation* of speed adaptation and its negative after-effect, it merely describes the phenomenon in more general terms so that it embraces a wider range of adaptive effects and after-effects. But it is useful in this respect because it shows that we are dealing with a general property of the nervous system, and not with some quirky 'one-off' illusion. To find an explanation for this phenomenon, we need to consider what goes on in the neural mechanisms involved in the visual perception of motion, and this we shall do below.

To make things simple, let us consider a situation in which an observer stares at a fixed point just behind which a pattern of black and white stripes moves across his field of view from right to left at a constant speed. This differs from the car driving situation in that the observer is stationary and the stimulus moves relative to him, but the adaptation effects are the same as when he moves relative to stationary objects in the outside world. The only important difference is that in the situation I have described above it is mainly the central portion of the retina which is stimulated, while in car driving the motion stimulation tends to fall more on the peripheral portions of the retina. But this does not materially affect the argument.

At the beginning of this chapter I stated that the nervous system codes the direction of motion by registering which of the direction-specific receptors in the retina were active, and velocity was coded by the rate at which the receptors fired off neural impulses to the brain. Let us assume that seen motion from right to left excites Type 1 receptors (in other words, that this direction constitutes the 'preferred direction' for these receptors); while motion in the opposite direction (from left to right) excites Type 2 receptors. Let us also assume (and this is supported by research evidence) that motion from right to left causes no alteration in the 'resting' discharge rate (i.e. the rate of firing that occurs when there is no motion present) of Type 2 receptors, while left to right motion evokes no change in the Type 1 receptors. Finally, let us state arbitrarily that the 'resting' discharge for both types of receptor is 100 firings per second. Now let us see what happens when we expose the moving stripes for a period of about thirty

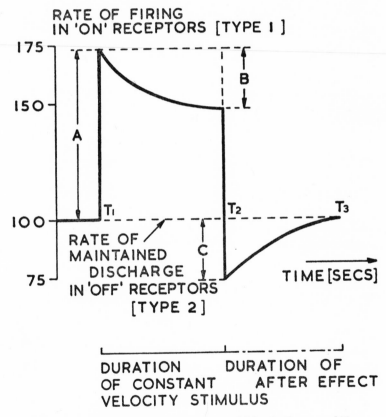

Figure 15 Graph showing the relative rates of firing in Type 1 and Type 2 receptors during and immediately after viewing a striped surface moving at a constant rate. For convenience, it is assumed that C = B. See text for further explanation.

seconds, and then stop them with the observer keeping his eyes on the same point throughout. The sequence of events is shown in Figure 15.

The vertical axis in Figure 15 shows the rate of firing in the Type 1 and Type 2 receptors in arbitrary units. The horizontal axis represents time in seconds. At T_1, the striped stimulus begins to move from right to left at constant speed, and it is stopped at T_2. T_3 marks the end of the after-effect. A is the initial rate of firing in the Type 1 receptors; B is the extent of the fall-off in this rate of firing at the end of the objective motion stimulus; and C is the subsequent mismatch in the rates of firing of the Type 1 and Type 2 receptors.

Prior to T_1, the striped stimulus is stationary, and so both types of receptor discharge at the same steady rate of around 100 firings per second (I say 'around' because in actual fact the rate of firing fluctuates around an average value). This rate of firing therefore constitutes a 'no-motion-in-either-direction' signal to the brain. At T_1 the motor driving the striped stimulus is switched on. Let us assume that it reaches its steady speed immediately. As soon as the stimulus starts to move, the rate of firing in the Type 1 receptors increases immediately from 100 to, say, 175 units of firing. This rate of firing in the Type 1 receptors in response to the stimulus is going to depend among other things upon the speed of the seen motion. Meanwhile, however, the rate of firing in the Type 2 receptors remains unchanged (indicated by the dotted line in Figure 15) because they are not receptive to right to left motion.

As the stimulus motion continues at its constant rate, the frequency of discharge in the Type 1 receptors begins to fall off, rapidly at first and then more slowly until no further reduction occurs. We have two sources of evidence for this: from physiological studies in which tiny electrodes are inserted into single retinal cells in a rabbit's eye;[9] and from psychological experiments in which observers are asked to indicate the gradual diminution in apparent velocity as they inspect a steadily-moving stimulus.[10]

It is highly likely that a similar fall-off in receptor firing rates is responsible for the impression of reduced speed after steady cruising along a motorway. After driving at a steady 70 mph for a while, the firing rates will fall to a level that, in an unadapted person, may well correspond to firing rates produced by an actual speed of around 50 mph. After exposure to a constant motion stimulus, the mental speedometer alters its calibration so as to make us less aware of the velocity of that stimulus. The upshot of this recalibration is that we tend to underestimate speeds in the direction along which we have been travelling. But there is a reverse side to this adaptational coin: should we (for some unlikely reason) suddenly decide to travel backwards in reverse, we would probably find ourselves overestimating our actual speed, at least for a while. We can appreciate how this happens when we go on with our consideration of the events depicted in Figure 15.

By the time T_2 is reached, the rate of firing in the Type 1 receptors has dropped to 150 firings per second, 25 units less than at T_1. When the motion of the striped band is stopped, the rate of firing in the Type 1 receptors drops by an amount equal to its increase at T_1, namely 175 units. This means that it falls to a rate which is 25 units less than the resting discharge of the Type 2 receptors. As far as the brain is concerned, this mismatch in the firing rates of the Type 1 and Type 2 receptors can only mean one thing: that the stimulus is moving from left to right at a velocity indicated by the difference in firing rates between the two types of receptor, namely 25 units. In other words, whenever the Type 2 receptors discharge faster than the Type 1 receptors, the brain interprets this as 'motion from left to right'; that is, in the preferred direction of the Type 2 receptors. All that the brain 'knows' of the outside world is communicated via these neural messages, and if they, for some reason, fail to correspond with the reality, then we perceive something that is not actually happening – as in the case of the motion after-effect.

As time passes the rate of firing in the Type 1 receptors gradually returns to its original resting discharge level, 100 firings per second. Thus, at T_3 both types of receptors are firing at their original equivalent resting rate, a state of affairs that means 'no motion' to the brain. At this point our perceptions once more correspond with the reality and we cease to perceive the illusion of apparent negative motion. These, then, are the neural events presumed to underlie the visual after-effect of motion, and, as we have seen, they provide an explanation both for the phenomenon of speed adaptation as it occurs in motorway driving and for the sensations of slipping backwards we sometimes experience on stopping. It is interesting to see how research into the visual after-effect of motion, which for many years seemed to possess nothing but academic curiosity value, can throw light on to the origins of a very real problem, namely our misperceptions of vehicle speed.

Finally in this chapter, we must consider how we can put this knowledge to some use. Will it, for example, give us any insight into the causes of the devastating multiple pile-ups that plague British motorways in conditions of reduced visibility? The police and the newspapers tend to have their own ideas about this: they attribute these accidents to 'motorway madness' – the lemming-like urge which is presumed to overtake drivers on foggy motorways causing them to hurtle to their doom at irresponsibly high speeds, despite warnings. While it is true that some drivers are indeed stupid and ignore the posted warnings because they feel that their ability to drive fast is not impaired by poor visibility, there may well be others who heed the warning signs but, in placing too much reliance on their mental speedometers, reduce their speed by too little and remain unaware of their natural error. Consequently when they see the brakelights of the vehicle ahead, they are likely to underestimate the required braking distance because they feel they are travelling more slowly than they really are. This type of misjudgement, common enough anyway in fog and poor visibility, is likely to be compounded by the effects of speed adaptation and by the 'slow-down' effect reported in the first study. It is clear, however, that even under conditions of perfect visibility, slowing down can be a very dangerous man-oeuvre if it is judged on the basis of subjective impressions alone. The moral of this chapter is therefore very clear: mistrust your mental speedometer at all times, but especially when you are reducing speed under conditions of poor visibility.

5 The Limited Channel

The information reaching the brain of the pilot or car driver needs to be acted upon at a much faster rate than the equivalent information received by a man strolling along at a steady three to four miles per hour. Not only that, increasing the speed of locomotion also increases the amount of information to be processed. Clearly the sheer speed and complexity of modern vehicles places an enormous demand on our natural capacity to handle information – a fact that can be verified by examining the formidable array of dials and instruments confronting the pilot of the modern jet aircraft (see Figure 19). Not only is the informational load heavier, but the consequences of failure are many times greater for the vehicle operator than they are in most cases of self-propelled motion. What is surprising, therefore, is not that pilots and drivers have accidents, but that they should have them so rarely.

Consider the following calculations made by a senior investigator at the Road Research Laboratory.[1] In 1969 there were some eleven million car owners in Great Britain spending approximately 3×10^9 hours of their waking lives in the act of driving. In the same period, it was estimated that the average driver made a claim on his insurance company for an accident once every six years. Studies carried out on London drivers indicated that in city traffic conditions they made approximately one control movement every second, or about a million a year. If we make two assumptions – first, that only half of a driver's insurance claims are the direct result of his own errors, and second, that each control movement reflects a separate act of decision – then we arrive at the somewhat startling conclusion that, on average, only one decision in twelve million results in an accident. Not a bad average, considering the vast amount of rapidly changing information that forms the basis of these decisions. So how do we manage to process all this information with so few errors of judgement?

Before trying to answer this question, I need to introduce some of the terms that are currently being used to describe the complex relationships existing between the man, his vehicle and the environment in which they operate. Since the late 1940s a tradition has grown up in which the driver and his car, the pilot and his aeroplane, the captain and his ship are studied not as distinct biological and mechanical entities, but as interacting elements in one overall system, the *man-machine system*. The basic components of this system are shown in Figure 16.

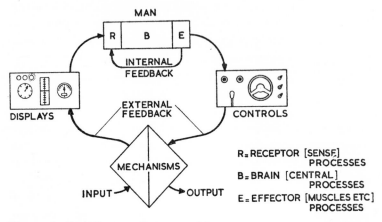

Figure 16   Basic features of a man-machine system.

This general diagram represents the essential features of any man-machine (or man-vehicle) system. In it the human operator is shown as an information-transmitting and processing link within the total system, connecting on his input side with the instrument display, and on his output side with the controls of the vehicle. The instrument display extends the range of his information uptake by providing him with data concerning, say, altitude, speed, engine revolutions, barometric pressures, and other 'vehicle-related' facts that are not immediately available to his unaided senses. The controls allow him to effect changes in the progress of the vehicle that could not be achieved by his hands and feet alone. Thus, the instrument display represents a logical extension of the operator's senses, while the controls represent an equivalent extension of his limbs and musculature.

One of the natural consequences of regarding the man as just another component of a total system is that it becomes meaningful to analyse his performance in the same terms that we use to describe the behaviour of the machine elements in the system. Not so long ago, any attempt to use machine models for man was doomed to failure because existing machines were not sophisticated enough to approach any kind of realistic simulation of human performance. But recent technological advances have been so dramatic, particularly in communication systems, servomechanisms (self-regulating machines) and electronic computers, that we can now build devices that not only behave like us in a number of important respects, but which can also outstrip us in certain areas of performance – for example, in computation and in the storage and rapid retrieval of large quantities of information. Keith Oatley put it well in his recent book:[2]

The reason why sublime properties of the mind have formerly seemed incompatible with the rather mechanistic processes of the body was not that we had too high a conception of the mind, but that we had too mean an understanding of the capabilities of mechanism. Machines that pump and propel may have few of the properties associated with mind, but the machines which control and calculate, the computers, have many.

Because of the existence of these 'new' machines, and their influence on psychological theorizing, the man in the man-machine system now tends to be described in mechanistic rather than in humanistic terms; in the language of engineering rather than that of traditional psychology.*

* It is worth pointing out that the far more common practice, at least in everyday language, is to describe machines in human terms, rather than the other way around. The earliest machines were regarded by the uninitiated as being powered by demons and spirits – usually malevolent ones at that. To some extent this belief still persists, although nowadays we more often tend to ascribe human rather than ghostly qualities to our machines. Machines, and especially vehicles, are regarded as having distinctive personalities: they have their likes and dislikes, their 'on' and 'off' days; they can be vindictive or benign, lively or subdued, and, as in the case of 'The Ship That Died of Shame', they can even be endowed with a moral sense as well.

Sexual overtones are frequently evident in the interplay between men and their vehicles. Presumably because they are capricious things, demanding of love and attention, we call ships, steam engines and a variety of other vehicles 'she'. To see

In these terms the task of the vehicle operator can be viewed as combining two machine-like activities – that of the computer and that of the communication channel. Signals from the display and the outside world arrive at the man's senses. On being transmitted to the central (brain) computer, they are transformed into other signals which elicit certain control actions. These actions alter the behaviour of the vehicle, and this change of state is detected by the vehicle's sensors and by the man's senses and so forms the basis of further control actions. And so it goes on. The whole man-machine system can therefore be analysed as one which receives, processes and emits information. In most vehicles this information is said to flow around a *closed-loop system*. That is, the information produced by the operator's actions is fed back into the system in a continuous stream. This is termed a *feedback loop*, and will be discussed again later in this chapter.

In order to reach a solution to the problem posed earlier – namely, how do we manage to process all the information necessary for handling a vehicle safely? – we first need to find the answer to another question: Does the human operator act like a *multiple* communication channel; that is, one capable of handling simultaneously a number of signals from different sources? Or does he behave like a *single* communication channel which needs to clear one signal through the channel before it can transmit the next one? Common sense and our personal experience suggest the

one's neighbours tending their cars at week-ends calls to mind gigolos ministering to the needs of insatiable, though often ageing courtesans. 'She's a little darling,' they say, caressing and patting the car with gestures more suited to a lover attending to his mistress. According to Dr Douglas D. Bond, a psychiatrist who served with the US Eighth Air Force during the Second World War, aviators are particularly prone to forming quasi-sexual attachments to their aircraft. Flying aircraft, he argued, provides gratification for certain unconscious needs that may extend far back into childhood. And for some men, this gratification may be so intense as to diminish or even supplant the more conventional sexual appetites. He illustrates his argument with quotations from flyers. 'After flying, my wife comes first.' 'Airplanes always took the place of a girl for me.' 'Every time an airplane landed or took off, you watched it the way sailors watch a woman walking the pier.' (D. D. Bond, *The Love and Fear of Flying* (New York, International Universities Press, 1952).) These sentiments reached their most poetic form in the writings of the French pilot and author Antoine de Saint Exupéry. 'The airman's profession is one of renunciation,' he wrote, 'he renounces the love of women. And by renunciation he discovers his hidden god.' (Quoted in S. Rodman, *The Poetry of Flight, an Anthology* (New York, Duell, Sloan and Pearce, 1941).)

former alternative: that man is, in fact, like a multiple-channel system. After all, it is easy to cite situations in which we cope with two different tasks at once – like holding a conversation while we drive, or knitting while watching television. But here, at least, the common-sense answer would turn out to be the wrong one. Yes, we can handle two activities at once; but only under certain circumstances – for example, when both tasks are highly practised, or when they involve a large amount of redundant information, as in a party where we manage to follow two conversations at once. But we do not achieve this by dealing with the two different kinds of information simultaneously. We process these various signals serially. In other words, we *time-share* between the two sources, clearing signals from one before admitting signals from the other. The evidence for these assertions comes from studies like the one described below.

In one of the earliest investigations of divided attention, people were instructed to listen for a bell and at the same time to watch a needle sweeping over the face of a dial with numbers around it like a clockface.[3] Their task was to call out the number the needle was pointing at when they heard the bell. At first sight, the results were very surprising. If the bell had sounded when the needle was actually pointing at, say, the number seven, the subjects, on average, reported that it was pointing at the number six. This was curious because it suggested that they had heard the bell *before* it actually sounded. However, there is another explanation. The subjects in this experiment were 'set' to attend to the bell rather than the face of the dial. When the bell sounded, it occupied their attention fully for a brief moment so that the information currently on the dial face was denied access to their conscious minds. Consequently, they missed the conjunction of the bell with the number seven on the dial face. When asked to say where the needle was at the moment of the bell, they responded with the number which had claimed their attention most recently, namely the one just *before* the bell rang.

This and a large number of related studies have shown that there is indeed some truth in the old saying about men having 'one-track minds'.[4] More specifically, we can state that the vehicle operator can be usefully regarded as behaving like a single rather than a multiple communication channel. We can also state that the capacity of this single channel for receiving, storing and acting upon information is limited by the characteristics of the human nervous system: hence the title of this chapter, 'The Limited Channel'. The notion of man acting like a single, limited-capacity, communication channel is central to the arguments presented in this and later chapters.

On the face of it, this single channel idea seems to complicate rather than simplify our problem of how the driver and the pilot cope so successfully (in the main, at least) with their heavy loads of information. Fortunately, this has not actually proved to be the case. What it has done is to focus interest on the input end of the single channel to find out how the skilled vehicle operator selects the important signals from among the vast number that impinge upon his senses. This rather than the possibility of alternative channels has become the key to understanding the behaviour of the skilled operator.

In order to come to grips with these issues, we need to consider in some detail the flow of information through the vehicle operator, and also the various operations performed upon that information between the time it enters his brain via his senses and the time it emerges in the form of control actions. I have chosen to use the car driver to illustrate these processes, although – for the most part, at least – these considerations apply equally well to other kinds of vehicle operator. To this end, I have represented the car driver in the form of a block diagram of the kind that engineers use to help them understand complex machine systems. This is shown in Figure 17 and will form the framework around which I shall structure the remainder of this chapter.

Compared to Figure 16, this diagram of the car driver may seem rather complex. But the two are essentially similar. All that I have done in Figure 17 is to elaborate upon what happens within the man part of the man-machine system.[5] Before looking at each of these separate subsystems in turn, I want to present an overview of the whole system. An indication of the quantity of information and its direction of flow is given by the arrows connecting the various boxes in the diagram. The first point to notice is that although a great deal of information enters the system through the senses, only one signal at a time gets through the bottleneck of the box labelled Input Selector, and hence into the Computer

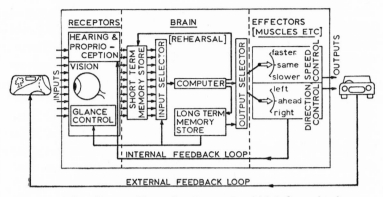

Figure 17   Flow diagram illustrating the way in which information is processed by the car driver. See text for detailed discussion of the various operations involved.

box. It is this latter which behaves like a single communication channel. Information that does not pass directly to the Computer is temporarily retained in the box labelled Short-Term Memory Store. But, as we shall see later, the capacity of this temporary store is itself extremely limited, both in regard to the amount of items it can retain, and the length of time for which they can be held.

At the output end of the Computer the driver's control actions fall into two kinds: those concerned with the guidance of the vehicle, and those concerned with its speed. Taking the diagram overall, therefore, it can be seen that while a great deal of information enters the system, only a comparatively small part of it forms the basis of the control decisions. To understand how the driver copes with his task successfully, we need to know how he manages to reduce the total flow of incoming information down to its bare essentials. Thus, the remainder of this chapter will be taken up with considering each component of the man, from input through to output. Before doing this, however, I need to comment on the two 'returning' arrows labelled Internal and External Feedback Loops.

Feedback loops

In the case of the car driver, the Internal Feedback Loop tells him where his limbs are at any one time. The information is signalled by sense receptors in the joints, muscles and skin, and is transmitted back to the brain along nerve pathways within the body. The External Feedback Loop is primarily visual: through it, the driver is able to see the consequences of his preceding actions.

In the very early stages of learning to drive a great deal of the information conveyed by the External Feedback Loop is of a kind which could be conveyed more economically by the internal loop. In other words, the novice driver needs to *see* where his hands and feet are in relation to the controls; he is not familiar enough with the task to achieve this by 'feel'. This, of course, is very wasteful of the Computer's limited capacity for processing information. If the learner driver is looking down at his feet to see if his foot is covering the clutch pedal, or looking at the gear lever to see that he is putting it into the right position, he is not able to attend to external factors dictating the appropriate speed or direction of the car. It is not uncommon, therefore, for the instructor to have to take over the steering of the car while his pupil is attempting to change gear. But with practice the learner driver comes to rely more and more upon 'feel', or internal feedback information, to monitor his own actions. And this gradual shift of emphasis from external to internal monitoring of one's own actions is one of the main indications of a developing skill.

In the case of the skilled driver the essential information conveyed by the External Feedback Loop is the discrepancy between what he intended and what the car actually did. As mentioned earlier, the task of driving can be broken down into two related tracking tasks: *speed control* achieved by the accelerator, brake and gear lever (to a lesser exent); and *direction control* achieved by the steering wheel. In the speed control task the external feedback frequently consists of the seen distance between the driver's own vehicle and the one in front. If the driver finds himself closing too fast with the car ahead, he can judge the effectiveness of his subsequent braking by the change it produces in the seen separation distance. Equally, visual feedback is vital to direction control. Amateur driving instructors often fail to appreciate that learners have to acquire gradually the knowledge of just how much a particular turn of the steering wheel affects the direction of the car. And they do this by seeing the consequences of their own steering adjustments. Any kind of feedback information provides what psychologists call 'knowledge of results', without which the acquisition of any skill would be impossible.[6] In car driving external feedback information – seeing the consequences of one's own control actions – is perhaps the single most important input to the Computer.

The senses

It is no accident that the box representing the senses contains a disproportionately large eye, and a relatively small subsection labelled Hearing and Proprioception (information about the body's own position conveyed by the internal feedback loop). The driver bases his judgements very largely upon what he can see. Additional information about the state of his vehicle (and occasionally about approaching vehicles) is obtained from what he hears and what he feels through his proprioceptors, but compared to sight this information is relatively imprecise and plays a very subsidiary role in directing his actions.

Before examining the ways in which the eye selects information, it is worth pointing out that a great deal of what a driver could see of the outside world as a pedestrian is excluded by the physical structure of the car as soon as he gets into the driver's seat. A walking man looking straight ahead can see something of his surroundings over a visual angle of about 180°, although he only has really clear vision over about two degrees of the central field of view. But only about 20 per cent of this scene is directly visible to the car driver including what is seen through the rearview mirror. The remainder is obscured by the bonnet, windscreen pillars, rearview mirror and the shape of the side windows (to say nothing of mascots and windscreen stickers).[7] In fog, of course, the driver's view is restricted to a few feet in any direction, while at night it is confined to the beams of his headlights, and to much less than that when he is dazzled by the lights of oncoming traffic.

Other limitations on what the driver can see are imposed by the physical operation of the eye itself. The ability to see clearly is dependent, in part, on the act of blinking which keeps the outer surface of the eye moist and smooth. Studies have shown that a single blink may effectively black out vision for as long as a third of a second;[8] but, to some extent, this loss of vision is compensated for by the fact that blinking frequently takes place during rapid eye-movements when the ability to see clearly is anyway non-existent. Interestingly enough, the mechanism of blinking seems to be organized in such a way as to minimize the loss of important visual information. During car driving, for example, the rate at which we blink is determined to some extent by the difficulty of the road conditions. An investigation of blink rate in drivers showed that blinking occurred fairly infrequently in heavy traffic conditions. But, on a quiet country road, the rate shot up to between seven and ten blinks per minute.[9] But despite the fact that blink rate seems to be organized so as to minimize information loss, when the vision lost through blinking is added to that lost in changing our gaze rapidly from one point to another, it turns out that we are effectively blind for about 10 per cent of our waking lives.

So much for the largely physical limitations on visual input. Now let us turn to the more psychological process of selecting *what* we look at, and in particular to the mechanism labelled Glance Control in Figure 17. I stated earlier that the human eye was only capable of making fine discriminations of shape and colour over a small part of the central field of view, amounting to about a two-degree circular region of the total. It follows from this that the kind of visual information which eventually reaches the Computer depends to a large degree on where the driver happens to be directing his gaze. However, it does not necessarily follow that only what is seen through central vision is important for the driving task. Most of the information reaching the driver's eyes will be seen outside of this central region by what is termed *peripheral* or *extra-foveal* vision. And it is the information detected by peripheral vision that largely guides his steering of the vehicle. It has been found, for example, that if the centre twenty-four-degree field of view is covered up, the driver's ability to control the speed and direction of his vehicle is only very slightly impaired. But when the driver can *only* see through this central field of view, he is unable to steer his car accurately.[10] Previously I mentioned that learning to drive a car involves a gradual shift of emphasis from external to internal feedback information. A somewhat analogous shift also occurs in the course of training from central to peripheral vision, as is shown by the eye-movement studies described below.

One way of determining where the driver is looking is by using an eye-marker camera which makes a continuous record of his search and scan eye-movements. Studies carried out at Ohio State University have shown that skilled drivers adopt quite different scanning techniques to those used by learner drivers.[11] Inexperienced drivers spend a lot of their time looking just ahead of their vehicle, presumably to ensure that they are positioned correctly in their lane. Within this 'near zone' of viewing, they also change their direction of gaze frequently and spend a fair proportion of their time looking at non-relevant features like lamp posts and guard rails. Experienced drivers, on the other hand, spend most of their time looking far ahead of their vehicles at or near the *point of expansion* described in the previous chapter; that is, the stationary point in the visual scene from which fixed elements appear to radiate outwards as we approach them, i.e. the phenomenon of motion perspective. Skilled drivers appear to rely on far-looking with central vision for directional information, and use peripheral vision to tell them where they are in relation to their correct lane position; consequently, they have little need to look just ahead of their vehicles as the learner drivers do.

In one study, the eye-movements of an experienced driver were compared with those of two novices over a straight and level run. It was found that while the skilled man stared well ahead of the car for nearly 100 per cent of the time, the two novices divided their scanning between near and far looking, spending only 60 per cent of the total time on the latter. The remaining 40 per cent was spent sampling the road just ahead of the car to establish their lane position. In addition, it was found that the experienced driver adjusted the extent of his forward focus to the rate at which he was travelling in order to give himself adequate warning time. The faster he went, the farther ahead he tended to look. But the novices failed to do this. They continued sampling close in to the front of their vehicles irrespective of speed. Another general characteristic of the novices was that, with the exception of looking straight ahead, they tended to look at any one point in the field of view for longer than did the skilled driver.

All of these findings point to the fact that unskilled drivers place more reliance on central (foveal) vision than do experienced drivers. At first, it appears that novices tend to make little use of the great deal of information detected by peripheral vision, presumably for the same reason that they are unable to make proper use of the internal feedback loop: because they have not yet learned to interpret its meaning adequately. But, analogous to the transition from external to internal feedback, they gradually learn to rely more and more upon peripheral vision for velocity and lane position information, leaving central vision free to seek for directional information, and also to cope with the unexpected.

An interesting feature of human skill is that, under stress, it tends to regress so that the behaviour of the skilled man comes to resemble that of the novice. Just as unskilled drivers place a great deal of reliance upon central vision, so also do skilled drivers who are fatigued or under the influence of alcohol. At Ohio State University, eye-movement measurements were made on drivers at two blood alcohol levels: at 0·04 and 0·08 milligrams of alcohol per cubic centimetre of blood.[12] Even at these relatively low concentrations, dramatic changes in eye-movement patterns were observed. At the 0·04 level there was some tendency to ignore peripheral information and to concentrate on central vision; but this tendency was especially marked at the 0·08 level. At this concentration of alcohol drivers clearly exhibited 'tunnel vision' – restricting their attention to a very limited area of the total field of view. For example, when drivers were sober, it was noted that they always looked at passing vehicles. But at the 0·08 level many drivers made absolutely no attempt to look at cars which overtook them until they were well ahead. This suggested that the drunk drivers had failed to detect the passing cars in peripheral vision. Their other marked characteristic was that, like the novices, they tended to stare at objects for much longer than sober drivers.

From these findings it would seem that, under the stress of alcohol, the driver redeploys his normal pattern of scanning so that he concentrates *only* on that part of the visual field which seems to him to convey the most information. This is something of the nature of an adaptive response. To compensate for his overall loss of efficiency he maintains some semblance of proper control by ignoring items in peripheral vision. The penalty he pays for this is that he loses the very useful capability of peripheral vision to act as an early warning system. When something moves in the 'corner of the eye', our natural tendency is to swivel our eyes to fixate the new object with central vision; an extremely important survival mechanism for primitive man, and one which has prolonged the life of many drivers and pedestrians as well. We will consider further effects of alcohol at a later point in the chapter.

An important question which emerges at this point is: what is the best search strategy for a car driver? Where should he look and when? One Dutch investigator concluded from a laboratory experiment that 'the best search method is no search at all'. And this is also borne out by the actual strategies adopted by the skilled drivers in the Ohio State University studies described above. In the Dutch experiment[13] subjects in a static situation were asked to detect brief flashes of light spread over a very wide field. It was found that flashes could be detected most quickly and with the least error when the subject was looking straight ahead. Can we conclude from this that the car driver ought to keep his eyes fixed straight ahead as far as possible?

The answer clearly depends on the road conditions at the time, and these may be either simple or complex. When we are driving down a straight road without intersections (as in the Ohio studies), looking straight ahead may indeed be the best scanning strategy. The most likely hazards in this simple situation are pedestrians stepping into our path, or slowly moving vehicles emerging from concealed drives. In either case their rapid detection is more likely when we are looking straight ahead. The radiating flow of visual elements from the expansion point of motion perspective provides a good background against which the independent sideways motion of a person or of a tractor emerging from a field will stand out clearly and thus be easily spotted in peripheral vision. As stated above, peripheral vision is specifically designed for such detection tasks, since one of its functions is to trigger a reaction whereby central vision 'locks on' to the new object.

However, this simple 'straight-ahead' strategy would no longer be appropriate if the road curved, or if the car was approaching an intersection. Under these circumstances, it is necessary for the driver to scan over a much wider area of the visual field. Vehicles approaching our track along intersecting roads need to be scanned with central vision in order to compute relative speeds and distances. Peripheral vision is unsuitable for this purpose, since it fails to give a reliable information as to the size or nearness of objects. And we need this information in order to decide upon the likelihood of a collision. Furthermore, under these complex road conditions, there is always the chance that another vehicle, moving towards the same point of intersection, may be obscured by the windscreen pillar and remain unnoticed if we simply look straight ahead.

The right scanning pattern for the prevailing road conditions develops, as we saw from the Ohio State University studies, as a function of driving experience. And this is indicated in Figure 17 by the arrow running back from the Long-Term Memory Store to the Glance Control box.

Now let us go one stage further into the system, and examine what happens to the information picked up by the man's sense organs. As Figure 17 shows, the next point along the line is the Short-Term Memory Store.

The Short-Term Memory Store

Sensory inputs that are not immediately processed by the Computer have to wait their turn in the Short-Term Memory Store which, as stated earlier, is extremely limited both in its overall capacity and the length of time for which items can be retained. These limitations are in contrast to the Long-Term Store, where a great deal of information may be retained indefinitely.

The presence of this Short-Term Store means that the driver forms his mental picture of the road situation not only upon what is being transmitted by his senses at that moment, but also upon what was registered by the senses a few moments previously. Forming a mental picture of the outside world is rather like watching a moving film where, at any instant, you can see not only the current frame but also some of the frames which preceded it. The significance of this is that we are able to act upon more than the *immediate* evidence of our senses. But how much more? And for how long?

The capacity of the Short-Term Store depends to a certain extent upon the kind of information being retained. For example, the memory span for letters is on average seven items, while the memory span for simple words is about five items. When letters are grouped into meaningful words or 'chunks' of information many more can be retained than when they are stored as individual letters. Similarly, people can remember eleven binary digits and eight decimal digits, though eleven binary digits can be represented by only four decimal digits. The capacity of the Short-Term Store is therefore limited to a few 'chunks' of information, although the number of separate items compressed into these chunks depends upon how they are linked together, and also the person's skill in forming them.

Information is lost from the Short-Term Store (and hence from being processed by the Computer) in a very short time. Estimates of this time vary, depending on the kind of information in the Store. In some cases it can be lost in a fraction of a second; in others the information may be retained for up to a minute. To a large extent the time of retention depends upon whether the item is rehearsed by passing it through the Computer. I shall elaborate upon this in a moment; but, first, let us consider what this Short-Term Store means to the car driver.

Imagine yourself waiting to enter a busy main road. You look one way and then the other, building up a composite mental picture of the road situation. But if you take too long about it, the 'picture' of where you are not actually looking at the present fades away, or else the road situation changes. More than half of all road accidents happen at road junctions, and elderly drivers in particular are prone to junction accidents. One of the reasons for this may be that short-term memory capacity appears to decline with increasing years. An elderly driver waiting to enter a busy main road may move out at the wrong time because he has lost the 'picture' of how the road situation was in one direction while he was checking the other way. Some older drivers may try to overcome this limitation by programming themselves to act in advance. In the case of one driver in his seventies, this policy led to an accident. Waiting to turn into a major road, he noted that the approaching stream of traffic contained seven vehicles – or so he thought. Instead of continuing his inspection of the oncoming traffic, he moved into the road as soon as he had counted seven vehicles passed. Unfortunately, he ran into a motor-cycle which had been concealed by the seventh vehicle on his first inspection. Laying down his actions in advance was one way of cutting down the time needed to inspect the road, but in this instance it turned out to be a dangerous procedure.

As I mentioned earlier, we can preserve items in the Short-Term Store by rehearsing them in our minds. This is indicated in Figure 17 by the arrow marked 'rehearsal' going from the output end of the Computer back to the Short-Term Store. The problem is that while we are 'rehearsing' what we have just seen on, say, a complicated road sign, we are occupying the limited capacity of the Computer so that other signals are denied access. This rehearsal process is like a man saying a new telephone number over to himself as he walks around looking for a pad and pencil. The same analogy can also be used to indicate the difference between long- and short-term memory storage. If in the process of repeating the number to himself the man is suddenly distracted by something else, the chances are that he will have forgotten the new number by the time the distraction is dealt with. But it is very unlikely that the distraction would have caused him to forget his own number, or that of his girl friend. These are firmly entrenched in the Long-Term Memory Store.

But in a crowded street, or at a busy intersection, too much information comes at the driver too fast for him to make use of rehearsal. It is a reasonable assumption, therefore, under these conditions, that if a piece of information is not acted upon almost immediately it will not be acted upon at all.

Input Selector

Instead of being forgotten, some items in the Short-Term Memory Store simply get delayed by the time it takes the Input Selector to switch from one class of stored events to another. This is shown by the results of an experiment which, although carried out in the laboratory, contained many elements in common with the driver's task.[14] A group of young men were given two jobs to perform at the same time. One task consisted of pressing a key with their left hands whenever one of three lights in the central part of the visual field went on or off. This is similar to the driver watching the road ahead and braking every time the brakelights of the car ahead come on. The other task involved monitoring four lights at the edge of the visual field – which is rather like watching out for pedestrians stepping into the road. When one of these peripheral lights came on, the subjects were told to forget all about the central lights and to operate something like a steering wheel with their right hands.

When they only had to perform the first task, the average time to react to the central lights was about 350 milliseconds. But when they also had to be on the lookout for the peripheral lights – even when they were not actually on – the time to react to the central task increased by about 40 per cent. This slowing of reaction was attributed to the time it took the Input Selector to switch from possible signals in peripheral vision to those actually occurring in central vision.

Further evidence for this delay caused by the Input Selector comes from accident statistics which show that the risk of a pedestrian being knocked down near to, but not actually on, a zebra crossing or traffic signal is at least three times higher than on the crossing itself.[15] It is, in fact, the most dangerous place to cross a busy street. When a driver approaches a pedestrian crossing or a traffic light, he has to divide his attention between the traffic state ahead and the end of the crossing (where a pedestrian may be waiting) or the traffic light. He cannot afford to keep looking straight ahead because events at the side of the road demand more than just peripheral vision monitoring; so he has to alternate his gaze between the two. Under these circumstances, somebody walking out in front of the crossing would be placing himself in double jeopardy. In the first place, the driver may be looking somewhere else. And in the second place, even if the driver was looking directly at him, he might not be able to brake or steer clear soon enough because of the time it takes the Input Selector to switch from one class of events to the other. To compound the hazard further, he is entering the road at an unexpected point – a fact which is likely to delay the driver's reactions by itself.

The manner in which the Input Selector operates is perhaps the single most important difference between the skilled and the unskilled operator. As a result of his experience, the skilled driver appreciates that much of the information reaching the Short-Term Store contains nothing new or important, and so can be safely ignored. This fact is embodied in the arrow coming back from the Long-Term Store to the Input Selector in Figure 17. Guided by the stored experience in long-term memory, the Input Selector is able to sift and order the incoming signals so that in the case of the highly skilled driver, the maximum amount of vital information passes through the limited capacity Computer channel in a given time. The skilled driver does not have a naturally greater capacity to process information than the novice, nor does he develop any additional channels. It is simply that experience has taught him how to minimize the built-in limitations of his nervous system through 'packaging' the information in the most efficient way for the job at hand.

Learning how to organize the input to the Computer is the key to the successful acquisition of any complex skill like car driving. Once the learner knows which are the genuinely important signals, he no longer has to overload the limited central channel by feeding through every piece of information that comes along. In other words, he learns how to filter out the redundant or useless information. Once he has begun to do this, he starts to have that most precious commodity for the execution of any skill: time to spare. Time in which to adjust his actions so that no single control movement is executed either too quickly or too slowly. And, most importantly, he gains time in which he can anticipate his future actions. The hallmark of the truly skilled operator is that he appears to have all the time in the world, and yet still responds quickly and effectively to all the task-relevant information reaching his senses.

Let me try to illustrate how these general principles of skill learning operate in a practical situation. When we start learning to drive, everything claims our attention – from the maker's name on the speedometer to remembering which foot is supposed to do what. Because of this, the learner driver has to work a good deal harder than an experienced one, and often feels that without an extra hand or foot the task is virtually impossible. Think back to the time when you made your first hill start. So much seemed to be demanded of you at once. Listening for the change in engine note as the clutch engaged; switching hands from handbrake to gear lever to steering wheel, and then one hand out of the window to signal; frantic scanning of rearview mirror and a glance over the shoulder just to be sure; trafficator signals; all culminating usually in the humiliation of a stalled engine or a slow roll backwards down the hill. But now you can do the same task perfectly while remaining virtually unaware of the individual actions. This observation brings us to another important aspect of human skill: with practice, many of the individual actions involved in driving (as in other skills) become semi-automatic, so that we are not always consciously aware of performing them. I will consider this process of *automization* further when we come to look at the operation of the Long-Term Memory Store. But first let us examine the function of the Computer.

Computer

Although the human brain has much in common with a modern digital computer, there are a number of important differences. For one thing, the brain functions more slowly than the computer. More than half the time involved in responding to a simple signal is taken up with mental processing time, the remainder being taken up with time required for the nerve signal to travel from the eyes to the brain and then from the brain to the appropriate muscles. If there are several possible signals, each requiring a separate response, as there is in the driving task, then mental processing time increases accordingly. This extra processing time is reflected in the braking distances recommended by the Ministry of Transport. The faster the car is travelling, the greater will be the 'thinking distance'; that is, the distance travelled by the vehicle while the Computer is occupied with selecting an appropriate action.

But, as I mentioned above, with increasing experience the Computer is able to translate incoming signals into control actions in an automatic way. And this is another point of departure from the digital computer. Although reaction time increases as a function of the number of signals to which a separate response is called for, this rule only appears to hold for unpractised individuals. Highly practised subjects can react almost as fast when there are many possible signals and responses to choose from as when there is only one signal and one response. Man is therefore adaptable in a way that the Computer is not.

When a particular road situation is anticipated, we are able to prepare the appropriate response *before* its initiating signal – say, the child running out from behind the parked vehicle – actually reaches the Computer. Seeing the child appear in the road ahead requires no conscious decision concerning the correct action. This has already been preformed, and is simply waiting to be triggered off as a whole. In other words, the highly skilled driver is very largely preprogrammed by experience to react in a particular way to a particular set of road conditions. The characteristic way a driver reacts – for better or for worse – constitutes his driving *style*, and we shall be examining consistent differences in style in Chapter 8.

But there are many circumstances on the road where an automatic reaction is both dangerous and inappropriate. In these situations the driver is forced to make a decision on the basis of weighing up the consequences of the alternative courses of action. And in many cases, such as overtaking, entering a busy road, or seeing an amber light, the time taken to reach the decision itself increases the hazards involved.

The decision-making behaviour of the overtaking driver was studied under both experimental and real-life conditions at the Road Research Laboratory.[16] Overtaking another car on a busy two-lane highway requires considerable skill and accuracy of judgement on the part of the overtaking driver. Somewhere between the long gaps that are perfectly safe and the very short suicidal gaps, there are critical gaps where on some occasions the driver will overtake, but on others, when the conditions appear much the same, he will hang back. The investigators called these critical gaps 'threshold conditions'; that is, one which on half the occasions leads to overtaking, and on the other half leads to refusals. Different drivers vary considerably in these 'threshold conditions', presumably reflecting their skill and their characteristic risk-taking behaviour. But regardless of whether a person is adventurous or cautious, the 'threshold condition' makes the greatest demands on the driver's decision processes. And this is reflected in the length of time it takes him to decide upon the course of action.

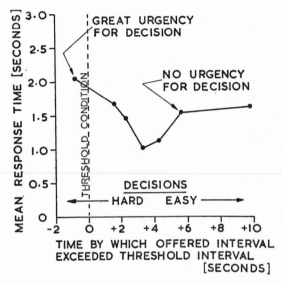

Figure 18 Graph showing the way response time varies as a function of the difficulty of the overtaking decision. Adapted from Moore (1969).

The results of the experimental part of this overtaking study are shown as a graph in Figure 18. From this, it can be seen that average decision times were about one second when the offered interval between the oncoming car and the overtaken car was four seconds longer than the subjects' threshold conditions. But it was up to two seconds when the offered interval was slightly less than their threshold gap. In other words, as the road conditions become more critical, the drivers took longer to reach a decision; and this occurred despite the fact that with these more critical conditions, a rapid decision was vital for safety. In short, the greater the need for speedy action, the more likely are drivers to dither over their decision-making. This conclusion conforms with the findings from laboratory studies on making decisions. In general, it has been found that decision time increases with the difficulty of the choice, and with the risks associated with the outcomes of the possible courses of action.

In the second part of their study, these Road Research Laboratory investigators watched overtaking drivers during a six-day period of British summer holiday traffic. These real-life observations tended to support the general conclusions of their experimental investigation. Pooling the information gained from both parts of the study, they made the following recommendations:

1. Drivers should not attempt to overtake if there is *any* doubt in their minds as to the safety of the manoeuvre. Doubt increases decision time, and this lost time could be disastrous if the driver finally decides to overtake.

2. Beware of overtaking vehicles travelling in excess of 40 mph. This is particularly dangerous because, not only is the vehicle's performance poorer at high speeds, but also road situations are less realistically assessed than at lower speeds.

Other things apart from high speeds can impair the driver's realistic assessment of a situation. The results of a series of ingenious studies carried out by Professor John Cohen and his associates at the University of Manchester clearly show that one of the major effects of alcohol upon the driver is to distort his assessment of the risks attached to a particular manoeuvre.[17] With only very small quantities of alcohol in his bloodstream, the driver exhibits a dangerous degree of overconfidence in his ability to handle the vehicle. In a situation where the real hazards of the situation were steadily increased, drunken drivers maintained the same subjective estimates of risk that they previously attributed to safer situations. Professor Cohen summed up the results of these studies as follows: 'The abundant evidence relating to the effects of alcohol on the driver points to one conclusion: alcohol brings disaster on the road less because of lack of skill than because of defective judgement *in relation* to skill.'[18] With a great deal of alcohol inside him, a man is simply not capable of driving at all. The real danger lies in the smaller doses that make him feel he is inviolate and capable of anything. As Professor Cohen points out, drink has a similar effect on driving as it does on love-making – it increases the 'disparity between aspiration and performance'.

Finally, with regard to the operation of the Computer, it is worth pointing out that certain control decisions make better use of its limited capacity by selecting the most rapid of a number of available actions. For instance, it is probable that a steering wheel response is made more quickly than a braking response. In one study it was found that drivers take, on average, 0·8 seconds to depress the brake pedal when they see a traffic signal change from green to amber.[19] It was estimated that 0·3 seconds of this time was taken up with shifting the right foot from the accelerator to the brake pedal. But other work at the Road Research Laboratory has shown that a corrective steering response can be elicited in as little as 0·25 seconds.[20] Even when the car was thrown ninety degrees off course by mechanical means outside the driver's control, the average driver was able to initiate corrective action in 0·6 seconds, and be back on the correct track in 1·6 seconds. In a number of circumstances, therefore, such as when a pedestrian steps out in front of the car, it is often better to steer out of trouble than to brake.

Long-Term Memory Store

When a skill is highly practised, it makes less demands on Computer processing time.* Something like an automatic programme

---

* William James made a similar point in 1892 with regard to habitual actions like dressing or washing: 'habit diminishes the conscious attention with which our acts are performed'. (W. James, *Psychology: The Briefer Course,* New York, Harper, 1961, p. 6.) In a chapter on Will in his larger work (*The Principles of Psychology,* vol. II, New York; Dover Inc.; 1950, first published 1890), he quotes from a Mr A. T. Dudley writing on the 'Mental Qualities of an Athlete' in the *Harvard Monthly*:

Ask him how, in some complex trick, he performed a certain act, why he pushed or pulled at a certain instant; and he will tell you he does not know; he did it by instinct; or rather his nerves and muscles did it of themselves . . . Here is the distinguishing feature of the good player: the good player, confident in his training and his practice, in the critical game trusts entirely to his impulse, and does not think out every move. The poor player, unable to trust his impulsive actions, is compelled to think carefully all the time. He thus not only loses the opportunities through his slowness in comprehending the whole situation, but, being compelled to think rapidly all the time, at critical points becomes confused; while the first-rate player, not trying to reason, but acting as impulse directs, is continually distinguishing himself and plays better under greater pressure.

This passage brings out an important point about skilled behaviour: namely, that once it has become fairly automatic, any attempt to monitor one's actions consciously often causes a disruption of the performance. Think of the times when you say to yourself while driving a car, 'I'm really going to make this a smooth gear change,' and then find that by paying too much attention to this particular for action has been built up in the Long-Term Store. This is taken account of in Figure 17 by the arrow running directly from the Long-Term Store to the Output Selector. Once this link has been established, the Input Selector and the Computer are left free to deal with other aspects of the driving task – such as predicting what will happen on the road ahead, and taking care of the unexpected.

To understand how this *automatization* of a skill occurs, it would be helpful to introduce two terms used by computer programmers.[21] Data-processing systems like digital computers are governed in their operation by *programs*, or sequences of instructions. Parts of these programs may be repeated many times over in one operation, and these relatively invariant sequences of instructions are called *subroutines*. These subroutines are under the control of higher-level instructions termed *executive programs*, and it is these that provide the overall logic and purpose for the whole set of instructions.

Human skills can be seen as showing the same hierarchical structure as computer programs. The executive program defines the goal to be achieved by the skill and determines the overall plan of the individual actions involved. Subroutines, on the other hand, consist of relatively unchanging sequences of movements which are called into play by the executive program at appropriate stages in the execution of the skilled activity. Consider the case of a man looking up a number in the telephone directory. The overall purpose, specified by the executive program, is to find a particular telephone number belonging to, say, John F. Doe. Finding the

---

'subroutine' of driving, you achieve a less smooth change than you would have done if you had allowed it to occur automatically. A more dramatic example is that of running down a flight of stairs two at a time ‿ you keep your mind on your goal – say, to answer the phone downstairs – and don't think about what your feet are doing, progress is usually fairly smooth; but if you suddenly concentrate on where you are putting your feet (i.e. upon a normally unconscious subroutine of the total act), then the chances are that you will begin to falter and stumble. Mrs Edmund Craster described this predicament exactly in her little rhyme about the centipede:

> The Centipede was happy quite
> Until the Toad in fun
> Said, 'Pray which leg goes after which?'
> And worked her mind to such a pitch,
> She lay distracted in the ditch
> Considering how to run.

number will involve a series of subroutines: picking up the book, turning pages until the right one is reached, running your finger down the list of names until John F. Doe is found and, finally, reading off the telephone number. Each of these subroutines is executed automatically, but they are all bound together as a purposeful series of actions by the executive program. Another simple example is that of swimming the crawl. The total program includes the subroutines of kicking, making arm strokes and breathing. The executive program co-ordinates and links these subroutines to produce the easy, smooth actions of the skilled swimmer.

Now if you think back over these examples, you will notice that each of the various subroutines mentioned above must once have been an executive program. To find a telephone number, for example, you must have needed an executive program to learn the alphabet. Subroutines do not arrive ready made. A baby has to learn to move his limbs as he wants them to move; the novice swimmer has to plan to acquire the right breathing pattern, and so on. Thus, subroutines can be thought of as 'has-been' executive programs. The simple act of tying a tie once required an executive program to govern the sequence of individual actions. But it then becomes a subroutine in the overall plan of dressing. With increasing practice at a skill, each repeated set of actions comes to be relegated to a lower, more automatic level in the total hierarchy. The more complex the skill, the larger the number of subroutines contained in the hierarchy. And, of course, the more instructions there are in the executive program.

In the very early stages of learning to drive each movement required continuous conscious monitoring. Put in computer language, we can say that each gear change, each turn of the steering wheel, each glance in the mirror, each depression of the brake or clutch pedals, each set of actions, in fact, once required a separate executive program. The subroutines governed by these many executive programs were the basic skills we had acquired earlier in life – skills like co-ordinating hand and feet movements, and moving our limbs in the way we intend them to go. With further practice these executive programs themselves become semi-automated subroutines. Some take longer to establish than others. Braking, for example, becomes a subroutine long before the many different actions involved in changing gear become automatic. As the skill becomes more and more proficient, so there are fewer and fewer executive programs to occupy Computer time. As we shall see in our later discussion of the Output Selector, there comes a stage in learning to drive where the trainee can subsume all of his actions under two separate executive programs, one relating to speed control and the other to direction control. But while he can perform each of these subtasks well enough by themselves, he cannot yet co-ordinate them under the control of one overall executive program. This only occurs in the final stages of skill acquisition.

Thus, the progress of learning to drive is characterized by a gradual decrease in the total number of executive programs as they become relegated to the status of subroutines. As this occurs, so the demands on the limited capacity of the Computer slacken off. Finally, of course, the act of driving becomes very largely automatic and occupies only a part of the total capacity of the Computer. The highly skilled driver is left with 'spare mental capacity', a notion I shall consider more closely in Chapter 7.

In case this should make us too complacent, it must be emphasized that this peak of driving skill takes several months of regular driving to achieve, much longer than the fifty hours or so that the average British driver needs before he passes his driving test. Although it is a slow and often difficult business to acquire, the fine edge of a skill is very quickly blunted by lack of practice, a fact which few 'week-end drivers' seem to appreciate.

Output Selector

In car driving, the final outcomes of the decision-making process carried out by the Computer are control actions relating to either the direction or the speed of the vehicle. In trying to simplify the task it is tempting to think of these as being two distinct subtasks which, though performed simultaneously, possess relatively independent features. But in the case of the skilled driver, at least, research shows that it is more accurate to regard steering and speed control as two aspects of the same unitary task which requires continuous integration by the man at the controls.

However, as I mentioned previously, there is good evidence to suggest that this integration within one overall executive program is a fairly late development in the acquisition of driving skill. In the intermediate stages of learning to drive novices appear to concentrate on one aspect of the total task to the neglect of the other. In other words, their behaviour is governed by two separate executive programs.

In a study carried out at the University of South Dakota[22] detailed measures of driving performance were taken while subjects with varying amounts of experience drove both a real car and a static car simulator fitted with a realistically moving visual display. The results showed some interesting differences in the overall control activity, and these were clearly related to the amount of previous driving experience. As might be expected, the experienced drivers exhibited consistently superior driving ability to either of the two novice groups. In particular they tended to drive at a higher average speed, and remained in the correct lane with comparatively few steering adjustments. In fact, they showed remarkably little variability in either speed control or steering. In other words, they appeared to achieve a high level of performance on both subtasks at the cost of relatively little physical effort.

The novice drivers with less than ten hours' experience, on the other hand, tended to work much harder at steering, making many more movements to achieve only marginal control of the car. But their speed varied very little – it stayed at a steady crawl! It seemed as though these very inexperienced drivers had simplified the task of driving by virtually ignoring one aspect of it, namely speed control. Their slow progress meant that there was little danger of a bad steering error. By 'load-shedding' in this way, they managed to keep their vehicles in the correct lane for about 70 per cent of the trip.

However, more experienced novices with more than ten hours' driving behind them showed an altogether different pattern of behaviour. Roughly speaking, their performance lay somewhere between that of the skilled drivers and the very inexperienced novices. Although they steered the car in much the same way as the inexperienced novices, their performance on the speed control aspect of the task differed considerably. Taken overall, their average speed was similar to that for the other novice group, but unlike them, their speed fluctuated wildly throughout the trip. Sometimes they moved at a snail's pace, while at other times they careered round the track at a breakneck rate. The findings of this study indicate that once a novice has acquired a certain degree of steering ability, he begins to 'flex his muscles' on the speed controls by accelerating madly on the straight sections of the road, and slowing overdrastically at the corners. In this way they are performing a more difficult task than the inexperienced novices, which suggests that their information processing has advanced to a point where they feel they have sufficient spare Computer capacity to experiment with speed control. Although this may well be a necessary developmental stage in the acquisition of driving skill, it is also likely to be a very dangerous one, as suggested by the accident figures. Drivers in their late teens have twice as many serious or fatal accidents as those in their early twenties, and these have twice as many as drivers in their forties. Experimenting with speed is clearly not the only reason for these age differences in accident risk, but it is likely to be an important contributing factor.

To reiterate the main theme of this chapter: the car driver can be meaningfully regarded as a single-channel communication system whose capacity for receiving, processing, storing and acting upon information is restricted by the limitations of his nervous system. The acquisition of driving skill is dependent upon two related processes. First, the reorganization or 'packaging' of incoming signals so that only new or important information is handled by the limited capacity Computer channel. Once the driver limits his attention to vital signals and ignores those which are redundant or irrelevant he begins to have time to anticipate what lies ahead, and so acquires the economy of action and accurate timing that is the very essence of skilled performance. The second process, closely tied in with the first, involves the gradual paring down of separate executive programs until the whole skill consists of a series of semi-automatic subroutines governed by one overriding executive program. Both processes lead to a lessening of the demands placed on the Computer.

But, as we shall see in later chapters, human skill is a very fragile affair, and readily breaks down when the vehicle operator is out of practice, fatigued or stressed by either too much or too little information. What happens when the vehicle operator is 'overloaded' by too much information or 'underloaded' by too little is the subject of the next chapter.

6 Overload and Underload

If we accept the view advanced in the previous chapter that the vehicle operator behaves like a single communication channel with limited capacity, then it should come as no surprise that the informational demands made by the speed and complexity of modern vehicles occasionally exceed the capacity of even the most skilled driver or pilot. What is less widely appreciated is that the human communication channel has a lower as well as an upper limit on its ability to process information, and that this too can be exceeded under certain conditions of vehicle operation with equally dangerous consequences. Just as our digestive system and metabolic rate set upper and lower limits on the body's food requirements, so the built-in characteristics of the human nervous system determine the optimal rate at which the brain can handle information. Going beyond these limits in either direction, whether by too much or by too little, can lead to a breakdown in normal brain functioning.

One of the by-products of the rapid growth of transport technology is that vehicles are increasingly able to carry man outside these optimum conditions into environments that either bombard him with too much information or deny him enough to sustain normal brain activity. And this is true not only of exotic space and undersea vehicles, but also of more conventional modes of transport such as cars, ships and trains. A car driver, for instance, on approaching a busy intersection, may be missing important signals from other vehicles, pedestrians and road signs because the total barrage of incoming signals exceeds his basic capacity to store and process it. But a few miles farther on he may find himself cruising at a steady speed down a straight stretch of empty motorway where the amount of information entering his brain is inadequate to maintain its proper state of alertness. Again, important signals are likely to be missed – not through fog or poor visibility, but because the driver's brain has been lulled into a condition of unpreparedness by the meagre nature of the informational input.

This chapter is concerned with the consequences of both too much and too little information, as they appear in various modes of transport. Since many aspects of the former problem have already been dealt with in the previous chapter, we will begin with only a relatively brief coverage of the causes and effects of *sensory overload*, and the bulk of the chapter will be devoted to the more theoretically intriguing problem of *sensory underload*.

Sensory overload

The problem of information overload breaks down into two related components: *speed stress* and *load stress*. Speed stress is a function of the rate at which signals from the environment impinge upon the man's senses, while load stress is related to the number of independent streams of signals or information sources. In an aircraft cockpit, for example, the degree of speed stress would depend upon the velocity of the aircraft, and hence the rate at which the displayed information on the instrument panel changes. Load stress, on the other hand, would depend upon the number of separate instruments that need to be monitored by the pilot in order for him to maintain adequate control over the aircraft.

An excellent description of how these two aspects of the pilot's taskload have increased during forty-five years of aviation development has been provided by Dr John Rolfe of the Institute of Aviation Medicine, and is summarized as a graph in Figure 19.[1] Through all these years, the pilot's intrinsic capacity to handle these stresses has, of course, remained unchanged. But, as we shall see below, there were some periods when the capabilities of the man and the aircraft were fairly evenly matched, and other periods in which the performance of the one outstripped the other.

The first point to notice in Figure 19 is that while the speed of a nerve impulse has remained constant at a little under 200 mph, the maximum speed of aircraft has increased exponentially with time – from around 120 mph in 1917 to beyond 1,300 mph in 1962. And

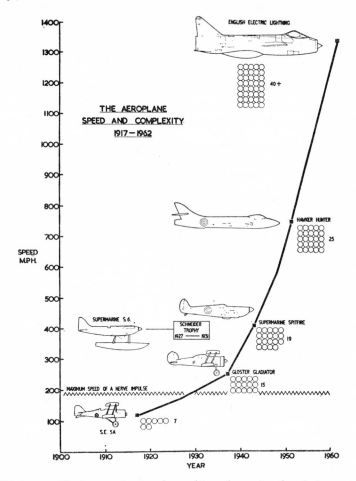

Figure 19   The increase in aircraft speed (speed stress) and cockpit complexity (load stress) up to 1960. Each circle represents one cockpit instrument.

here we are only considering a limited sample of fighter aircraft that have been in squadron service with the Royal Air Force. Today, of course, the maximum speeds are even faster, the informational loads greater, and the gap between the performance of military and civil aircraft has virtually been eliminated by the advent of the supersonic transport aircraft.

It can also be seen from Figure 19 that this increase in aircraft top speed is closely matched by the increase in information load;

that is, the number of flight instruments confronting the pilot. The forty-plus instruments of the English Electric Lightning is a far cry from the seven primitive dials in the cockpit of the SE5, a First World War fighter plane. This shift in the balance of power between the two principal components of the man-machine system – the pilot and the aircraft – has been illustrated by Dr Rolfe in the following example:

Consider the case of a pilot flying an [SE5] aircraft at its top speed near the ground. If through haze, high ground should appear directly ahead and about two miles distant he would have ample time to detect and avoid it visually, but if he took too violent an avoiding action his aircraft might disintegrate. The man in this case was the most efficient component in the man-machine system. In the same situation . . . the pilot flying a Spitfire at about 350 mph sees the hill and both man and machine work together to climb above the obstacle. At this point in time, man and machine are in unison, their limits are almost equal, man can react and machine can respond to all that man demands. But now consider a contemporary aircraft flying at 1,400 mph. The aircraft is master and if there were no mechanical and electronic extensions to the pilot's senses the aeroplane would crash into the hill before the pilot had time to recognize the approaching danger.[2]

The instrument designer can partially ease the overload problem for the pilot of a high-speed modern aircraft by providing him with instruments which, instead of merely informing him of some aspect of the aircraft's state (like a conventional altimeter, or air-speed indicator), actually *command* him to make specific control actions. These so-called *command instruments* simplify the pilot's task by displaying only the amount of error between his actual and the desired flight path. Instead of having to make this calculation mentally from a number of different instruments, and then work out some appropriate corrective action, all the pilot need do is move the controls so as to minimize the displayed error signal. In other words, the necessary information reaches his brain in a 'predigested' form, thus allowing it to be acted upon more rapidly.

Unfortunately, when the information is prepackaged in this way, there is a natural tendency for pilots to concentrate solely upon the command instrument to the neglect of the normal cock-pit drill of cross-checking with other dials to establish that all are working correctly. Some years ago, a jet airliner, fitted with a take-off monitor instrument (a command instrument which displays the discrepancy between the actual angle of climb-out and the desired one for the prevailing conditions), crashed shortly after take-off. The subsequent investigation revealed a minor mechanical failure of this instrument which caused it to indicate (that is, command) too steep an angle of climb. Although this command instrument was faulty, both the captain's and the co-pilot's conventional flight instruments were working perfectly. Both of them had only to glance at their artificial horizons or airspeed indicators to see that they were approaching a stall (a situation in which there is insufficient airflow over the wings to maintain lift). At that time, however, they were also preoccupied by the failure of one engine, a situation which by itself was not sufficient to cause the crash, but it distracted their attention from cross-checking with other instruments. As a result, the captain continued to climb at the dangerously steep angle indicated by the command instrument, and the co-pilot failed to notice the approaching catastrophe until it was too late. Here, then, is a good example of how overloading can conspire with other factors – in this case, the 'fascination' of the take-off monitor – to cause the loss of several lives.

Speed and load stress affect the car driver as well as the aircraft pilot. Indirect evidence for the former is the effectiveness of speed limits in reducing road accidents. The only year in which the casualty rates on the road fell appreciably in Britain was in 1935, when a 30 mph speed limit was first imposed in built-up areas. And other countries have had similar experiences. Even now, the visible enforcement of existing 30 mph speed limits brings about a substantial reduction in road accidents. The Road Research Laboratory investigated the effects of increased police patrols, kerbside 'radar traps' combined with additional warnings and prosecution of offenders upon driving behaviour and road accidents on six roads in different parts of the country.[3] During the twelve-month period of the experiment, injury accidents dropped by 25 per cent on the restriction-enforced roads. In addition, accidents in the surrounding areas fell by 7·5 per cent as compared with the national trend for speed-restricted roads. Although all types of road user had fewer casualties, drivers and passengers were most affected, with more than a 50 per cent reduction.

In December 1965 a 70 mph speed limit was imposed on all British roads. A subsequent investigation by the Road Research Laboratory showed that this had brought about a 20 per cent reduction in motorway casualties.[4] In human terms, this meant something like sixty lives saved and five hundred fewer people injured. The investigators claimed that the speed limit had reduced the number of vehicles exceeding 80 mph on the motorways by 75 per cent. There were also fewer accidents caused by skids and tyre bursts. In the United States, one investigator estimated that a 20 per cent reduction in speed limits on American highways would result in an annual saving of 25,600 lives, 77,000 permanent disabilities and two million injuries, and 51,000 fewer people would suffer bereavements.[5] The financial saving derived from the lower accident rate was calculated to be in the region of four billion dollars. Against this has to be set the fact that such a reduction in speed limits would add, on average, eleven minutes per day to each driver's travel time. And, of course, it would also increase the cost of road haulage and law enforcement. If we divide these figures by five, we get a rough idea of what a similar 20 per cent reduction in speed limits would mean for Great Britain.

However, it should not be assumed from this that the relationship between road accidents and vehicle speed is simple and direct. Studies in both the United States and Great Britain have shown that there is a U-shaped variation of accident rate with speed.[6] That is, the vehicles which are moving at the average speed for the prevailing road conditions have the lowest accident rate, and the rates for the very slow and the very fast vehicles are much higher. In the case of the American study, it was found that the slowest drivers had a greater risk of accidents than the fastest drivers. One explanation for this might be that slow driving is associated with certain types of driver and car, such as elderly drivers, women drivers, learners and so on in old or poorly maintained vehicles, and that these combinations of car and driver are more prone to accidents irrespective of their speed. But to set against this possibility is the fact that a motoring survey undertaken by the Government Social Survey in 1961 revealed that these particular classes of driver and vehicle have a lower than average accident rate – probably because they do not travel so far or so frequently as other road users. However, this does not entirely eliminate the possibility that certain personality traits are correlated with slow driving (for example, indecisiveness, excessive caution and so on), and that these are more conducive to accidents than slow vehicle speed by itself. We will be examining these driver traits in some detail in Chapter 8.

Figure 20   Three road signs that are too complex to grasp while driving. From Walker (1961).

An important set of factors contributing to the car driver's load stress are the design and location of road signs. Although recent years have seen some improvement in the readability of directional signs, many remain that are better suited to the days of the horse and buggy when a man could get out and examine the signpost at his leisure without holding up a line of traffic. Research at the Road Research Laboratory[7] has shown that even a simple road sign displaying only two or three destinations can take as long as three seconds to read when driving in traffic. At 30 mph this means that the car has travelled almost fifty yards while the driver is taking in the sign and not the other sources of information competing for his limited attention. With more complicated signs, the reading time is much longer. In a laboratory experiment complex signs like those shown in Figure 20 were exposed for a brief time while the subjects were simultaneously engaged on a tracking task comparable to steering a car. With an exposure time of twenty seconds the reading errors ranged between 50 and 70 per cent, and completely correct readings were hard to obtain even when the signs were exposed for an indefinite period. Faced with signs like these the experimenter concluded that the driver would have as good a chance of going the right way if he simply guessed at random. At least that would have the merit of keeping his eyes on the road. To make things even worse, most road signs are located at points of maximum information load, like busy intersections and roundabouts, when the task of manoeuvring the vehicle safely places an already heavy burden on the driver's limited capacity. To a large extent this problem could be overcome by good traffic engineering. Signs need to be simple, large and sited well ahead of the road junction away from competing information sources. The driver can then share his attention between the road ahead and the contents of the sign more comfortably, and if the sign is large enough he will be able to sample it over a period which is sufficient to take in all the salient facts.

As mentioned above, busy road intersections are by themselves a considerable source of load stress. Some evidence that the driver's capacity may not always be adequate to cope with this stress is provided by the accident figures. The accident liability of a stretch of road twenty yards either side of a junction (and including the junction itself) is about ten times greater than that of an equal length of road without an intersection. Furthermore, the degree of road stress varies with the driver's intention. On entering a major road in Britain, where we drive on the left, there are six possible collision points associated with a right turn, three in going straight ahead and two when turning left (see Figure 21).

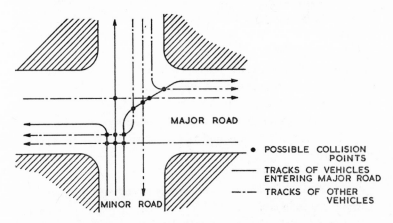

Figure 21   Possible collision points for drivers entering a major road. Adapted from Moore (1969).

In order to guard against these hazards, the driver must scan for vehicles on a potential collision course over a 180° field of view covering right, straight ahead and left. Load stress also depends on the number of roads which join. In Great Britain, for instance, 22 per cent of all road junctions have four or more intersecting roads.

Man is not particularly good at handling a number of different sources of information over a wide visual angle. And this is especially true when the content of these separate messages is continuously changing. While he is attending to one source, the information retained from other sources gets 'out of date' – for example, a previously empty road now has a fast car approaching along it – or it is simply lost from short-term memory. When drivers waiting to enter a major road were studied with a film camera,[8] it was found that a considerable amount of complex eye and head movement went on before any move was made, indicating that a great deal of information was being selected and processed. The overall inspection times ranged between five and ten seconds, although some of this was taken up with waiting for a favourable break in the traffic flow. Because of the need to keep rechecking, the lead driver at an uncontrolled junction will sometimes miss his opening, and the frustration this produces combined with the real or imagined impatience of the drivers waiting behind may well goad him into making an ill-considered move. Considering how many ingredients for disaster are present in this situation, it is hardly surprising that road junctions are accident 'black spots'. What is more surprising is that accidents happen so comparatively rarely, even under these conditions.

How do we cope with speed and load stress? When faced with an overload of information we may adopt a number of different strategies so that we can still maintain some level of appropriate output. These strategies have been identified by Dr J. G. Miller of the University of Michigan,[9] and the more important ones are listed below:

(a) *Omission* – when there is an excess of incoming signals, we simply ignore some of them.
(b) *Error* – processing the information incorrectly and not making the necessary output adjustments.

(c) *Queueing* – delaying responses during peak load periods and then catching up during the lulls.

(d) *Filtering* – the systematic omission of certain categories of information, according to some kind of priority scheme (ignoring signals in the periphery, for example).

(e) *Approximation* – an output mechanism whereby the less precise or accurate response is given because there is no time for precision.

(f) *Escape* – leaving a situation entirely, or taking other steps that effectively cut off the flow of information – like closing one's eyes and praying.

Dr Miller observed that once people had become familiar with all of these 'coping' strategies, certain ones were preferred depending on the rate of information input. At moderately high loading rates, all of them were tried wherever possible. But at high rates, filtering and omission were the most frequently used strategies. Even under excessively high rates, it has been found that the human operator can keep going, even if it means omitting something like 98 per cent of the incoming signals.*

If road engineers accept that the driver is not all-seeing and omniscient, and assume that he will, at times, be unable to process all the available information, they may be able to improve his lot by redesigning the road environment so that the least dangerous of these defensive strategies is called into play in a particular road situation. For instance, it has been suggested that essential road features, signs and signals should be arranged in a hierarchy 'such that the most important are simple in design, bigger, brighter, more conspicuous and more meaningful than other signals or signs'. [10] If this recommendation were carried out, it would certainly aid the driver in arranging his signal priorities so that only

* Nehemiah Jordan of the RAND Corporation, writing in the *Journal of Applied Psychology*, 47: 161 (1963), pointed out that the primary difference between men and machines is that men are more flexible – they cannot be depended upon to perform in a consistent manner, but they are capable of modifying their behaviour to suit altered circumstances. Machines, on the other hand, can generally be relied upon to perform consistently, but – except for the most sophisticated of them – they are largely inflexible. One of the consequences of his greater flexibility is that, under stress, man's performance breaks down gradually rather than precipitately. As Jordan put it: 'Machines can either do the job as specified or they botch up; man degrades gracefully.'

the relatively unimportant sources of information get filtered out. Another suggestion is that drivers should be provided with a clearly defined fixation target that will tell him the most important place to look in a particular traffic situation. On entering a motorway, for example, the driver frequently tries to scan three lines of traffic by craning his head over one shoulder. But, initially at least, he only needs to look at the traffic approaching in the slow lane. If a distinctive target was placed in this region, the eye would be directed towards it and thus to the most important source of information. Similarly, on curved roads, a marker placed in an appropriate position might help the driver detect other vehicles approaching the bend. There are clearly many ways in which the driver's road environment can be modified to minimize his informational load. But this can only be achieved effectively when the driver's natural limitations are fully understood, and we are still a long way from this understanding at the present time.

So far in this chapter we have examined what happens when the vehicle operator has too much information demanding his attention. Now we turn to the other extreme, and consider the effects on his performance and state of mind when he has too little information reaching his senses.

Sensory underload

Psychologists have traditionally studied the problem of sensory underload under two general headings: *vigilance performance* and *sensory deprivation*. The first area of research is concerned with the ability of the human observer to detect infrequent, irregular and often indistinct signals in monotonous and boring surroundings. The second area involves studying what happens to a man when he is cut off, either partially or completely, from meaningful sources of stimulation. Both of these research areas have given us an insight into hitherto mysterious breakdowns in human performance and mental functioning, particularly as they occur in vehicles which carry men into empty and featureless environments.

Research into vigilance performance began in earnest during the Second World War when it was realized that airborne radar operators, on the look-out for enemy submarines, were unable to sustain their initial level of vigilance throughout their watches. After about half an hour or so on duty, they showed an increasing tendency to miss important signals. The watch periods were lengthy and the job tedious, consisting mainly of waiting for 'nothing to happen'. The radar man worked largely in isolation, and no regular check was made on his efficiency. The object of his search – a small blip of light, often only a millimetre in diameter – was hard to find under the best of conditions, and it remained on his screen for a relatively short time. To make his task even more difficult, he had to detect the submarine echo against a background of random signals reflected back from the waves, so-called 'wave-returns'.

The job of finding out what caused this fall-off in vigilance was given to Dr N. H. Mackworth of the Applied Psychology Research Unit at Cambridge. His first step was to try to simulate all the important characteristics of the radar man's job in controlled laboratory conditions, and this he did by constructing a simple yet ingenious piece of apparatus called the Clock Test. In this test, the subject watched a pointer moving around a clockface in regular jumps at the rate of one jump per second. At infrequent and irregular intervals, this pointer was programmed to make a jump of double the normal length. This double jump was equivalent to a submarine 'echo' on the radar screen, and when he saw it the subject had to respond by pressing a key.

The subjects were required to work at this task for two hours at a stretch, equivalent to a two-hour radar watch in a RAF Coastal Command long-range aircraft. When the results were compared in half-hour periods, it was found that 85 per cent of the signals were correctly detected in the first half-hour period, but this fell to 74 per cent after one hour, and finally to 72 per cent after two hours. The general pattern of these findings fitted in fairly well with the actual performance of radar operators in Coastal Command, which eliminated the possibility that this deterioration in performance, or *vigilance decrement* as it came to be called, was not simply a unique feature of the laboratory task. Since that time a large number of experiments have been performed on the same phenomenon, and although there have been many theories to explain it, the facts of vigilance decrement are well supported.[11]

The main conclusion to be drawn from this work is that men do not make very good watchdogs – particularly when they are required to sit in boring surroundings and keep a lookout for signals which arrive in no predictable sequence, which are generally hard to discriminate and are, anyway, few and far between. However, the same research has also shown that a man's detection rate is much improved if somebody takes the trouble to give him knowledge of results; that is, to tell him immediately after a signal has occurred whether or not he identified it correctly. But his performance also improves dramatically if he is simply rung up for a chat during the doldrums of his watch. Similarly, having someone else in the room, even when he is not helping on the task, can prevent the vigilance decrement. These results, and others like them, suggest two possible explanations for the fall-off in vigilance. The first we can call the *expectancy theory*, and the second, the *arousal theory*. Although these two theories are by no means mutually exclusive, I will consider them separately and see what insights they can give us into the origins of some rather strange transport accidents.

Put simply, the expectancy theory states that if the signal frequency is low, the observer's expectation of a signal arriving in, say, the next two or three minutes, will also be low. This creates something of a vicious circle. If the observer is not expecting a signal, he will be less vigilant. Instead of keeping a close watch on the signal source, he will be daydreaming or studying his finger-nails, or generally trying to pass the time as best he can. As a result he is likely to miss more signals as time passes, and the effect of this is to make him *expect* even fewer signals in the future. And so his vigilance continues to decline. But when, as in some of the Mackworth Clock Test experiments, the observer is told at what point a signal occurred and whether or not he spotted it correctly, the vicious circle is broken since he now has accurate information on which to base his expectations of future signals. That is, he has a true indication of the overall signal rate, and so can maintain an appropriate level of attentiveness throughout the watch.

Another finding that fits in with this general idea is that when one signal occurs very soon after another – a fairly rare occurrence, but possible due to the irregular spacing – it has a particularly high probability of being missed. Having just dealt with one signal (presuming that he spotted it), and knowing that they are fairly rare events, the observer does not expect the second of the two signals so soon after the first, and chooses that period to 'switch off' his attention or divert it elsewhere.

The notion of expectancy conforms with the general psychological principle that there is more to perception than mere sensation – or, to put it another way, there is more to seeing than meets the eye. All perception – our mental picture of the world – is the outcome of a subtle interaction between the information coming in through our senses from the outside world, and the internal information stored in the form of preconceptions; what our previous dealings with a particular situation tell us *ought* to be 'out there'. Even when there is plenty of stimulation reaching us from our surroundings, we still tend to mould it so that what we actually perceive conforms more to what we expect than is justified by the sensory evidence. Think of the occasions you have waited for somebody outside the ticket barrier on a railway station. How often do you think you see their face in the crowd before they actually arrive? And the later they are, the more often you think you can see them – because your need to see them becomes greater the longer you wait.

But when external information is lacking, or is in some way ambiguous, these built-in expectancies play an even greater part in shaping what we see or hear. The tendency to project your preconceptions and needs into the outside world is always present, and it takes on a dominant role when the opportunity to make an adequate test of the reality is missing, as it is when external information is sparse. More often than not, of course, what we think is 'out there' and what is actually 'out there' are the same thing; but sometimes they add up to two quite different things, and when this happens it is often the thought rather than the sensory evidence that finally determines what we see.

Professor Russell Davis, now at the University of Bristol,[12] has described a number of railway accidents in which the primary cause appeared to be an inappropriate expectation, or what he calls 'false hypothesis', held by the train driver. A false hypothesis is a preconception of the world that does not fit the facts. Normally it becomes modified or abandoned as the result of further transactions with reality. But sometimes it can persist in flagrant disregard for the sensory evidence. Or else it continues to hold sway because the information entering the senses is insufficient to challenge it. In either case, it can lead to a totally inappropriate response. An engine driver, for instance, who has made the same journey many times, quickly develops a strong set of expectations about events and signals farther down the line. At the beginning of the run, he is likely to be on the alert for departures from the expected. But as the journey progresses and he becomes tired or anxious about making up lost time, he may neglect a signal which he does not expect, or misinterpret one that jibes with his preconceptions. Two railway accidents appear to bear out this point.

In the Ludlow train collision of September 1956 the driver ran past a caution signal and two stop signals at danger without slowing down. In the official report it was suggested that the driver 'may have been lulled to some extent, through his long experience of working over the line, by the expectation of a clear run through Ludlow as is usual with this train'. Another accident, this time at Lewisham in the following year, could be attributed to a similar cause. Once again the driver passed a number of cautionary and stop signals without reducing speed. At his trial he remarked that he had expected a green 'go' signal 'because I have never been stopped there in the whole time I have been travelling'.

It has also been suggested that false hypotheses are particularly likely to be acted upon just after some period of stress or high anxiety. When some emergency or hazard has been successfully negotiated, there is a tendency to relax prematurely. Similarly, towards the end of a long trip, one often feels 'as good as home', which again can lead to a decline in alertness and proper caution. An accident that illustrates the consequences of this 'nearly home' effect is the Harrow and Wealdstone train crash of October 1952. The driver of a train from Perth was approaching the end of his journey when he passed a colour signal at caution and two semaphore signals at danger without reducing speed. At the official inquiry it was estimated that this lapse of attention must have lasted for at least a full minute. It may be supposed that after a difficult journey, during which he had been delayed by fog and a late start, the driver was lulled into a false sense of security by the clearance of the fog and the prospect of an easy, uninterrupted run into the London terminus. So strong was this expectation that he failed to register a series of perfectly visible warning and danger signals. A similar kind of 'end deterioration' was noticeable in ferry pilots during the Berlin Airlift. After flying several missions in one day, a number of pilots simply 'let go' when they found themselves over their base airfield. Only the prompt action of other crew members saved them from disaster. The same kind of premature relaxation seems to have occurred in the case of a motorist who, on returning home from a long journey, swung into the identical driveway of his neighbour's house and hit a tree which, as far as he was concerned, 'just couldn't have been there'.

I stated earlier that a false hypothesis can be retained even though there is a mass of evidence to the contrary. When this happens, we can only assume that the vehicle operator simply rejects from his mind all the pieces of evidence that fail to support his erroneous expectation. Einstein once said, 'If the facts don't fit the theory, the facts are wrong', and this is especially true of false hypotheses. How else can one explain the following incident described by a police sergeant patrolling the Hertfordshire stretch of the M1:

We coned off an accident for 200 yards. There were two police cars with blue flashing lights, two breakdown trucks with amber flashing lights, two hazard lights working in advance of the accident and one set of blue spinning lights 400 yards ahead – and a Hillman came through everything at 60 mph, right over the top of a red light on one of the cones. When I stopped him he said he thought the lights were advertisements. Yet 5,000 other drivers had known what they were.[13]

As mentioned before, the *expectancy* and *arousal* theories of vigilance decrement are not necessarily in conflict; rather they emphasize different aspects of the vigilance task. While the expectancy theorists concentrate on the low signal rate and the irregular intervals between them, the arousal theorists look to the monotony and uneventfulness of the total situation for their answers. The term 'arousal' is variously defined, but as it is used here it refers to a continuum of nervous activity anchored at one end in sleep and at the other by extreme agitation and frantic excitement of the sort associated with overpowering feelings of fear or anger. Thus, an individual's level of arousal is, as one psychologist laconically put it, 'the inverse probability of falling asleep'.[14]

Let us look briefly at the neurophysiological ideas underlying the notion of arousal. It is believed that wakefulness is maintained by a neural centre in the base of the brain called the *ascending reticular formation*. This brain centre is strategically placed so that nearly all the ingoing and outgoing nerve pathways to and from the higher centres of the brain (the cortex) pass through it. When active, it sends up a barrage of nerve impulses to these higher centres which, within certain limits, keep them functioning efficiently. But when these limits are exceeded, either by too much (as in the case of extreme emotion) or by too little (as in very boring surroundings), then the cortex ceases to operate at maximum efficiency. This fall-off in brain functioning is manifested in the speed and accuracy of overt performance. These, in very simple terms, are the neural mechanisms underlying the notion of arousal. So how do they explain the missed signals in, say, the Mackworth Clock Test?

When background stimulation is low and signals few and far between, the level of arousal – and with it vigilance – begins to decline because the quantity and variety of the sensory inputs reaching the reticular formation are insufficient for it to carry out its job of maintaining cortical efficiency. But knowledge of results, a chat on the telephone or the presence in the room of someone else prevent the vigilance decrement because they boost the overall level of arousal and so keep the mind alert.

Interestingly enough, many of these antidotes to vigilance decrement were unwittingly present on the footplate of the old steam locomotive. In between shovelling coal, the fireman would sit opposite the driver and help him with the identification of signals, train speeds and other problems connected with driving the engine. These procedures developed out of tradition and custom rather than deliberate planning, but it is obvious that this system carries with it at least two advantages. First, it kept the driver alert through additional auditory stimulation and the presence of someone else in the cab. Second, it provided the driver with confirmation of any unexpected signal. Also the fireman was usually a younger man learning the trade of engine driver (who, on some American railroads, was never younger than forty-one, and quite often in his seventies). Without being specifically planned for, the inevitable diminution of visual acuity, dark-adaptation, colour vision and so on, that begins after fifty in most people, was nicely compensated for by the keen senses and fast reactions of the younger man. Unfortunately, the advent of the diesel engine broke up this happy partnership. As the operational and mechanical facilities of the diesel locomotive increased, many trains began running with only one man in the cab. Since the most prestigious trains usually went to the most senior drivers, it often happened that, on some American railroads, the oldest driver finished up driving the fastest locomotive over the longest distance.

Mackworth also found that a short rest period produced fewer missed signals than when no break was given in a two-hour watch. And this held even if it meant that some signals were missed while the man was away from the task. This point is evidently appreciated by legislators in some American states who compel drivers, if they have been travelling for a certain number of hours, to leave their cars and take an enforced rest before continuing their journey. However, the results of recent experiments indicate that the benefits of a break largely depend on how the person occupies himself. If he just sits and does nothing, the rest fails to bring about any marked improvement in his vigilance once the watch is resumed. But studies at the University of Illinois[15] show that if the rest is spent in conversation or in doing some mild exercise, then subsequent vigilance is considerably improved. Now if it was just a question of dissipating the fatigue built up on the task, any sort of rest would probably do; but these results suggest that some kind of 'arousal jag' is needed. That is, an event which stimulates the activity of the ascending reticular formation and so increases cortical efficiency. Further evidence for this is that a change, even to another fairly boring task so long as it is sufficiently different, can sometimes be as good as a rest. Novelty and variety, as well as an increase in the overall level of stimulation, can provoke the alerting 'arousal jag'.

Driving down straight stretches of uneventful motorway which demand little or no change of speed and little steering activity, flying straight and level through featureless blue sky at high altitude, standing watch on the bridge of a ship in a calm empty sea – all these and many more transport situations share the essential 'de-arousing' ingredients of the Mackworth Clock Test, and they have similar detrimental effects on alertness and vigilance. As arousal ebbs, the nervous system becomes increasingly less responsive to external stimulation. Signals need to be brighter, louder, or in some way more 'attention-grabbing' in order to be spotted. And even when they are detected they only elicit a fairly sluggish response because the reactivity of the entire nervous system is damped down.

When we prepare for sleep we make ourselves comfortable, darken the room, close our eyes, relax our muscles and think soothing thoughts. We do this deliberately to reduce our level of arousal, and so hasten the onset of sleep. It is not surprising, therefore, that when a similar kind of sensory underload is imposed upon us from outside it achieves a similar effect. That is, the nervous system begins to 'wind down' in preparation for sleep. But when we do not initiate this process ourselves we are less aware of its consequences. How many times have you come to with a start during the course of some boring lecture or tedious sermon to find that you had dozed off without knowing it?

It is the insidious build-up of its 'de-arousing' effects that makes sensory underload so dangerous; particularly since, almost by definition, it only occurs when things seem to be going safely or smoothly. Not only does a diminished flow of information make us less attentive, and our reaction time longer, it also inhibits the mental processes which, under wide-awake conditions, continually evaluate and update our expectations. As a result, we tend to cling more tenaciously to our 'false hypotheses'. And when the quantity of sensory information entering the nervous system falls below a certain critical level, the breakdown process can go one stage further. Instead of simply misinterpreting the facts of our surroundings, like the driver who mistook the crash warning lights for advertisements, or missing important signals because we are convinced they should not be there, we move into the perilous hinterland between normality and psychosis where we may see and feel things that have no basis in reality. Rather than just distorting the world to fit our preconceptions of it, we begin to people it with the figments of our imaginings – as we do on falling asleep. When this happens the simple information-processing model of the driver or the pilot reveals its limitations. These mechanistic notions are helpful up to a point, but when it comes to understanding the effects of *sensory deprivation*, the language and training of the psychiatrist are more useful than those of the engineer. The sensory deprivation effects considered in the final section of this chapter are essentially human ones, and have no counterpart even in the most sophisticated of machines.

If you have ever sat completely motionless in pitch darkness and felt the silence pressing on your ears, you will have some idea of what psychologists mean when they talk of *isolation* or *sensory deprivation*.[16] The first experimental study of isolation was carried out at McGill University in Canada in the early 1950s under the direction of Professor D. O. Hebb. The impetus for this study came from several sources: from Hebb's own theoretical ideas; from the reports of bizarre mental disturbances experienced by shipwrecked sailors, arctic explorers, submariners and prisoners held in solitary confinement; and, particularly at that point in time, from the political and military interest aroused by the reports of the 'brainwashing' and 'thought control' of American and United Nations prisoners-of-war during the Korean conflict. Whatever its origins, however, the dramatic findings of the McGill study captured the interest of psychologists in many countries, and other studies of isolation soon followed.

The conditions of 'isolation' have been achieved in many ways. The most extreme involve an almost complete shutting off of external stimulation. This has been achieved by suspending a man in a tank of water at constant temperature while wearing a 'wet suit' and a blacked-out skin-diver's mask for breathing. In the McGill study, however, the investigators were primarily concerned with eliminating any meaningful patterning or variety of sensory stimulation. Volunteer subjects were confined to a small soundproof room where they lay motionless on a bed with cardboard 'cuffs' over their hands and forearms to cut out tactile stimulation. They also wore goggles which let through light but removed any structuring of the visual input. You can achieve a similar effect by cutting a table-tennis ball in half, and placing the two halves over your eyes. Later studies have involved even less deprivation as a rule; in some cases, the effects were simply achieved by placing the subject in an ordinary 'iron-lung' machine.

What actually happens to people under these conditions is still a little confused. But in the McGill and water-immersion studies, the most dramatic finding was that subjects experienced vivid and often extremely disturbing hallucinations. In the McGill study, 86 per cent of the student volunteers reported some kind of hallucination, and these occurred at any time between twenty minutes and seventy hours of confinement. Typically, the hallucinations progressed from simple flashes of light to complex moving pictures. The latter were so compelling that some subjects actually claimed to have felt motion sick. One subject, who claimed to be wide-awake at the time, saw rabbits with knapsacks on their backs marching across a field; another saw a tiny space-ship firing pellets at him, and also felt their impact on his skin.

The evidence of these and later studies suggests that the bizarre consequences of sensory deprivation have little to do with the reduction in the amount of physical energy reaching the senses. Rather, it appears to be the removal of the meaningful structure or patterning of the sensory messages which is the crucial factor. For instance, subjects may be listening to a loud but constant level of background 'white noise' (a sound rather like fat spitting in a frying pan) through earphones and looking at a fairly bright but constant level of illumination through translucent goggles (like the table-tennis ball halves), and yet still suffer these effects of sensory deprivation because of the *lack of information* conveyed by either source of stimulation. Nor, as I indicated earlier, is it necessary to go to such lengths as the McGill investigators in cutting down informational input before the consequences of sensory deprivation are felt. A number of examples drawn from vehicle operation will serve to bear out this point.

An American study of long-distance truck drivers[17] revealed that more than half had experienced some kind of hallucination, particularly during the hours of darkness while driving on long, straight roads. One driver reported that he had 'seen' a calf standing on the road ahead of him, and in swerving to avoid it had overturned his vehicle. On being questioned further, the same driver admitted that on previous occasions he had frequently 'seen' herds of mules in glittering harness standing on the road. A survey of some two hundred motorists and lorry drivers carried out at the University of Manchester indicated that visual illusions and hallucinations were equally common even on British roads. Fatigue and darkness seemed to be the most important factors, but they could also become interwoven with features of the landscape, lighting systems, hedges, overhanging trees and so on. These reports and our own personal experiences – there are likely to be few drivers who have not at one time or another experienced some kind of perceptual distortion due to reduced sensory information – suggest that it is not always necessary to be shut up in a 'small black room' before the effects of sensory deprivation make themselves known. Simply driving through a monotonous or dark landscape can sometimes be enough.

The problem of sensory deprivation is even more acute in high altitude flight. In 1956 Dr Brant Clark and Dr Ashton Graybiel of the US Naval Aerospace Medical Institute, Pensacola,[18] investigated the incidence of what they called the 'break-off phenomenon' among naval aviators. They defined this as a 'feeling of physical separation from the earth when piloting an aircraft at high altitude'. What prompted them to this inquiry were reports from pilots describing feelings similar to those expressed by an American test pilot in his book, *The Lonely Sky*:[19]

Fifty-nine thousand, sixty thousand, reeling off sixty-one thousand. I have left the world. There is only the ship to identify myself with, her vibrations are my own, I feel them as intensely as those of my body. Here is a kind of unreality mixed with reality that I cannot explain myself. I have an awareness that I have never experienced before, but it does not seem to project beyond this moment . . . And with this adrenalin inflicted state floats the feeling of detachment.

Of the 137 pilots interviewed, 35 per cent had experienced the 'break-off' effect, and 12 per cent of the pilots who had not themselves gone through this experience had heard it discussed by other pilots in the crew-room. Only a third of those who had had the break-off effect had discussed it with other pilots. Many of them expressed the view that the experience was too personal, and not the sort of thing they could readily talk about to other flyers. A number of the younger pilots were, in fact, relieved to hear that other people had shared this experience. They were reluctant to mention it to other pilots for fear of being thought peculiar.

Because the experience is so idiosyncratic no consistent picture emerged as to its form or subjective content. The one common set of characteristics was the feeling of being isolated, detached, or separated physically from the earth: a kind of 'other-worldliness'. A few first-hand reports illustrate this. 'It seems so peaceful; it seems like you are in another world.' 'I feel like I have broken the bonds from the terrestrial sphere.' Some pilots found the experience intensely pleasurable. 'I have had the feeling of being detached . . . it's really a tremendous feeling.' 'I feel something like a king.' 'I feel like a giant.' For others, it is the reverse. Some 38 per cent of those who experienced 'break-off' described feelings of fear or anxiety associated with it. One pilot's report went as follows. 'He feels alone, light, remote and insecure. He is unhappy until he gets to a lower altitude. He feels the need to have an important objective to take his mind off it.'

Another feeling commonly associated with 'break-off' is loneliness. This was reported by 70 per cent of the pilots who had experienced the effect. For example: '. . . you do have a feeling of separation and loneliness'. 'It's lonely alone at high altitude.' These feelings can become extremely disturbing should the flyer momentarily lose radio contact with the ground.

That some form of sensory underload was responsible for these effects is suggested by the pilots' replies when asked what factors contributed to 'break-off'. Many factors were mentioned, but the three most commonly cited were being alone, being at high altitude, and not being particularly busy in controlling the aircraft. The effect could occur anywhere between 15,000 and 45,000 feet, but the most typical height was somewhere around 33,000 feet. When asked 'Did your feelings help or hinder your ability to operate the plane?' 55 per cent of those with experience answered 'neither', and 21 per cent felt that it helped. The remainder regarded it as a hindrance, or had no opinion.

A more recent British study[20] of 'break-off' considered five cases in which isolation in flight gave rise to disturbing feelings of confusion, sometimes leading to near-disasters. All the cases occurred at high altitude, in flyers who were either solo or physically separated from other crew members. The author of this study, Dr Hastin Bennett, likened the pilot's condition to that of subjects in sensory deprivation experiments. He gives the following description of the pilot's environment in high level flight:

When the aircraft is flying straight and level the aviator has very little to do, and there are only slight appreciable changes in the instruments, which are the only things that might move in the cockpit. The pilot is strapped into his seat and cannot move about; often he cannot see the wings behind him or the nose of the plane sloping away in front. The background noise of the engines and of the oxygen system is monotonous and unvarying. Outside there is an unchanging vista. At 45,000 feet the horizon is over 200 miles away, and the eye cannot detect any movement over the earth's surface, supposing that it is visible and not obscured by haze or cloud. The aviator is suspended in his transparent canopy in the sky.

To date, I know of no reports of hallucinations associated with 'break-off'. This does not mean that none have occurred, since pilots are notoriously reluctant to talk about such things. Nor does it mean that sensory deprivation is not the primary cause, since many of the more recent experiments have failed to confirm the high incidence of hallucinations reported by the McGill subjects. For example, investigators at the Aerospace Medical Laboratory, Ohio,[21] reported hallucination-like phenomena in only two of their sixty subjects. But with or without hallucinations, 'break-off' is a potentially dangerous state – regardless of the euphoria that may accompany it. Any marked changes in the pilot's emotional state, whether it be towards delight or apprehension, can adversely affect the performance of his complex task. At a very practical level, it can, for example, lead to overbreathing which, in turn, makes increased demands on the oxygen supply. Breathing too great a concentration of pure oxygen can, by itself, lead to a fall-off in efficiency, or it can enhance the emotional 'high' (or 'low') associated with the break-off effect.

Although hallucinations are not a common occurrence in high-level flight, many have been reported by seafarers – less taciturn than flyers, and with a greater delight in the strange and wonderful. While many of the world's great sea monsters may owe their existence to an excess of rum, or to the sailor's well-known love of a 'tall story', some at least may have a basis in the hallucinations of a solitary mariner keeping watch while becalmed in a leaden sea that merges imperceptibly into a grey, overcast sky. Joshua Slocum describes the following 'apparition' that came to him shortly after his sloop *Spray* had left the Azores *en route* to Gibraltar: '. . . looking out of the companionway, to my amazement I saw a tall man at the helm. His right hand, grasping the spokes of the wheel, held them as in a vice. One may imagine my astonishment. His rig was that of a foreign sailor, and a large red cap he wore was cockbilled over his left ear, and all was set off with shaggy black whiskers.'[22] This gentleman later introduced himself as Columbus's pilot, and proved very helpful (according to Slocum) in getting the *Spray* back on to the correct course. Slocum himself attributed the presence of this apparition to an excess of white cheese and plums eaten at his last port of call, but it is not inconceivable that his solitary state may have had something to do with it as well.

Finally, what of the astronauts and cosmonauts, the men to whom 'other-worldliness' is a reality? So far, the laconic and matter-of-fact remarks of these men have revealed no hint of any experience comparable to that of 'break-off', nor of any other sensory deprivation effect. Is it that they are not prone to such phenomena? Hardly likely, considering that many of them are recruited from among naval aviators who, as we have seen, are far from immune. It is more probable that the job of manning a space capsule is still too demanding and too 'arousing'. Not only that, most space flights have been watched by the television-viewing world, and if there is one thing likely to inhibit the onset of sensory deprivation effects it is probably the feeling that you are standing in the middle of a world stage. However, this state of affairs is changing. Public interest in space exploration is waning fast; the novelty is gone and the outcome seems all too predictable. It took something like the near-disaster of Apollo 13 to re-awaken the great interest shown in the earlier missions. How many people were watching the progress of Apollo 13 before things went wrong? Far fewer than watched afterwards.

So what will become of the men who will circle the earth for months on end in orbiting laboratories, or those who will take part in a manned flight to Mars where the shortest round trip is likely to take in excess of a year? Once the 'world's eye' is no longer watching their every move, it seems probable that disturbing feelings of separation from the earth, particularly when they correspond to reality, are going to become not only more frequent than those reported by earthbound aviators, but also more intense, and from the psychiatric point of view more dangerous. 'Other-worldliness' is a relatively unexplored dimension of human experience, and one that we are likely to hear a great deal more of in the future.

7 Fatigue and Stress

'Fatigue' is one of those awkward and overworked terms that abound in psychology, terms which through being inherited from everyday speech convey some meaning to almost everyone, but which are too vague to be of much use to the scientist. More than fifty years ago it was recommended that the word should be banished from scientific discussion and more precise terms substituted, but it still survives, and so do the problems of definition that faced the early investigators. The trouble is that while 'fatigue' appears to refer to a single entity it actually embraces a wide range of different psychological and physiological processes, and perhaps the only thing they have in common is their causal relationship to prolonged performance.

Just what are these fatigue processes? In trying to answer this question, the first thing we encounter is the distinction between the subjective and objective aspects of fatigue. That is, between the subjective awareness of tiredness and the objective effects of prolonged work on some measurable index of performance, such as speed or accuracy.

If you ask people what they mean by the word 'fatigue', they will usually refer to the feelings of tiredness, the muscular aches, the crick in the neck, the drowsiness and the irritability that make up the sensations of fatigue. And these, after all, are the most obvious signs to most people. But we clearly cannot limit ourselves simply to the reports that only the driver or the pilot can make about his feelings of tiredness. Quite early on in the scientific study of fatigue it became evident that almost any kind of subjective statement can be made in relation to almost any kind of objective performance. In other words, there is virtually no correlation between the two; and where there is, it is quite likely to be in the opposite direction to what one would expect. For instance, one person may complain of excessive tiredness and yet show no measurable decline in performance; whereas another may claim to be perfectly fresh and yet handle his vehicle in a dangerous or otherwise inadequate fashion.

But even when we confine ourselves to objective measures of work output or quality of performance, we still have problems. Different kinds of sustained activity can produce quite different, even contradictory, fatigue effects. For instance, where an activity is simple and repetitive, but involves hard physical work – like rowing a boat, or shovelling coal in a steam locomotive – the most obvious indication of fatigue is a reduction in the total amount of activity. But in a task like driving a car or flying an aeroplane, something which calls for comparatively little in the way of muscular effort yet demands persistent concentration and a high degree of skill, the effect of prolonged activity is likely to be the reverse of that seen in the simple repetitive task. Instead of doing less, the tired driver or pilot may actually do *more work* than when he was fresh.

Prolonged performance of a complex co-ordinated and accurately timed activity like flying or driving produces a number of subtle effects that cannot be explained in terms of simple muscular fatigue. What deteriorates under these conditions is not so much the physical ability to perform the required control actions, but the mental ability to integrate these actions into the kind of co-ordinated sequence that is essential for the successful execution of any highly skilled activity. As we shall see below, one major effect of 'skill fatigue' is that it disrupts the *organization* of a skill; and it does this primarily by eroding the 'packaging' of information that was so painfully acquired during training, and which permitted the single-channel 'mental computer' (described in Chapter 5) to handle the incoming sensory signals essential to the task.

Pilot fatigue

The principal effects of pilot fatigue have been shown most clearly in the classic series of experiments called the 'Cambridge Cockpit Studies' carried out during the Second World War under the direction of Sir Frederic Bartlett, then Professor of Psychology at the University of Cambridge.[1] The experimental situation was as follows: a standard Spitfire cockpit, complete with instrument panel and flight controls, was rigged up in such a way as to simulate the conditions of blind flying or instrument flight (i.e. in cloud or poor visibility). That is, the instruments – displaying among other things airspeed, sideslip, heading and altitude – responded in a realistic way to the movements of the control column, rudder bar and throttle while the subjects, 140 pilots with wartime flying training, carried out a series of prescribed manoeuvres. The deviations from the intended 'flight path' were automatically recorded, indicating both the extent and the nature of the pilots' errors. The main purpose of the experiment was to study the changes that occurred in the pilots' behaviour as the result of two hours' continuous 'flying' in the simulator.

To ensure that fatigue rather than boredom or some other factor was influencing performance, certain selected pilots volunteered to continue flying the simulator until they were exhausted. In some cases these extended sessions lasted for as long as six or seven hours, and the results obtained indicated that the effects observed in the two-hour test were, in fact, caused by fatigue rather than anything else.

The results of the two-hour tests showed that the pilot's ability to maintain a desired airspeed and to prevent sideslip (unbalanced flight) deteriorated by nearly 50 per cent in relation to initial, fresh performance. But the maintenance of a desired altitude and direction was little affected by prolonged work; indeed, there was even a gradual improvement with practice which tailed off towards the end of the session.

Although it was more likely that the correct rather than the incorrect response would be made, even towards the end of the two-hour session, the most noticeable deterioration was in the *way* these responses were executed, particularly with regard to their timing. There was clear evidence to suggest that timing – the ability to co-ordinate a series of actions into a smooth and economical sequence – suffered more and more as fatigue developed. The main cause of this seemed to lie in the fact that instead of responding to the instrument panel as a unified whole, and extracting the information in a coherent 'chunk' (as they had been trained to do), tired pilots tended to react to each separate instrument individually. Thus, instead of communicating a single message, the display 'split up' into several discrete 'bits' of information.

As indicated earlier, an experienced pilot acquires the skill of scanning separate units of information and then integrating these into a single 'mental picture' of what the aircraft as a whole is doing. However, as time goes on, this process of integration begins to break down and the tired pilot resorts to a simpler though less efficient style of responding. That is, he regresses to the stage where he concentrates his attention on each individual instrument in turn and tries to maintain a particular component of his flight path, say, airspeed, at the expense of the other related components. But as he follows the fluctuations of the airspeed indicator with his controls, errors build up unobserved in the other instruments – for example, height begins to slip away, or the aircraft starts to sideslip, or goes into a gradual roll. When he finally notices these discrepancies, he has to make large corrections to eliminate them, and these in turn lead to other errors, and so on. Eventually he finds himself in a progressively losing race trying to catch up with these separate, accumulating errors. The upshot is that he loses both the timing and the economy of action that derives from a highly organized mental picture; and he has to work a good deal harder – rather like the trainee pilot – simply to maintain a barely adequate level of performance.

Thus, pilot fatigue accumulates in a vicious circle: being fatigued makes the pilot do more work, which in turn makes him feel more tired and anxious about his performance, until eventually the point is reached when the flying skill breaks down completely. But until a very great level of fatigue is reached, this process may not reveal itself as gross deficiencies in performance, particularly in the highly-skilled man for whom the business of flying has become automated through years of practice. On the face of it, a tired but very experienced pilot may appear to be flying as well as ever, but the mental effort of maintaining this level of performance is likely to be much greater than when he was fresh, and this additional effort may well reduce his ability to handle an emergency, or to make rapid and accurate decisions in an unexpected situation.

This fragmentation of the instrument panel into separate, almost unrelated sources of information is further accentuated by the fact that fatigue, like many other forms of stress, brings about a marked reduction in the *span of attention*, or the amount of information we can take in at a single glance, a phenomenon which has been called 'tunnel vision'. This does not mean that vision is restricted only to the foveal part of the retina (see Chapter 4). What happens is that there is an increasing tendency to narrow one's attention down to that area of the visual field – central or peripheral – from which important signals are expected to come. While it may actually improve one's vigilance in that particular area of the visual field, it also causes one to neglect or disregard important signals that fall outside this area. Another way of describing it is to say that we become less flexible in the way we *deploy* our focus of attention.

In the Cambridge Cockpit study, for example, pilots were instructed to make regular checks of some fuel gauges situated at the edge of the instrument panel; and one of the earliest signs of fatigue was that these periodic checks were omitted. By the end of the two-hour period, some 60 per cent of the subjects were paying no attention to these peripheral instruments – a fact which could have led to disaster if they were actually flying a real aircraft. Many of us will have noticed a similar tendency at the end of a long car drive. The more tired we become, the greater is the likelihood that we will confine our attention to a small area of the road ahead, so that we pay scant attention to – or even fail to perceive – events occurring on either side of the road.

This tendency to ignore peripheral signals is probably also related to the gradual loss of capacity in our short-term memory store (see Chapter 5) that is known to be characteristic of fatigue in skilled tasks. Forgetfulness was perhaps the most noticeable psychological change observed in aircrew after twelve hours of flying in Catalina Flying Boats.[2] For example, about four minutes before a change of course was required the navigator passed a slip of paper to the pilot on which was written the new course and the time of the course change. A fresh pilot experienced no difficulty in changing his heading at the correct time. But after several hours of flight he sometimes forgot to alter course for several minutes after the change was due.

Another important finding in the Cambridge Cockpit experiment was that self-imposed standards of flying accuracy gradually deteriorated with prolonged performance. For example, when the pilots were fresh the sideslip needle was considered to be within satisfactory limits if it deviated no more than two or three degrees from the vertical (no-slip) position. But as the men became more fatigued these acceptable error limits widened, first to five degrees either way, and then ten degrees or even more in some cases. Similarly, at the beginning of the session, speed was kept to within five to ten knots of the desired rate, but towards the end, the standards became so lax that stalls were not uncommon.

Because he is usually unaware that he is relaxing his flying standards the tired pilot often thinks he is actually performing more efficiently as the task progresses. In fact, this only appears so because his error limits are widening, allowing previously unacceptable errors to go uncorrected. As we said earlier, therefore, the tired pilot's account of what is happening to him becomes increasingly less reliable as the flight progresses.

In addition to becoming more unreliable in his judgements, he also becomes more irritable and short-tempered. What happened to the Cambridge Cockpit pilots has been graphically described by Bartlett:

... this experiment demonstrated conclusively that the everyday observation which associates growing irritability with increasing fatigue ... is correct. When the operator began, absorbed in his task, he was usually silent. As he went on, sighs and shufflings emerged from the machine. Then mild expletives took the place of sighs. By the end of the experiment ... most operators kept up a flow of the most violent language they knew. And all the time their handling of the controls became more and more rough, so that they were doing more work and not less, as the task went on. It was at this stage that the tendency to project all errors on to the experimenter or the machine reached its height.[3]

When the acute stages of fatigue are reached, Bartlett also noticed that for some individuals 'dogged fortitude ... will carry a man through to a kind of second wind.' This raises an important but often neglected question: How do motivational factors interact with the effects of fatigue? Most of us have experienced situations in which a stubborn determination to keep going – a quality, incidentally, which only the Finns appear to have a single word for, namely, '*sisu*' – has effectively postponed the onset of fatigue. This is the kind of motivation that keeps long-distance runners on their feet for the last few yards of the race, after which they often collapse into a long-overdue and complete state of exhaustion.

A similar thing can show itself at a much more mundane level: in running for a train, for example. Dr Robert S. Schwab stood on a Boston railway platform and estimated the average distance a commuter was prepared to sprint after a departing train before he gave it up as missed.[4] He watched for three separate trains, the 4.31, the 5.21, and the 5.45 – which was the last train out of Boston for the day. Motivation to catch the first of these trains was not particularly high, as there were two later ones, and the commuters who missed it were only prepared to jeopardize their dignity to the extent of sprinting after it for about twenty yards. But missing the last train carried with it much higher penalties, a five- or ten-dollar taxi ride, or the alternative of spending the night in Boston with the problem of getting the wife to believe the story. This produced considerably higher motivation, and those who arrived on the platform when the train was departing went to much greater lengths to get aboard. Throwing dignity to the winds, wheezing commuters would run flat out for an average distance of seventy yards (as compared to only forty yards for the penultimate train), crying out and gesticulating wildly in the hope that someone would see them and stop the train – which actually happened in several cases.

Schwab also carried out a very similar experiment using a horizontal bar. He asked people to hang there for as long as they could. With instructions to hold on 'as long as possible', the average length of time before letting go was less than a minute. With strong urging and suggestion, the time lengthened to just over a minute. But with an offer of five dollars for improving their previous efforts, subjects managed to cling on for an average of nearly two minutes.

Of course, this motivational coin has its reverse side as well. A short walk through dull streets is often more tiring than a longer walk through pleasant and interesting surroundings. Similarly, driving down a straight stretch of featureless motorway makes one feel more fatigued than driving the same distance through country lanes. Even though it allows us to make good time, we frequently long to be off a motorway, into traffic even, just to be rid of the monotony of mile after mile slipping by, each indistinguishable from the last. Monotony and boredom can exacerbate the effects of fatigue, just as a short 'arousal jag' can alleviate them – up to a point, at least.

In their study the Cambridge investigators found that they could bring about a temporary but quite marked improvement in a tired pilot's performance by changing the experimental instructions to make the flying task more difficult. In an actual flight experiment, continuous recordings were made of altitude and heading during chosen intervals of a fifteen-hour flight in an RAF Shackleton aircraft.[5] There were two pilots per crew, and during each flight these two pilots stood four watches of approximately two hours each. But they only piloted the plane manually for approximately one hour of the two-hour watch. One interesting finding in this study was that during their first two watches, pilots tended to fly more accurately and consistently in rough air (due to turbulence) than in calm air. In other words, during the early part of the flight, the 'arousal jag' due to the increased demands of flying through turbulence brought a remission of fatigue symptoms just as the harder instructions did for the Cambridge Cockpit subjects. However, during the last two watches of the flight, their performance was adversely affected by turbulent air. Thus, the benefits of increased arousal were only evident during mild fatigue; at a more advanced stage of fatigue, an 'arousal jag' makes matters worse.

So far we have concentrated on the immediate effects of sustained flying on the pilot's performance, and most of our evidence has been drawn either from the Cambridge simulator experiment or from studies conducted aboard long-range maritime aircraft. While much of our knowledge gleaned from experiments with crews of relatively slow-moving, piston-engined aircraft is generally applicable to the pilots of high-speed, high-altitude jet aircraft, there is quite a lot of evidence to suggest that the *degree* of fatigue suffered by the contemporary jet pilot is probably greater than that experienced by his propeller-driven predecessors. In a recent survey carried out among jet pilots, for instance, it was found that 93 per cent of them regarded flying fatigue as a major problem. What makes jet flying so much more tiring?

David Beaty, airline pilot and author of *The Human Factor*,[6] has listed some of the additional stresses associated with flying the modern jet airliner, any one of which is going to contribute to the fatigue experienced by the captain and crew. First, the aircraft is much larger. The jumbo jets now in service carry nearly five hundred passengers, and inevitably this additional responsibility will weigh heavily on the captain. Combined with this there is the greater risk of mechanical failure invariably associated with a new type of aircraft.

Second, the modern jet airliner flies much faster than its predecessors, and calls for faster decisions and greater activity on the part of the pilot. Apart from the fact that the critical phases of take-off and landing are much closer together in time, the business of checking in at radio stations, sending position reports, and altering course has become almost a continuous operation for the pilot – to say nothing of the need to cope with the increased hazard of collision over crowded airports where an aircraft may remain 'stacked' for hours waiting for an opportunity to land. No matter how rapid the flight, however, the time of maximum fatigue always coincides with the period in which the greatest demands are made upon the pilot and crew; namely, during the let-down and landing.

Unlike the captains of ten years ago, the contemporary airline pilot has little or no chance to stretch his legs by walking back and fraternizing with the passengers, something which used to provide a brief respite from the stresses on the flightdeck. Not only is the workload greater, but the number of crew members available to handle it is less than that on smaller piston-engined aircraft. In the cockpit of a jet airliner like the Boeing 707, the captain will usually be accompanied by two other pilots: a first officer with considerable co-pilot experience, and a relatively inexperienced second officer. Either the first or second officer will handle the navigation, and, in addition, there will be a flight engineer on board. Although this reduction in the flightdeck crew has been made possible by technological advances in radio and navigational aids, it still compares unfavourably with the operating crews carried on the smaller, piston-engined airliners like Constellations or Stratocruisers, where there are two pilots, two engineers, a radio officer, and a navigator on board. As David

Beaty points out, a large crew carries with it two additional safety factors: there are more people on the flightdeck to monitor one another, and there are more officers on board to handle emergencies when they arise.

Jet airliners fly much higher than piston-engined aircraft, and the supersonic transport (SST), soon to be in service, will fly even higher than the present generation of subsonic transports. Among other things, higher flight means that the airline captain may have to spend up to eight hundred hours a year in a cabin pressurized to about six thousand feet above sea-level, and breathing very dry air. Recent research at the RAF Institute of Aviation Medicine has shown that environmental conditions like these, previously regarded as having no effects on mental function, can bring about quite a significant deterioration in the performance of a complex decision-making task, as well as marked loss of subjective well-being.[7] It is also known that even a mild diminution in the oxygen content of the air can hasten the onset of fatigue.

Finally, there is the problem of 'multiple timezone travel' which stems from the rapid transit times of jet airliners – becoming even faster, of course, with the advent of the SST. Anyone who has travelled over several timezones in a few hours will appreciate how long it takes to 'reset' the built-in, twenty-four-hour, 'body clock' to local time. While the natives are composing themselves for sleep you are pacing around looking for the action, and when the locals awake refreshed you are finally sliding into a fitful slumber. Research suggests that the period necessary to resynchronize the traveller's twenty-four-hour rhythm after a long-distance flight depends on both the number of timezones crossed and also on whether the flight was in an easterly or westerly direction. A general rule of thumb, however, is that most travellers adjust to a timeshift at the rate of one hour per day. On average, therefore, it takes three to four days to resynchronize the 'body clock' after crossing four timezones, as for example in flying across the United States from coast to coast. After a transatlantic crossing, covering five or six timezones, it takes about five to six days for complete readjustment to occur. And after crossing twelve timezones, involving a complete reversal of the day–night cycle, readjustment may take up to twelve days. During this time, most people experience some discomfort. As

Dr Hubertus Strughold (sometimes called the 'Father of Space Medicine') put it: 'They become hungry, sleepy or wide-awake at the wrong time in relation to the new local time. Their head clocks, their stomach clocks, and their elimination systems are confused.'[8]

In a recent study carried out by West German investigators at the Aerospace Medical Institute in Bad Godesburg,[9] the efficiency of experienced pilots unaccustomed to multiple timezone travel was tested before and after flying as passengers on a rapid scheduled flight from Germany to the United States. After a seventeen-day stay in America, they returned to Germany, again as passengers on a scheduled jet flight, and were tested at different hours of the day for several days after both journeys. The time-shift for both the outgoing and return trips was eight hours. The efficiency test involved flying a supersonic transport simulator under instrument flying conditions with some unexpected emergencies thrown in for good measure by the experimenters. In addition to measuring overall efficiency in flying the simulator, a number of physiological indices – like heart rate and oxygen consumption – were also recorded.

The results showed that for both the westbound (outgoing) and eastbound (return) trips, the time needed for the pilots' twenty-four-hour rhythm to resynchronize with local time was, on average, about five days – which conforms with the rule of thumb mentioned earlier. But the results relating to changes in pilot efficiency associated with this 'catching-up time' were less clear-cut. They depended a great deal upon the individual pilot, and upon the time of day or night at which he was tested.

In some pilots the decrement in performance after rapid transportation was as much as 40 per cent in comparison with their preflight (control) performance on the SST simulator; while in others the effects were quite negligible. In general, though, the overall performance level was lower when tested during the day than when tested during the night – a complete reversal from the preflight sessions where there was sometimes a 75–100 per cent decline in efficiency at four in the morning as compared to three in the afternoon.

The one definite finding with regard to efficiency was that for all pilots the general decline in flying performance after the return eastbound trip (where they 'lost' eight hours) was much greater than after the westbound flight (where they 'gained' eight hours). Since they stayed for seventeen days in the United States, this difference could not be explained by the effects of the outgoing flight 'carrying-over' to compound the effects of the return flight, because the recovery time for the 'biological clock' was five days both ways. To some extent this difference could be accounted for by the fact that the return flights were more fatiguing in that they invariably departed from the United States during the evening and arrived in Europe in the early morning, leaving the passenger with another twelve or fifteen hours before he could decently go to bed. When he did finally try to get to sleep, he was often prevented from doing so because his body clock was slow relative to local time.

Although a number of studies have now shown that the period of readjustment is more disturbing after an eastbound rather than a westbound flight, there is far from general agreement on this point. For instance, Dr Aschoff at the Max Planck Institute in West Germany found quite the reverse.[10] He simulated west-bound and eastbound flights in finches and humans by keeping them in an underground bunker and artificially altering the light–dark cycles. In one experiment he found that both men and birds adjusted more rapidly after an eastbound 'flight', requiring only about three days to recover from a six-hour shortening of the day–night cycle, as opposed to nearly six days to recover from a corresponding lengthening of the cycle (equivalent to a west-bound flight). Recovery in this case was measured by the resynchronization of body temperature, which is known to bear a close relationship to efficiency of performance.

These contradictory findings are characteristic of the considerable variation, both between and within people, that is apparent in the effects of multiple timezone travel. Some people, for example, feel that they readjust more easily after returning home to familiar surroundings and routines, irrespective of whether this involves an eastbound or a westbound flight. There is also some evidence to suggest that people travelling alone take longer to readjust than those travelling in groups. And, as mentioned earlier, there are very wide individual differences: some individuals appear to be unaffected by multiple timezone travel, others are considerably disturbed. The same variation is observed in the way people adjust to different working shifts. There are also age differences. During the first three months of life, babies show little or no effect; while, for the elderly, readjustment to a new day–night cycle is a slow and frequently uncomfortable business.

We still need a lot more careful research before we can fully understand the effects of crossing many timezones in a few hours. However, it is quite clear from existing studies that these unnatural changes in man's twenty-four-hour rhythm – a rhythm which was evolved through millions of years as an adaptation to life on earth – will reduce a pilot's efficiency if he is required to fly again soon after landing from a long-distance trip, and it will do this mainly through the effects of impoverished sleep and the resultant accumulation of chronic fatigue. To combat this some airlines, like Air France, have adopted the sensible expedient of requiring their crews to maintain their home routine of sleeping and waking during short stays in other timezones.

But even within the same timezone, a pilot's ability to carry out a complex task like flying will fluctuate widely over a twenty-four-hour period. For example, as I mentioned earlier, the German SST simulator tests carried out before the transatlantic flights showed that even when the pilot is fresh at the beginning of a particular test session (in the sense that he had not missed his sleep), his performance at four o'clock in the morning can be as much as 75 to 100 per cent worse than it is at three o'clock in the afternoon. Although there are wide individual differences in the consistency of this cycle, and in the times of maximum and minimum efficiency – for instance, intraverts reach their peak efficiency earlier in the day than extraverts – these general findings relating quality of performance to time of day provide strong support for the widely held idea of a 'night flying risk'. Studies carried out by the United States Civil Aeronautics Board and the Flight Safety Foundation have shown that the relative risk of aircraft accidents is much greater at night than during the day.[11] Although part of this higher night accident rate is likely to be due to reduced visibility, it is also likely to be the result of reduced pilot efficiency as well. When the number of fatal airline accidents in United States domestic airlines occurring between 1938 and

1949 were plotted against time of day, it was found that the greatest number of accidents happened between two o'clock and four o'clock in the morning – a period which according to the German simulator experiments coincides with the lowest ebb of pilot performance.

There seems little doubt that susceptibility to fatigue during night operations will be much greater than during the day. Even when the pilots flying at night have slept beforehand, they are unlikely to obtain the full benefit from this sleep unless they have become fully adjusted to a reversal of the day–night cycle. And this, as we have seen, can take several days during which both the amount and the quality of sleep, and particularly the latter, are likely to be less than they ought to be – a factor which is not always taken into account in the scheduling of airline flight crews.

If serious disturbances can arise from the rapid transit of time-zones on earth, the problem for the space traveller is even more acute. Spacecraft can orbit the earth in between 90 to 130 minutes. In this situation the customary twenty-four-hour day–night cycle has been replaced by an erratic sunlight-shadow cycle which is less than one-tenth of the day–night cycle on earth. But the space traveller, like his pre-neolithic ancestors before him, has his body clock set to a terrestrial time scale, and this has revealed itself in the sleep experiences of some astronauts and cosmonauts in orbital flight. Gordon Cooper, for example, showed a very disturbed sleep pattern in space. He dozed off for a series of one-hour 'catnaps' totalling about four hours in a flight of just over thirty-six hours. The second Russian cosmonaut, Gherman Titov, had some initial difficulty getting off to sleep in weightlessness (whenever he dozed off, his arms floated away from him and this woke him up; he solved the problem by tucking his arms under his seat belt), but after this his sleep periods closely coincided with Moscow night-time. On later missions, like the fourteen-day orbital flight of Gemini 7, life was made easier for the astronauts by artificially darkening the windows of the spacecraft at certain periods to provide a day–night cycle in tune with what they had been used to before blast-off at Cape Kennedy. In general, the sleep patterns of astronauts and cosmonauts have continued to reflect the twenty-four-hour cycles of their point of departure.

Astronauts and even aircrew have teams of scientists working on their sleep–wakefulness problems, but how can we, the average earthbound traveller, minimize the discomfort caused by multiple timezone travel? According to Dr Strughold, there are at least three things we can do which will either avoid throwing the body clock out of phase, or else will shorten the readjustment time. First, there is the method of preflight adaptation. If you need to be on top form immediately upon arrival at some distant location, you can avoid the adverse effects of timeshift by pre-setting the body clock some days before the flight. For an eastbound trip you can go to bed an hour earlier each night and wake an hour earlier the next day until you are in phase with local time at your destination. For a westbound trip you reverse the procedure: go to bed an hour later and get up an hour later each day prior to the flight. Second, there is the method of postflight adaptation. If it is at all possible, you can fly to the distant place several days in advance of the important event or meeting. This gives the body clock time to adjust before the critical or demanding engagement. This method is frequently used by heads of state flying to important summit meetings on another continent. Finally, you can take some mild medication to help you to adjust to the new day–night cycle at your destination. This is probably the most convenient method, although perhaps it is also the least satisfactory of the three.

Next, we turn to the more widespread, yet curiously elusive problem of driver fatigue. Although not fundamentally different from that of pilot fatigue, it does – as we shall see – tend to show itself in less obvious ways, and to be promoted by somewhat different factors.

Driver fatigue

While most people would agree that sustained driving, like prolonged work at any skilled task, is likely to impair the driver's performance, there is surprisingly little research evidence to indicate that such a deterioration actually occurs. True, there have been many studies – particularly in the United States, involving long-distance truck drivers – which have demonstrated that a lengthy period at the wheel can reduce a man's score on laboratory tests measuring such things as reaction time, co-ordination, speed of tapping, the ability to discriminate flicker in a light source, body sway, and hand steadiness. But this is not the same thing as showing a decrement in *actual* driving ability.

Although some investigators have claimed, on the basis of such tests, that long hours of driving reduce efficiency and increase the likelihood of accidents, they are voicing opinion rather than fact, since we have no real evidence that performance on these laboratory tests has any direct bearing on a man's ability to handle his vehicle safely. In other words, the fact that a tired truck driver produces, say, a slower reaction time when tested at the end of his trip under laboratory conditions is no guarantee that he would have stamped on his brakes any the less quickly if a child had run out in front of his truck while he was actually on the road. In any case, we cannot assess the quality of a man's skill by testing him on a number of simple and isolated tasks like those described above. The essence of a skill is that it forms an integrated whole which is more than the sum of its constituent actions.

Unfortunately, our understanding of driver fatigue has not been greatly advanced by those studies which have measured the effects of prolonged driving on the driver's actual performance behind the wheel. For example, two American investigators observed the performance of bus drivers over a three-and-a-half-hour scheduled passenger route.[12] When they compared driving performance during the first and last thirty-minute periods, the most noticeable finding was that, during the last half hour, the drivers made considerably fewer steering wheel movements than they did during the first half-hour – probably because this aspect of the task involved a good deal of muscular effort in the days before power-assisted steering when this study was done. But when they examined all the other different measures of driving proficiency, they found no significant deterioration in any of them. This absence of any gross decline in driving ability is a fairly typical finding for those studies which have attempted to show the effects of prolonged driving on vehicle-handling performance. Either the fatigue effects were too insignificant to be shown up in the first place, or – which seems more likely – the investigators were concentrating on the wrong aspects of driving performance. We will consider this latter possibility in further detail at a later point.

Another direct way of tackling the problem of driver fatigue has been to look at the number of hours a man had been driving before he was involved in an accident or a near-accident. But here again no clear evidence of a fatigue effect emerges. In 1938 the US Public Health Service examined accident rates among inter-state truck drivers and found that the greatest number of 'driver-responsibility' accidents occurred after only five to six hours on duty. Only about 12 per cent of all accidents involved drivers who had been on duty for ten hours or more. In 1949 the accident-prevention departments of two large insurance companies reported that 60 per cent of all long-haul trucking accidents occurred during the *first* three and a half hours of a trip. They also found that the most likely period for a driver to cause an accident through falling asleep at the wheel was between four and five hours after the last sleep. In 1954 a study was reported in which seventeen long-distance truck drivers on a total of twenty trips, averaging 250 miles per trip, were checked for near-accidents by an observer riding in the cab. Of the forty-eight near-accidents noted, 46 per cent occurred within the first two hours of the trip, and 67 per cent during the first four hours of what was usually a nine-hour drive. Far from indicating that long hours of driving increase the risk of near-accidents, these data suggest that the risk diminishes as the hours of driving increase. The pattern is similar to that found in the earlier studies, cited above, which restricted themselves to actual accidents.

Yet most of us feel subjectively that long hours of driving reduce our efficiency, and increase our tendency to make silly mistakes, or to see things that are not there while missing the things we should have seen. So why should the effects of driver fatigue be so difficult to specify, and so hard to pin down?

It may have something to do with the fact that compared to flying, driving a motor vehicle is a relatively *self-paced* activity. The driver is more of a free agent than the pilot. The length of time a pilot spends at the controls is largely determined by external factors such as what was in the flight plan he filed before departure, the nature of the route, the availability of diversion airfields, and so on. By comparison, the driver is usually able to adjust his rate of work, and the length of time he drives without a break, to suit his own feelings. Outside of traffic jams, motorways and other restricted parking areas, the private motorist, at least, can take a rest, a 'catnap' even, almost whenever he considers he needs a break. In some American States such periodic breaks are enforced by law. Even the commercial driver has his regular 'pull-ins', cafés and lay-bys along the route. The same is not true, however, for the bus driver, constrained as he is by a fixed route and a rigid timetable, and this may be one of the reasons why London bus drivers, as a group, have more than their fair share of hypertension and other cardiovascular stress disorders.

To the extent that driving a motor vehicle is a more self-governed activity than flying an aeroplane, it is reasonable to expect that the effects of 'skill fatigue' will show up more readily in flying than in driving. For instance, being a generally simpler task and less rigidly determined by external factors, driving is less likely to show the marked errors of timing and perceptual disorganization that were characteristic of the early stages of pilot fatigue.

If the effects of driver fatigue are more covert than those of pilot fatigue, then it is probable that the earlier studies of the effects of prolonged driving failed to show any noticeable deterioration because they focused exclusively on the overt aspects of driver behaviour. Recent researchers have suggested that the elusive effects of driver fatigue may reveal themselves in a number of more indirect ways; namely, as (a) changes in emotional arousal or 'stress fatigue', (b) as a loss of 'spare mental capacity', and (c) as an increase in the frequency of lapses of attention or 'involuntary rest pauses'. We will consider each of these factors in turn.

Dr Alan Crawford of the British Road Research Laboratory believes that, in driving, the number of hours spent behind the wheel may be less important in producing fatigue than the cumulative emotional effect of all the stresses and annoyances created by traffic conditions and the behaviour of other road users.[13] Instead of manifesting itself directly in the way we handle our vehicle, this 'stress fatigue' affects us by increasing – at least at first – our overall level of emotional arousal. One of the well-known characteristics of increased arousal is that relatively mild stimuli tend to call forth disproportionately large reactions, particularly emotional ones. As we know from our everyday experiences, an agitated person tends to be overly sensitive, perceiving slights and threats where none was intended, and taking umbrage where none was given; and to all of these things he reacts with a kind of emotional overkill. The same thing, Crawford argues, is true of the motorist suffering from the first stage of stress fatigue.

At the beginning of a drive the mild frustration created by, say, the car ahead being slow off the mark at a green traffic signal, is (depending on temperament) usually accepted philosophically as 'one of those things'. But the gradual accumulation of these petty irritations steps up the driver's level of arousal until, eventually, the same kind of incident will trigger an excessive torrent of muttered abuse and pent-up tension.

Thus, the tired driver reveals his fatigue – according to Crawford – not so much through his actions as through his emotions. Of course, actions like changing gear and stepping on the accelerator are likely to be coloured by emotional arousal, but not necessarily to an extent that would make the driver totally mismanage his vehicle.

If this primary stage of stress fatigue is sustained, it is likely to be overtaken by a second stage that is comparable in many respects to a mild form of battle fatigue. Emotionally exhausted by the excesses of arousal of the first phase, the tired man becomes increasingly *less* responsive to external stimulation, and this is also accompanied by an attitude of indifference that makes it difficult to elicit any kind of emotional response at all. It is comparable to that 'drained' or 'washed-out' feeling that overwhelms us after a harrowing and protracted emotional experience. It can be regarded as a form of defence mechanism: something that prevents our emotional reserves from being depleted too far.

In the case of the motorist, both the primary and secondary stages of stress fatigue are likely to increase his risk of accident. But, from the accident figures discussed earlier, it seems probable that the first stage of over-arousal is more dangerous than the second stage of emotional indifference. However, the second stage may also take its toll, as the following study indicates. Psychologists at the University of South Dakota have recently carried out an experiment which provides some support for this idea of stress fatigue.[14] They investigated the effects of an artificially-induced stress – mild electric shocks contingent upon driving errors – on performance in a car simulator. Fifty-four male students were assigned to one of three experimental groups: a 'stress' group who received a mild shock on their forearms whenever they made a steering error in the simulator (i.e. touched the sides of the 'road'); a 'random shock' group who received the same mild shock but at random intervals with no relationship between shock and driving performance, and a control group who received no shocks at all. All the subjects 'drove' the simulator for a period of six hours, and measures were taken of their steering ability, speed maintenance, reaction time and vigilance in spotting occasional lights (comparable to brakelights) and the occasional deflections of a needle on a meter dial.

It was found that the 'stress group' did not differ significantly from the other two groups in their overall steering ability. The tracking performance of all three groups declined gradually over the six-hour driving session. However, at each point in time the stress group made more errors than the other groups – although the difference was not very marked except towards the end of the session.

According to Crawford's theory, stress fatigue comes in two stages: a first phase in which increased emotional arousal leads to oversensitive behaviour characterized by strong reactions to mild irritations; and a second phase in which sustained arousal leads to a reduced intensity of response together with a general indifference to irritation. The American investigators predicted that the onset of this second phase would reveal itself primarily in a decline in the driver's vigilance: that is, he would tend to miss more of the occasional signals that were subsidiary to the main driving task. The results tended to support this prediction. During the fourth hour of driving, the stress group showed a very sharp fall-off in vigilance compared to the other two groups. The reaction times of the stress group also became considerably slower and their speed maintenance more erratic.

These results suggested that, for this kind of task at least, the second phase of stress fatigue takes about four hours to develop. The effects of the first phase were less marked than those of the second, although there was a general tendency for an increased level of arousal in the stress group (as measured by skin resistance) to produce somewhat poorer performance on all aspects of the task.

Another problem associated with studying fatigue on the roads is the difficulty of establishing the driver's level of concentration from his actual behaviour. A number of studies have shown that if the basis of comparison is simply how the driver handles his vehicle, it is impossible to distinguish a man who has been driving continuously for hours, but who is concentrating hard on his task, from the man who is completely fresh and driving with only a moderate level of concentration. But common sense and personal experience tell us that the man who has been driving for a long period is likely to be the worse driver in that he is probably less able to cope with the unexpected.

In Chapter 5 we pointed out that the human operator behaves very much like a single-channel communication system with a limited capacity for handling relevant information. However, the highly-skilled and wide-awake car driver probably has a greater capacity for handling necessary information than would be called upon in the normal run of driving. In other words, he is likely to possess some 'spare mental capacity' upon which he can draw in an emergency, and which partially compensates for increased fatigue or difficulties in the driving task. But information-handling capacity is limited, and if a person continues to drive for a long period he is likely to use up his reserve of spare capacity so that there will come a time when some unexpected event will do for his single-channel system what the proverbial straw did for the camel's back. We need to know the state of this reserve capacity *before* it gets used up; but we cannot determine this simply from watching the way a person drives. Therefore, we need some additional way of 'tapping' this spare capacity.

Dr Ivan Brown and his colleagues at the Applied Psychology Research Unit in Cambridge, England, have devised a method of assessing spare mental capacity which can be used in the real driving situation. What they have done is to measure the driver's performance on a secondary task while he carries out the primary task of driving. These secondary tasks have included such activities as mental arithmetic and listening for a particular combination of numbers in a series of tape-recorded digits.

In an initial experiment[15] Brown demonstrated that a driver's performance on a secondary auditory task was sensitive to changes in traffic density. When traffic was thick and driving difficult, more errors were made on the secondary task than when traffic was light and driving easy. These preliminary findings were encouraging for they suggested that the secondary task was, in fact, measuring spare mental capacity. Unfortunately, this early promise has not been borne out by later studies aimed directly at measuring the effects of prolonged driving. So far, these Cambridge investigators have failed to find any significant decline in either the primary task of driving or in a secondary task after eight and twelve hours of driving duty. Indeed, in one experiment using police drivers, performance on the secondary task was better for one group of drivers at the end of a spell of duty than it was for another group at the beginning.[16] It is worth taking a closer look at this peculiar finding, since it will give the reader some insight into the problems facing the experimental psychologist when he attempts to pin down these subtle and elusive effects of driver fatigue.

In this particular experiment all the drivers were tested at the same time of day – the late afternoon – when one group of police drivers were coming off watch and another group just starting. They were tested at the same time to eliminate any possible 'time-of-day' effect, discussed earlier. However, it was found on questioning that irrespective of whether they started their duty at eight in the morning or four in the afternoon, both groups got up at the same time, and those on the late afternoon shift filled the early part of the day with domestic chores like gardening or house-decorating. Thus, the strong possibility existed that the fatigue accumulated during these off-duty chores transferred to the driving situation, making these drivers more tired at the beginning of their watch than others who had been on driving duty since eight in the morning. It is just this kind of 'behind-the-scenes' factor which makes driver fatigue studies so difficult to execute and so inconclusive in their results.

Yet another indirect way in which driver fatigue could reveal itself is by an increase in the frequency of spontaneous lapses of attention termed 'involuntary rest pauses' or 'blocks'. In 1931 a psychologist named Bills presented subjects with a series of colours which he asked them to identify by name.[17] As soon as the subject had named the colour, a fresh one was presented, so that the subject worked at his own pace. Bills measured the time between the presentation of the colour and its naming by the subject, and he noticed that after working for some time, people began to produce occasional, unduly long response times. As the task went on, the frequency of these extra long responses increased, although the normal-length responses remained as short as ever. He also observed that after one of these lengthy pauses, people would frequently make a mistake in naming the colour. Bills called these unduly long response times 'blocks' (subsequently called 'Bills' blocks').

Other experiments have confirmed the existence of these intermittent blocks in a wide variety of tasks. They apparently occur sooner and more frequently in self-paced than in externally-paced activities. You can perhaps demonstrate them for yourself in the following simple experiment: take a sheet of newspaper and cross out all the 'e's' you can find. When you check your performance (or better still, when somebody else checks it), you will probably find that the occasional 'e' has been missed, presumably because it coincided with an involuntary rest pause or block. You may also notice a certain regularity in the occurrence of these omissions, and there will probably be more of them in the second half of the sheet than in the first.

A number of theories have been put forward to explain these occasional mental blocks. One theory suggests that if we are instructed to attend to a certain class of stimuli – like the 'e's' on the piece of newspaper – our attentional 'filter' will occasionally switch automatically to another class of stimuli in order to select fresh information. As we have said many times before, the human nervous system is a change-detector, and gets 'bored' with a steady state of affairs.

Another theory employs the notion of 'reactive inhibition' – a fatigue-like nervous process which accumulates as the result of mental activity and which, when it reaches a certain level, will enforce an involuntary rest period. During this rest the reactive inhibition will dissipate of its own accord and afterwards the person will continue to pay attention to the task in hand until the next involuntary rest period intervenes.

Although these blocks may only last for a few seconds, it is not hard to see how they could contribute to accidents – particularly those accidents which defy obvious explanation, like the motorist who runs into a tree in broad daylight on an empty road, or who leaves the road because he failed to steer round a perfectly obvious bend in good visibility. They may also contribute to the 'missed signal' railway accidents that we discussed in Chapter 6. Certainly, there is good evidence to show that the likelihood of involuntary rest periods is increased by the kind of monotonous stimulation encountered on railways and modern motorways. Unfortunately, they are not readily amenable to investigation. In those accidents where we may suspect their influence, the only person who can tell us anything is usually dead, and even if he were alive he could tell us little since these blocks come and go without advertising themselves to the conscious mind.

There is some evidence to indicate that extraverts tend to develop reactive inhibition more quickly and more strongly than introverts.[18] If the reactive inhibition theory were correct, this would make the extravert more liable to road accidents resulting from involuntary rest pauses. For the same reasons, elderly people are more likely to have 'blocks' than younger people. In certain types of people, therefore, the occurrence of these blocks constitutes a definite safety hazard. And their likelihood is increased by depressant drugs like alcohol or antihistamines.

One final point relating to both pilot and driver fatigue, and one which helps to distinguish this kind of fatigue from that produced in non-transport activities, is that it is likely to be exacerbated by the fact that the repetitive vestibular stimulation produced by the motion of a vehicle acts on the central nervous system very much like a sleeping pill. It is no coincidence that the baby falls asleep when it gets rocked. Although the mechanism is not fully understood, there is little doubt that nervous impulses coming in from the vestibular receptors act directly on the sleep centres of the brain in a way that increases drowsiness. This is something that needs to be taken more account of in future studies of transport fatigue than it has in the past.

If there is one overwhelming impression to be gained from the contents of this chapter it is that the psychologist has a great deal more to learn about the nature and causes of pilot and driver fatigue. Indeed, it may be that we have not yet begun to frame the right questions, let alone obtain the right answers. But the problem of fatigue, like many other human-factor problems in transport, is one that is increasing rather than decreasing with technological progress.

8 Style, Personality and Accidents

Although the *kinds* of action involved in controlling a particular car or aircraft are more or less uniform, no two drivers or pilots ever perform these actions in exactly the same way. It is rather like handwriting. If we ask a group of people to write down the same words, the verbal content of the passage will be identical; but the *way* it is written, the *style* of the handwriting, will vary from person to person. And so it is with driving or flying. Each person acquires his own individual style, a characteristic way of doing things that colours all his actions; and even when these actions achieve the same end-result as those of a hundred other people, their manner of execution remains idiosyncratic and distinct.

An individual style of handling a vehicle can be moulded by many factors, but our main concern in this chapter is with the influence of personality. The term 'personality' tends to mean different things to different people, but as used here it refers to those relatively stable and enduring features of the individual which distinguish him from other people and, at the same time, form the basis of our predictions concerning his future behaviour.

Very crudely, we can say that 'personality differences' are what remain after we have eliminated all the other obvious sources of individual variation. For instance, if we select a group of drivers or pilots of the same age, experience, level of intelligence, quality of previous training and sex, and then ask them to execute the same manoeuvres in the same vehicle under the same conditions, any differences in style that emerge can reasonably be put down to the influence of personality factors. Needless to say, we rarely achieve this degree of control in reality.

G

In the early days of travel, accidents were often attributed to bad luck or to a fit of divine pique. Later, during the infancy of mechanized transport, accidents were usually blamed – with some justification – on a failure of the machine. But nowadays we cannot escape the fact that the behaviour of the man controlling the vehicle is responsible for most transport accidents. In 1969, for example, 56,500 people were killed on American roads, and 4,700,000 were injured. Of these, approximately 82 per cent of the deaths and 87 per cent of the injuries could be attributed to the actions of the drivers involved. A breakdown of these actions is shown in Table 7. When reading this through, it is worth keeping in mind that three out of four people killed or injured were travelling on dry roads in clear weather.

TABLE 7   AMERICAN ROAD CASUALTIES DURING 1969
(ATTRIBUTABLE TO DRIVER ACTION)*

Driver action	No. killed	Per cent	No. injured	Per cent
Exceeding speed limit	18,700	40·5	1,056,000	25·5
On wrong side of road	6,300	13·6	236,000	5·7
Did not have right of way	5,800	12·6	795,000	19·2
Cutting in	50	0·1	12,000	0·3
Passing on curve or hill	100	0·2	8,000	0·2
Passing on wrong side	1,100	2·4	83,000	2·0
Signalling errors or failures	150	0·3	25,000	0·6
Drove off roadway	7,100	15·4	575,000	13·9
Reckless driving	5,500	11·9	1,267,000	30·6
Miscellaneous	1,400	3·0	83,000	2·0
TOTALS	46,200	100·0	4,140,000	100·0

* Taken from *The Travelers 1970 Book of Street, Highway, and Interstate Accident Facts* (Hartford, Conn. 1970).

The aim of the present chapter is to consider the following questions: Are some styles of driving or flying more conducive to accidents than others? If so, can we identify these styles? And are they associated with a particular type of personality? Such questions take us inescapably into the quagmire of arguments and counter-arguments that surround the vexed issue of *accident proneness*. So I will begin by summarizing how the notion of accident proneness developed and what its status is today.

The notion of accident proneness

In 1919 two British investigators, Major Greenwood and Hilda Woods, published an account of the accidents sustained by workers in a munitions factory during the First World War.[1] If a group of people work under equally risky conditions for a long period of time then, by chance alone, it is to be expected that some workers will have no accidents, some will have one, some two, some three, and so on. But Greenwood and Woods found that a small minority of workers had more accidents than would be expected if only chance factors were operating. In other words, some workers had more than their 'fair share' of accidents.

A few years later another British investigator, E. M. Newbold, followed up this work by studying the accident records of a large group of workers in thirteen different factories.[2] Her findings also showed that a few people tended to have most of the accidents. For instance, in a sweet factory where a group of ninety-eight girls were engaged in dipping nuts into hot caramel, the chance hypothesis would have predicted that over a period in which there were 136 accidents, twenty-four girls should have had no accidents, and only one or two girls should have had more than four accidents. Actually, forty-three girls had no accidents and five girls had more than four. Newbold, herself, drew very cautious conclusions from these and similar observations. She wrote: 'It is not possible in a mass examination of this kind to find out how much of this may be due to individual differences in the conditions of work or how much to personal tendency, but there are many indications that some part, at any rate, is due to personal tendency.'

Later writers took up this notion of 'personal tendency', but they abandoned the caution that characterized the pioneers in the field. In 1939 two more British investigators, E. Farmer and E. G. Chambers (who, incidentally, coined the term 'accident proneness'), examined the accident records of a large group of drivers, and once again found that a few had a disproportionately large number of accidents.[3] But then they went a stage further. They gave a series of psychological tests – including personality tests – to a group of drivers designated as 'accident-free', and to another group of so-called 'accident-repeaters'. Although these tests failed to distinguish between the two groups in any clear-cut fashion, Farmer and Chambers were confident enough to go beyond their evidence and proclaim: 'Accident proneness is no longer a theory but an established fact.'

So far we have retraced three distinct stages in the development of the accident proneness idea. First, Greenwood and Woods report the statistical fact that some people are accident-repeaters. Second, Newbold confirms this for a much larger group of workers, and tentatively suggests that some people may possess a 'personal tendency' which makes them more liable to accidents than others. Third, Farmer and Chambers again find an unequal liability to accidents, this time among drivers, but then they go on to *explain* the descriptive fact that some people have more accidents than others by coining the term 'accident proneness'. As an explanation of repeated accidents in certain people, accident proneness refers to a personality characteristic that is possessed by these individuals, and which causes them to have mishaps *regardless of the environmental circumstances*. And it is this use of the term that has provoked all the controversy.

The idea that some people carry within them the seeds of their own misfortune was greeted with tremendous enthusiasm by scientists and laymen alike, and the term 'accident-prone' has achieved a lasting place in the English language. The idea dominated accident research for nearly thirty years. And the reasons for this great popularity are not hard to guess at.

In the first place, the belief that some people are especially vulnerable to misfortune is firmly rooted in folklore and mythology. The first well-documented case of accident-repeating is probably that of poor Job in the Bible. The story of Job and his so-called comforters is interesting since it illustrates a common tendency to blame misfortune on to some characteristic of the victim. In Job's case it was wickedness; today the labels have a more scientific ring to them, but the tendency is the same.

The notion of accident proneness was also born at a time when engineers were finding it increasingly difficult to reduce industrial accidents any further by conventional safeguards. Consequently they were very much attracted to the idea that the man rather than the machine was primarily responsible – or, to be more specific, the accident-prone man. To some extent they were supported in this view by the appearance of the new Freudian concept of the 'death wish', the self-destructive urges deep in our unconscious which Freud was prompted to add to his psychoanalytic theory of personality by contemplating, among other things, the senseless slaughter of the First World War.

If one accepted the idea that some people were cursed with an 'accident-prone personality', the next step was clear. Make a careful study of accident-repeaters, find the common personality type, and the solution is at hand. Simply put all workers and applicants for driving or flying licences through a battery of personality tests, screen out all those people whose personality profiles coincide with that of the 'typical' accident-prone person, and you have eliminated the accident problem. The objective is laudable and obvious. But what happens when you fail to identify the 'typical accident-prone individual'? Because that is what actually turned out to be the case.

Many researchers hunted diligently for this elusive personality type. In the end, they came up with several – the aggressive, the maladjusted, the inconsiderate, the excessively hostile, the timid, and many more besides. It soon became obvious that a list of attributes as extensive and as varied as that could not possibly refer to a single type of individual. To make matters worse, no two cases of accident-repeating appeared to be exactly similar. For example, in a study of fifty motormen with high accident rates in the Cleveland Railway Company,[4] the primary causes were found to be extremely varied, as shown in Table 8.

Studies like this sounded the deathknell for the attractive idea that there was such a thing as a clearly defined 'unsafe' personality. And if we cannot identify the 'accident-prone personality', there is little point in clinging to this idea as an *explanation* of unequal accident liability. So where do we stand at the moment?

Today we do not deny that some people are more liable to have accidents than others, but we are more cautious about the extent to which this liability remains a characteristic feature of the individual. Examination of accident-repeaters over a lengthy period indicates that they are members of a club which is continuously changing its membership. New people are added, while long-standing members cease to qualify. It is possible that in some people accident proneness is a passing phase, while in others it is more enduring. The one thing that is certain, however, is that the whole business is a good deal more complicated than was first imagined. There is more to accident liability than was ever dreamt of in the simple philosophy of accident proneness.

TABLE 8   PRIMARY CAUSES OF ACCIDENT-REPETITIVENESS
AMONG FIFTY MOTORMEN

Judged cause	Per cent
Faulty attitude	14
Failure to recognize potential hazard	12
Faulty judgement of speed and distance	12
Impulsiveness	10
Irresponsibility	8
Failure to keep attention constant	8
Nervousness and fear	6
Defective vision	4
Organic disease	4
Slow reaction	4
High blood pressure	2
Senility	2
Worry and depression	2
Fatiguability	2
Improper distribution of attention	2
Inexperience	2
Miscellaneous	6

Another feature of contemporary thinking is the rejection of the sharp distinction formerly made between 'personal' and 'environmental' contributions to accident liability. As two South African scientists, Arbous and Kerrich, have pointed out:[5] '. . . our attempts to oversimplify the accident-causing situation by seeking to subdivide it into "personal causes" and "environmental causes" tends to lead us nowhere . . . Surely the essence of accident-causation is the rather intricate interrelationship which exists between the individual and the environment and the influence of the one cannot be appreciated without considering its interaction with the other.' Thus, different characteristics of the individual may contribute to accident liability in different situations. It is reasonable to assume, therefore, that each person has a *range of behaviour*, any part of which may be safe or unsafe depending on the type of hazards to which he is exposed. This does not mean that we should give up looking for relationships between accident liability and personality factors, only that we should not expect to find any *single* type of 'unsafe' individual.[6]

In the early studies of accident proneness there was a tendency for investigators to neglect differences in on-the-job style. They jumped straight from the accident statistics to the personality measures without carefully examining how accident-free and accident-repeating individuals actually carried out their jobs. If consistent relationships had been found between accident liability and well-established personality traits, this omission would not have mattered so much; but no such consistent relationships were found. So, in recent years, investigators have tried a different tack. Instead of concentrating on personality measures – or any other kind of psychological test for that matter – they have focused their attention on individual differences in style. And these, as we mentioned earlier, are likely to reflect the influence of many other factors apart from personality.

Thus, psychologists have attempted to differentiate drivers and pilots on the basis of the characteristic way they handle their vehicles. Only *after* these stylistic types have been identified (if at all) are personality tests administered. The advantage of this approach is that even if no relationships are subsequently found between style and personality, it is no great loss because these stylistic differences can exist in their own right providing they are sufficiently consistent and distinct. The fact that we are unable to pin a familiar personality label to them does not make them any the less useful for predicting accident liability.

For the remainder of this chapter we shall be looking in some detail at two kinds of stylistic difference in handling a vehicle. The first has been labelled the *inert-overactive continuum,* and has been repeatedly identified in a number of well-controlled experiments using both drivers and pilots. In addition to proving itself of some value in predicting accident-liable people, this stylistic continuum is also found to be related to the personality factors of extraversion and neuroticism.

The second kind of stylistic difference that we shall be

considering has been identified recently at the British Road Research Laboratory, and is concerned with the phenomenon of *dissociation* in car drivers. So far, it appears to be unrelated to any established personality type, but the work is of such interest and potential value in reducing accidents that it is well worth the detailed attention it will receive below.

Inert and overactive individuals

These stylistic differences were first observed during the Cambridge Cockpit experiments mentioned in Chapter 7. These studies were designed to elucidate the effects of fatigue on the performance of a highly-skilled task – in this case, that of 'flying' a prescribed series of manoeuvres in a fixed-base aircraft simulator (actually a mock-up of a Second World War Spitfire cockpit) in which the information displayed on the instrument panel was realistically linked to the movements of the controls. The task was like that of flying in cloud, except that the pilots received no feedback through their position and motion senses. However, the experimental situation was sufficiently like the real thing for most subjects to regard it as an exercise in instrument flying.

An incidental finding in the first experiment (the main results relating to the fatigue effects have already been described in Chapter 7) was that some of the pilots failed to cope with the simulated flying task. As time passed, and their fatigue increased, their performance was characterized more and more by the unusual way in which they carried out the necessary control actions. These unusual reactions fell into two groups: the *overactive* and the *inert*. They were distinguished not so much by the quantity of the error but by its quality. The overactive pilots tended to make a large number of rapid, almost agitated, corrective movements, while the inert pilots were quite the opposite: they allowed an error of, say, heading or height to become quite large before they bothered to correct it, and when they finally got round to making a correction they did so with a large, slow control action. These characteristic response styles caught the attention of the psychiatrist on the research team, Dr Russell Davis, and he designed a second 'cockpit' experiment specifically to study these individual differences.[7]

Thirty-four pilots took part in the second experiment, and once again wide and consistent differences were observed in response style. A typical overactive pilot made a large number of rapid control movements, frequently overcorrecting for errors which, in turn, called for more control activity. Overactive subjects also felt 'excited and under strain, tense and irritable, and sometimes frankly anxious. They felt that correction was urgent and made it impatiently.' These pilots were highly motivated to do well on the test, and remained preoccupied with their performance long after the experiment had finished.

The typical inert responders, on the other hand, made comparatively few control actions, and allowed very large errors to build up before they were corrected by extensive and unhurried adjustments of the controls. Instead of feeling stressed and anxious, they felt mild boredom which increased as the task progressed. 'In contrast to the restless striving of the overactive class, the pilots in the inert class gave the impression that they had lowered their standards of performance to a level well within their powers.' Unlike the overactive subjects, they were generally indifferent as to their performance on the test and appeared to forget about it as soon as it was over.

Russell Davis followed up these findings with a third experiment, this time using a much simpler task (subjects were asked to align a pointer with a line to the right or left, according to the brightness of two lights flashed on at both sides), and a much larger number of subjects. These included 355 normal pilots and thirty-nine who were undergoing treatment for at least two kinds of neurosis: in particular, acute anxiety states and 'hysterical' neurosis (which contrary to popular opinion is not associated with screaming and 'carrying on', but is characterized by a general inhibition of response, often taking the form of a paralysis). Later research by Professor Eysenck at the Maudsley Hospital has shown that 'anxious' neurotics (or dysthymics) tend to be introverted, while 'hysterical' neurotics are extraverted.[8] The distinction is important as we shall see later on. The results of this third experiment are summarized in Table 9.

The important thing to notice about these results is that the neurotic pilots showed a larger proportion of overactive and inert responses than did the normal pilots. Thus, to put it crudely,

TABLE 9   CHARACTERISTIC RESPONSE STYLES OF NORMAL AND
NEUROTIC PILOTS (FIGURES ARE PERCENTAGES)

Subjects	Normal	Overactive	Inert (reactions)
Normal pilots (N = 355)	75	17	8
Neurotic pilots (N = 39)	33	28	38
Acute anxiety state	43	50	7
Hysteria	12·5	12·5	75
Other diagnoses	35	18	47

abnormal reactions were often more associated with abnormal pilots. The second thing of interest is that the type of neurotic disorder was related to the kind of abnormal reaction. Anxious pilots were more likely to produce overactive than inert reactions, while the opposite was true for the hysterical pilot (there was only one pilot in this category, so we cannot make much of it). Now it was mentioned earlier that acute anxiety neurosis was associated with introversion and hysterical neurosis with extraversion, so these findings – albeit very tentative ones – provide grounds for supposing that where normal individuals show these extreme stylistic reactions there will be a tendency for introverts to display overactive reactions and extraverts to display inert reactions.

This possibility was examined by Professor P. Venables, now at Birkbeck College in the University of London.[9] He devised an ingenious piece of apparatus that incorporated some of the important features of a driving or flying task, but from which it was a good deal simpler to assess characteristic differences in response style. The subjects' task involved moving a pointer from a central position to either of two side positions along a groove. The direction and rate of movement was dictated by light signals situated immediately above the two side positions. The task was in three phases: (a) an 'easy' phase in which movements were demanded at only two-second intervals, and where the direction of movement was clearly signalled; (b) a 'stress' phase in which the rate of movement was more rapid, and the direction signals considerably more difficult to interpret – this phase of the task was almost impossible to accomplish accurately; and (c) another 'easy' phase, like the initial one. As in the Russell Davis study, both 'normal' people (210 male trainees for the job of bus conductor) and hospitalized neurotics (eleven hysterics and eleven acute anxiety cases) were used as subjects.

The results were fairly clear-cut. The hospitalized hysteric patients presented an inert type of response during the initial 'easy phase', and then maintained the same kind of performance throughout the two subsequent stages. In other words, their degree of inertia was not affected by the 'stress phase', but remained at its initial high level throughout the entire test. However, the same was not true of the hospitalized anxious patients. During the initial 'easy phase', their response style was indistinguishable from that of the normal subjects; but during the 'stress phase', their reactions shifted dramatically in the over-active direction. During the final 'easy phase', they returned again to their initial moderate level.

Normal extraverts and normal introverts, on the other hand, could only be distinguished by their reactions to the 'stress phase'. When the pressure of the task increased during the second phase, the extraverts showed a marked tendency to shift their performance in the inert direction. The introverts showed the reverse tendency. They responded to the stress by becoming more over-active, but the effects of the 'stress phase' were not so dramatic as those produced in the anxious patients. After the stress had passed, both extraverts and introverts returned to something like their initial type of performance.

These results support the hypothesis that individual differences along the inert-overactive continuum are related to the personality dimension of extraversion-introversion. However, among normal people, these tendencies appear to be evoked *only* during periods of stress. Whereas for the hysterical patients, at least, extreme inertia is a characteristic of their performance regardless of whether stress is present or not, cases of anxiety neurosis, on the other hand, are distinguishable from the other subgroups by their extreme overactivity during periods of stress.

In another experiment Venables studied car-driving performance.[10] He showed that drivers who obtained high scores on a personality test which measured both neuroticism and extraversion tended to be more inconsistent in their speed and directional control of the vehicle than those who obtained relatively low scores for these two factors. He explained this result by suggesting that the inertia associated with a combination of extraverted and neurotic characteristics would make for lax driving. And one obvious way in which this laxity can show itself is by the erratic fashion in which these individuals repeat manoeuvres calling for the same actions, such as slowing to a halt or steering round a particular corner.

Although we have little direct evidence, it is reasonable to assume that inertia of this sort would increase accident-liability in those people for whom it is a stable characteristic of their driving performance. Certainly, Russell Davis found that whereas both overactive and inert pilots had an unusually high accident liability, the latter were more likely to become involved in fatal aircraft accidents. However, these observations were made during wartime when large numbers of undertrained and otherwise incompetent pilots were taking to the air; this means that we should be cautious about extrapolating these findings to contemporary aviators whose standard of selection and training are very much higher. But the same stringency does not apply to contemporary car drivers!

How can we explain these stylistic differences? One theory advanced by Russell Davis is based on the notion of *anticipatory tension*. This is something akin to anxiety, which is produced by the anticipation of some future, challenging event. In car driving, for instance, it could be evoked by the sight of a dangerous bend in the road ahead, or by a sign warning the motorist of imminent roadworks. For most people, anticipatory tension is a normal and healthy 'keying-up' reaction which dies down once the hazard has been safely negotiated. But – Russell Davis argues – in the chronically overactive, the level of tension is so high that the anxiety remains even after the hazard has been passed, and may persist although no further hazards are anticipated. In the inert responders, on the other hand, the level of tension is too low or absent entirely. Passing a potential hazard safely leaves them unmoved because they either fail to perceive it as such, or else are indifferent to it in the first place. As we shall see below, these individuals appear, on the face of it, to have a lot in common with the 'dissociated passive' drivers identified by researchers at the Road Research Laboratory.

The 'dissociated' drivers

In recent years a number of very interesting studies of driver behaviour have been carried out at the Road Research Laboratory under the direction of Mr Stewart Quenault.[11] The object of this research has been to discover if there were any significant, measurable differences in the driving styles of what we might loosely call 'good' and 'bad' drivers. The 'bad' drivers, in this case, were defined initially by purely legal criteria; that is, by the possession of a conviction for careless driving. Although this in itself was hardly enough to label a person as a bad driver, especially in view of all the difficulties associated with any kind of legal definition of competence, it provided a starting point from which a number of more reliable categories of 'bad driving' were later identified.

In the first study two groups of drivers were tested: a C group of fifty drivers with their licences endorsed for careless driving during the preceding three years; and an R group of fifty drivers selected at random at same time and from the same geographical area as the C group. A careful examination of the make-up of the two groups revealed that there were no significant differences between them with respect to age, driving experience, type of car owned, sex and marital status. However, it was found that drivers in the C group did on average twice the annual mileage of the R group, had three times as many accidents, and six times as many convictions for careless driving. In addition, more of the C group than the R group used their cars for business as opposed to purely private purposes

Both groups were put through the same four test procedures:

1. A picture test in which the subjects were asked to classify photographs of actual road conditions into three groups: situations regarded as dangerous for the driver; situations regarded as frustrating for the driver; and situations that were neither dangerous nor frustrating.

2. A twenty-item intelligence test (the Shipley Abstraction Test).

3. A forty-eight-item personality test designed to measure extraversion and neuroticism (the Maudsley Personality Inventory).

4. A driving test in which each subject drove around a pre-determined route in his own car under normal traffic conditions. He was accompanied by two observers, one in the back seat to check the driver's mirror usage, and one in the front seat who communicated particular aspects of the subject's car handling and driving into a tape recorder,* using a 'close-speaking' microphone so that his remarks were not overheard by the subject. Neither observer had any idea from which group the subject was drawn, so there was no chance of their biasing their observations in the light of this knowledge. Eleven different driving indices were noted, but only the four set out below proved of any value:

(a) A/M: the ratio of the number of times the driver used his rearview mirror during a manoeuvre to the number of manoeuvres executed. (Manoeuvre = turn right or left, overtake, pass stationary vehicle, slow or stop.)

(b) O/T: the ratio of the number of times the subject overtook other vehicles to the number of times he was overtaken.

(c) UM: the number of unusual manoeuvres performed by the subject. These included such things as signalling on bends, or slowing down at the sight of oncoming traffic.

(d) NA: the number of near-accidents, where this was defined as behaviour leading to an emergency stop or avoiding action.

Other driving indices included such things as the average speedometer readings in restricted and derestricted speed zones, driving posture – whether it was tense or relaxed – and the time taken to cover the route. The important thing about all of these measures was their objectivity – something of a novelty in an area for so long dominated by the subjective and unqualified assertions of numerous medical, legal and psychological pundits. The measures in this case were such that no matter who was making the observations, the scores for each subject would have remained more or less the same.

When the results were analysed, it was found that of all the tests used only the four indices from the Driving Test – A/M, O/T, UM, and NA – differentiated significantly between the C and the R groups. These differences led to a classification of the drivers into four groups: safe, injudicious, dissociated active, and

---

* In later experiments, a special scoring sheet was used.

dissociated passive. The logic behind these classifications is set out below:

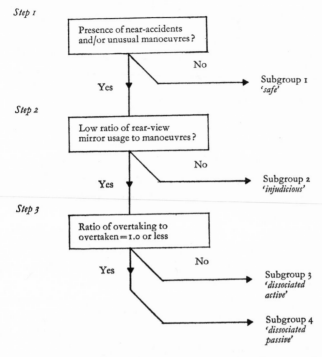

Step 1

Presence of near-accidents and/or unusual manoeuvres?

No → Subgroup 1 *'safe'*

Yes

Step 2

Low ratio of rear-view mirror usage to manoeuvres?

No → Subgroup 2 *'injudicious'*

Yes

Step 3

Ratio of overtaking to overtaken = 1.0 or less

No → Subgroup 3 *'dissociated active'*

Yes → Subgroup 4 *'dissociated passive'*

Thus 'safe' drivers were characterized by the absence of near-accidents or unusual manoeuvres. These drivers appeared to be fully aware of all the relevant information, and used it to keep out of trouble. 'Injudicious' drivers did everything correctly most of the time, that is they used the available information and did not overtake excessively, but every now and again they made a bad error of judgement which resulted, on occasion, in near-accidents mainly connected with overtaking and passing. They were also characterized by the presence of such 'unusual manoeuvres' as wide passing, and steering with only one hand on the steering wheel.

The term 'dissociated' was used by Quenault to identify 'those drivers who appear to drive with a degree of awareness of the relevant presented information below that necessary for safe driving'. This lack of regard for information relevant to the driving task showed itself in a number of different ways. For example, mirror usage by dissociated drivers was either very low (as compared to safe drivers), or non-existent. Dissociated drivers generally failed to take any notice of junctions to the right or left as they drove along main roads: they simply stared fixedly to the front all the time. This lack of adequate visual scanning was particularly noticeable at roundabouts, where they sailed straight through, looking neither to the right nor the left. They were also characterized by lack of intelligent anticipation of future road situations, and by their poor judgement in summing up the conditions ahead. Thus, they frequently pulled out to pass parked vehicles in the face of oncoming traffic, or they overtook on blind bends, and attempted to overtake on a three-lane highway despite the presence of two lanes of oncoming traffic. When near-accidents did occur, the dissociated drivers maintained an apparent unconcern as if nothing dangerous or untoward had happened – needless to say, the observers riding with them were terrified.

Quenault summed up the distinguishing features of the dissociated driver as follows: 'From work done to date, it appears that dissociated drivers are not readily identifiable from appearance, social background or responses to some paper and pencil tests. It is only when they get behind the steering wheel that this pattern emerges.' This reaffirms the point I made earlier, namely that we need to identify the accident-risk individual on the basis of stylistic rather than personality, intelligence or social characteristics.

The next thing to consider is the difference between the 'dissociated active' (DA) and 'dissociated passive' (DP) driver. Quenault identified four features which appear to distinguish between these two kinds of dissociated driver. The first was overtaking behaviour. DA drivers overtake many more times than they are overtaken, while the reverse is true for the DP driver. In the first study, for example, the DA drivers overtook four times as much as they were overtaken. By contrast, the DP drivers were overtaken five times as much as they overtook.

The second distinguishing feature was the type of 'unnecessary manoeuvre' they executed. The most common DA unnecessary manoeuvre was variation in speed for no apparent reason. 'For example, a DA driver travelling along a clear derestricted road at, say, 56 mph may suddenly drop his speed to 40 mph for a short period and equally suddenly return to 56–58 mph for no reason obvious to the observers.' In the case of the DP drivers, the most commonly observed unnecessary manoeuvre was that of 'locking on' to another vehicle. That is, they followed behind the vehicle ahead for long periods and adjusted their speed to match it, even when there was plenty of opportunity to pass. Sometimes this 'tailing' behaviour went as far as 'locking on' to a bus and stopping behind it at bus stops despite a clear road ahead and behind.

The third distinction lay in the type of risk taken. DA drivers took risks actively and consciously, the most common one being overtaking in very dangerous circumstances, such as on a blind bend, the brow of a hill, or in the face of oncoming traffic. DP drivers, on the other hand, did not take risks actively. Instead they put themselves at risk passively because of their failure to appreciate the hazards implicit in a particular action or traffic condition. A typical DP risk situation is depicted in Figure 22. Here, a DP driver approaches a roundabout with the intention of going right; but his lane positions within the roundabout are such that they are likely to give rise to quite a different interpretation of his intentions in the eyes of other drivers (X, Y and Z).

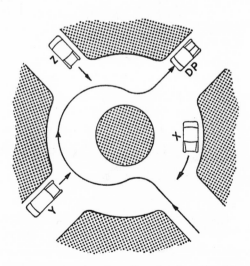

Figure 22 Typical risk situation for a dissociated-passive driver. Adapted from Quenault (1968).

The fourth distinction was the kind of near-accidents experienced by DA and DP drivers. In both cases the near-accidents arose originally from their failure to take account of all the relevant information, but they differ in the way they were brought about. In the case of the DA driver near-accidents tended to result from behaviour initiated by the DA driver himself in carrying out a manoeuvre in the presence of information that would cause a safe driver to hold back and reject the action as foolhardy. For the DP driver, on the other hand, near-accidents 'happen to him' because he persists in a style of behaviour that is no longer appropriate for the prevailing or impending road conditions. In his case, therefore, they are due to rigidity rather than rashness. Typical DA and DP near-accidents are shown in Figures 23 and 24.

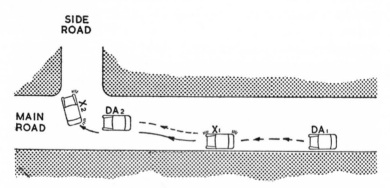

Figure 23   Typical near-accident for a dissociated-active driver. Adapted from Quenault (1968).

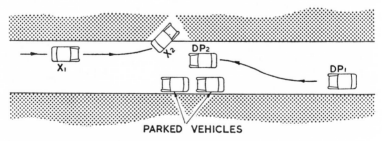

Figure 24   Typical near-accident for a dissociated-passive driver. Adapted from Quenault (1968).

In Figure 23 the DA driver has been following the car X for some time. As X approaches the road junction, he signals his intention to make a right turn and begins to change lane accordingly. But, as he does so, the DA driver begins to overtake, resulting in a near-accident at DA_2, X_2.

In Figure 24 DP is ambling along at his characteristically steady 30 mph towards a line of parked vehicles on his side of the road (DP_1). At this point both observers in the DP car notice the oncoming vehicle at X_1. It is immediately apparent to them that X will arrive opposite the parked vehicles at the same time as DP, if the latter continues at the same speed – which he does, being completely oblivious of his oncoming competitor for the one-car gap. And so, at point DP_2, X is forced to take violent avoiding action (X_2) – which he does, much to the relief of the observers. DP, however, continues at his unchecked speed of 30 mph, apparently unmoved by the whole business.

To summarize: the DA driver tends to be impatient and unpredictable, doing different things in situations that call for the same actions, or similar things in situations that call for different responses. On one occasion, for instance, he may, on approaching a main road, go through the correct scanning drill and then edge out slowly and safely; yet at an identical T-junction a little farther on, he may drive straight on to the main road without a pause for signalling or checking right and left. The DP driver by contrast tends to be stolid and patient. He is predictable to the extent that he prefers to drive within a narrow range of speeds, and if a particular item of unusual behaviour – such as slowing at the sight of oncoming traffic on the far side of the road – shows itself early in a drive, it will tend to be repeated several times throughout the test session. The DP driver is also someone who is inclined to be 'set' in his driving ways; he will maintain a particular speed or direction when the road situations demand more flexible behaviour. Similarly, he is content to trail other vehicles, or remain in queues even when the conditions are safe for overtaking.

Let us now turn back to the original careless driver (C) and randomly selected (R) groups, and see what proportions of safe, injudicious, dissociated active and dissociated passive drivers were found in each. The percentages, given in Table 10 below, are taken from two separate studies in which there are fifty drivers in each of the C and R groups, making a total of a hundred for each group.

TABLE 10 PERCENTAGES OF SAFE, INJUDICIOUS, DA AND DP
DRIVERS IN THE C AND R GROUPS

Subgroup	Careless group	Random group
DA + DP	52	27
DA	20	7
DP	32	20
Safe	36	69
Injudicious	12	4

It can be seen from these figures that there were more DAs and DPs among the group with convictions for careless driving than among those drivers selected at random. To some extent, therefore, these results validate the notion that more 'bad' drivers are to be found in a group selected by the legal criterion of a conviction for careless driving than in a group chosen at random from a similar driving population. And this is despite the obvious fact that the charge of careless driving is a very ill-defined one, and that both citations and convictions for this offence vary widely both within and between different areas of the country.

When the accident records of safe, injudicious, DA and DP drivers in both the C and R groups were examined, it was found that one-eighth of the safe drivers, one-quarter of the injudicious drivers, one-half of the DA drivers and one-third of the DP drivers had had at least one previous accident. However, as Quenault himself pointed out, these figures must be treated with caution since they rely on the driver's own statement of his accident record. Human nature being what it is, there is a high probability that the true accident histories for all of these groups were more extensive. But even allowing for this general underestimate, there is evidence to show that the DA driver is the least safe, closely followed by the injudicious and DP drivers.

To date, something like two thousand drivers have been put through a somewhat streamlined version of the test procedure described for the first experiment. Although not all the results have yet been fully analysed, the four-part classification into safe, injudicious, DA and DP continues to be upheld by the later work.

Moreover, this typology appears to be a fairly consistent one, in that drivers who have been retested on a number of occasions almost invariably remain in their initial classification – a classification, I hasten to remind the reader, which depends not upon the opinions of the observers, but upon the scores obtained by the drivers in various aspects of the driving task.

Currently, Quenault and his colleagues are tackling the important question of driver retraining. Is the dissociated driver stuck that way for life, or can his driving behaviour be modified by remedial instruction? The method presently in use is to retest the driver, then for the observers to go through his test results with him afterwards, indicating how his performance differed from that of safe drivers. One result of this retraining programme is that the drivers concerned often show marked improvements in such things as mirror usage. Whether or not lasting improvements can be achieved, and the unsafe rendered safe, is still impossible to judge. This aspect of the research is still very much in its early stages; but the preliminary results, at least, are encouraging.

In the early part of this chapter I discussed the concept of accident proneness, and presented evidence which suggests that there is no such thing as a clearly identifiable personality type associated with accident liability. In the light of this failure of conventional psychological methods, I argued that it would be more meaningful to attempt to identify the accident-liable person, not on the basis of psychological tests, but from the way he actually performs the task of handling a vehicle. In other words, we should attempt to identify consistent *stylistic* differences between people in the way they drive cars or fly aeroplanes, and then see how these relate to their accident records. Ultimately our goal is to predict *future* accident liability on the basis of present performance.

The latter part of the chapter described two moderately successful attempts to isolate meaningful stylistic differences in vehicle handling: inert and overactive responders, and dissociated and non-dissociated drivers. This work suggests that if the notion of accident proneness has any meaning at all, it is in relation to the characteristic style with which a person performs a *particular* task. Thus, those stylistic features that contribute to a person's accident liability in, say, driving need not necessarily increase his risk of accidents in another task like operating a lathe or working on a production line. Nor, for that matter, need they show any significant relationship with well-established psychological dimensions like, for example, extraversion–introversion, so long as they are sufficiently consistent in their own right.

9 Reconciling Man and Vehicle

This book has dealt with some of the psychological problems that arise when we allow ourselves to be transported by something other than our own two feet. That is, when we expose ourselves to the unnatural circumstances of passive motion by taking a ride in one of the wide assortment of vehicles that our technology has created to carry us on land, over and under the sea, through the air and into space.

Most of these problems can be classified under two broad headings: those related to the gathering of sensory information, particularly by our position and motion detectors; and those concerned with the way this information is processed by the brain. The former were considered in Chapters 1–4, while the latter were discussed in Chapters 5–8.

For the most part the information-gathering problems are the *direct* result of being moved in a way that is quite alien to the kind of active locomotion for which our senses were adapted by the process of evolution. But the information-processing problems show a more *indirect* relation to vehicle motion. In this case passive motion does not create the problem; instead, it creates situations in which certain natural limitations of our 'mental computer' are brought into greater prominence. In other words, it accentuates existing weaknesses in the operation of our central nervous system, rather than causing them directly.

For example, the fact that vehicles carry us at much faster rates than we can naturally propel ourselves accentuates the limited capacity of our single-channel mental computer for handling and storing information. The result is that the system becomes overloaded and we cease to process incoming signals effectively, or fail to respond to them altogether. At the other end of the informational continuum, the same vehicles are also capable of transporting us into environments that deprive the brain of sufficient information to keep it functioning efficiently; a state which leads to a decline in alertness or vigilance and, in extreme sensory deprivation, to perceiving things that have no basis in reality. Moreover, the job of the vehicle operator often involves long hours of work and emotional stress, both of which can erode the complex organization of sensory-motor skill through which the limited capabilities of the man are matched to the demands of his vehicle.

Clearly there are many different ways in which we can tackle these problems. I have discussed some of them already. Logically they fall into two categories. We can either modify the vehicle to make the best use of man's natural capabilities and to minimize the effects of his known limitations; or we can attempt to modify the man so that he is better able to meet the unnatural and often excessive demands of the vehicle.

In this final chapter I shall be discussing two general remedial measures that fall into the latter category of modifying the man rather than the vehicle. For want of better terms, I shall call them 'knowing the problem' and 'adaptation'. I am aware that by concentrating attention on these two I am ignoring a wide variety of possible remedial measures. However, since the emphasis throughout this book has been upon 'built-in' psychological problems, it seems appropriate that it should conclude with a consideration of some 'built-in' solutions.

Knowing the problem

For many of the problems discussed in this book, and particularly the sensory deceptions produced by vehicle motion, the first step towards a solution is to make people aware that a problem exists. At first sight this may seem a little strange, for it could be argued that if a person has failed to notice a problem for himself then it can hardly be much of a problem. But as we shall see there are a number of good reasons why such an argument does not apply in this particular case.

While it is apparent to everyone that the conditions in space, say, or on the moon, or at very high altitudes, or in the depths of the sea, are alien to our physical make-up, it is by no means immediately obvious that driving at a steady 70 mph down a motorway, for instance, is alien to our psychological make-up. But the experiments described in Chapter 4 show that it is. We readily accept that the astronaut and the aviator need sophisticated life-support systems to sustain them, just as we accept that the diver needs air cylinders to keep him alive under water; but it is not generally appreciated that the car driver needs something more than the evidence of his own senses to tell him how fast he is travelling. Yet he needs this other source of velocity information for the same basic reasons that the astronaut needs his spacesuit or the diver his air supply: that is, because he is doing something that human beings were just not designed to do.

One factor that tends to disguise the inaccuracy of our motion detectors when we are being moved passively is that they work extremely well during the course of the natural, self-propelled locomotion for which they were evolved. A lifetime of satisfactory service under natural conditions has given us few previous grounds for doubting their reliability when we ride in a vehicle. Particularly when, on the face of it, vehicle motion seems nothing more than a mechanized extension of our own powers of loco-motion – at least in the case of land vehicles. Riding in a vehicle has become as familiar to us as walking; for some, possibly more so. There are no obvious signs to indicate that active and passive locomotion are fundamentally different from a biological point of view. But they are, simply because we were built for one and not the other.

Strong evidence that people are generally unaware of these perceptual difficulties, particularly in driving, is provided by the way the newspapers and the authorities respond to the seasonal rash of motorway deaths caused by multiple collisions in fog and bad weather. The immediate reaction has generally been to blame these disasters upon 'criminal negligence', or what the newspapers have dubbed 'motorway madness'. The assumption is that these accidents are caused by delinquent motorists who refuse to heed the warnings and continue to drive at dangerously high speeds out of reckless bravado or sheer bloody-mindedness. While this may indeed be true of some, it is also highly probable that many of these accidents result from the drivers' inability to make accurate subjective estimates of their speed – a fact that was amply demon-strated by the studies discussed in Chapter 4. Unfortunately, the error is most commonly in the direction of feeling that the vehicle is travelling more slowly than it really is, particularly in smooth-sprung modern cars, and this in turn will cause the driver to underestimate his safe-braking distance when he is called upon to halt suddenly.

As a regular sequel to these winter pile-ups, there has been a wave of public and press indignation against the criminal folly of certain drivers. The remedies offered include demands for higher penalties in the courts and high-minded appeals to the motorist's sense of responsibility. But, as Dr Ivan Brown has pointed out, '. . . normal human perceptual characteristics will inevitably tend to produce overfast driving and inadequate headway in fog . . . [so] it is irresponsible to dismiss all resulting motorway crashes as criminal negligence and to rely on moral exhortation to change drivers' behaviour.'[1] This kind of reaction is liable to do more harm than good. For one thing, it clouds the true nature of the issue – which is perceptual rather than moral. For another, motorists can hardly change the underlying cause of these misjudgements; namely, the fact that their central nervous system is biased towards detecting novel stimuli and is generally unreceptive to the *status quo* – created artificially in this case by constant-speed motorway driving. The irony is that this same nervous system characteristic has great survival value in man's natural environment.

Clearly, the most effective solution to this kind of problem would be to relieve the driver of the need to make subjective speed judgements. This could be done by attaching his vehicle to an automatic guidance system built into the motorway, governing speed and station-keeping along a given carriageway. Although such systems are technically feasible – indeed, cables for this purpose are being installed in some motorways presently under construction – they are still a long way off. In the meantime it would pay those concerned with road safety and the training of drivers to take note of how the flying training organizations have dealt with the comparable problem of pilot disorientation. This is a hazard that has been recognized and taken seriously since the early days of flight.

It is widely accepted that the best way to prevent accidents arising from pilot disorientation is to educate aircrew in the sensory causes of spatial confusion so that they can recognize the symptoms, and also the flight situations in which they are most likely to occur. Trainee pilots are not only informed of the mechanics of the vestibular system, they are also placed in flight situations in which they can gain first-hand experience of these sensory deceptions. For instance, a flying instructor may take a student into cloud and ask him to estimate the aircraft's attitude without reference to his flight instruments. The discrepancies that almost invariably exist between these subjective assessments and the true attitude of the aircraft provide convincing proof of the limitations of flying by the 'seat of the pants' in the absence of a clear horizon. These lessons can also be consolidated on the ground by putting the student pilot on a rotating chair and demonstrating to him the illusory nature of his vestibular sensations when he moves his head out of the plane of rotation, or when the chair is stopped abruptly after a period at constant angular velocity. He can then be told of the type of flight manoeuvres that are most likely to cause similar illusory sensations – for example, turning the head during a steeply banked turn, or recovering from a prolonged spin.

The object of these exercises is to convince the pilot that when he is deprived of clear external reference he must reject the evidence of his earthbound senses and believe only what he sees displayed on his flight instruments. But this involves two rather difficult processes. In the first place he must put aside the habit of a lifetime and disregard what his senses tell him. And secondly he must acquire an entirely new skill: that of translating numbers and pointer positions on a bewildering array of dials into a single integrated mental picture of what the aircraft is doing at that moment. After continual practice at instrument flight, most pilots are able to disregard their sensory impressions almost entirely. In fact, the research evidence suggests that these misleading vestibular signals are filtered out at a preconscious level, so that very experienced pilots fail to notice them even when they have been specifically directed to attend to them.

However, like other recently acquired aspects of human skill, this filtering process is extremely fragile. In times of acute stress, or when not in current flying practice, or even when mildly 'hungover', these defence mechanisms crumble, leaving the pilot at the

mercy of his erroneous sensory impressions. In these circumstances the experienced pilot – like the novice – is faced with two
competing and often contradictory sources of information: his
instruments, which his training tells him must be right, but about
which there is always the nagging doubt that they might have
suffered some mechanical failure; and his sensory impressions,
which his training tells him are probably wrong, but which are
backed by the authority of a lifetime's usage. Under stress, the
latter frequently predominate, and that is when accidents are
likely to occur. But even when the sensory impressions are not
believed, the conflict imposed by these two contradictory sources
of information can bring about a marked deterioration in the
quality of flying performance, and this too can lead to trouble.

In addition, episodes of spatial confusion can be quite unpredictable in their onset. They can occur 'out of the blue' in both
the literal and the metaphorical sense. Dr Alan Benson, a specialist
in pilot disorientation, has written: 'aircrew should be warned
that disorientation may appear quite unexpectedly even on routine
flights which have previously been carried out many times without
incident or difficulty.'[2] And he goes on to specify the remedy:

On these occasions, as at other times, the main protection against
control of the aircraft being either disorganized or governed by the
false perception is for the pilot to disregard his own sensations completely and direct his attention to his instruments. Having checked that
these function normally, he must then believe them implicitly. The ease
with which this can be done depends largely upon the skill of the pilot
in instrument flight and it is of prime importance that proficiency in
this art should be maintained at a high standard by frequent practice.

There is little doubt that drivers would benefit from being made
aware of their perceptual limitations in a similar way to that
described for pilots. As with aircrew, drivers – and particularly
learner drivers – could be told of the form their misjudgements
are likely to take, and also the kind of road conditions in which
they will occur. Drivers under instruction could be taken as
passengers on the motorway and asked to make speed judgements
with the speedometer concealed from them. The essential thing is
that they should be allowed to experience the misjudgements at
first hand. Moreover, it may even be possible to assess understanding of these difficulties, along with other technical knowledge,

by requiring applicants for driving licences to pass a short written paper before they take their driving test. Written tests are now an integral part of the licence-gaining procedure in many American states and European countries, so there is nothing new in this aspect of driver assessment.

What would be the purpose of this kind of instruction? For one thing, it could be used to instil in a driver the habit of making regular checks on his speedometer in the same way as he would check his rearview mirror. These speedometer checks should be made just before and just after a manoeuvre involving a change of speed. Of course, this procedure is not without its problems. The act of checking the speedometer may consume as much as two seconds of precious road-scanning time. But nevertheless, under most road conditions, the loss of external information that this speedometer check entails is probably more acceptable in terms of safety than the belief that one is travelling at, say, 20 mph slower than the actual speed of the vehicle.

Now let us turn to a problem which is usually of more concern to the passenger than to the man at the controls, that of motion sickness. Can knowing about the factors which cause motion sickness be of any help to the sufferer? Yes it can. Knowledge of the sensory conflicts that produce this disorder can allow the susceptible passenger to act in such a way as to keep the symptoms within tolerable bounds, or even to prevent them altogether.

In nearly all circumstances where motion sickness occurs, the passenger can exercise a wide measure of control over his susceptibility through his own behaviour. He is to a large extent the master of his own well-being. If he does the wrong thing he can make matters a good deal worse than they need have been; but if he does the right thing and obeys a few simple rules, he can greatly reduce the likelihood of his becoming sick. What are these rules?

First and foremost: *move the head as little as possible while riding in a sick-making vehicle.* As we saw in Chapter 1 there is a great deal of research evidence to show that independent movements of the head superimposed upon those of the vehicle tend to magnify the sick-making properties of the total stimulus. As a general rule, therefore, passengers are strongly advised to keep their heads as still as possible while travelling. In a car head restraint is most comfortably achieved by using a headrest attached to the seat; but if this is not available, try to restrain the head voluntarily. On a ship head movements can be minimized very effectively by lying flat on a bunk – preferably amidships, where the motion of the vessel is least severe.

The second rule: *try to match up as far as possible the various sources of motion information available to the brain.* Motion sickness occurs whenever the information signalled by the vestibular receptors fails to corroborate that signalled by the other motion senses, particularly the eyes. In a car the best advice is to imitate the action of the driver. After all, he is rarely if ever disturbed by the motion. Concentrate attention on the road ahead, just as the driver does. This gives the visual and inertial motion senses a better chance of telling the brain the same story. It also helps to maintain the position of the head – it is hardly likely to move very much if attention is directed straight ahead through the windscreen. Do not attempt to read a map or book. Do not keep looking round to see what the children are doing on the back seat. These actions will exacerbate existing symptoms, or initiate them if none exist: they are self-imposed sensory conflicts.

In a ship or an aircraft it is not always possible to avoid sensory conflict. In a ship, of course, the only way the various sources of motion information can be made compatible is by looking at the horizon or some visible landfall. Where some sort of conflict between the visual and inertial senses is inevitable – as when no view of the horizon is available – the best strategy is to close the eyes. At least that is a fairly natural way of shutting out visual information, and experiments have shown that it is reasonably effective in reducing susceptibility.

A third useful rule: *occupy the mind with something other than the state of the stomach.* There is strong evidence to suggest that mental activity, involvement in some demanding task, tends to reduce a person's proneness to sickness. In Chapter 1 it was suggested that this occurred because the brain has only so much capacity to process the sick-making sensory signals, and when it is fully engaged in some other activity, the available pathways may well be preempted. Whatever the reason, however, the effect does occur and the implications are clear-cut. If you are in a car, play word games with the children (without looking round at them). Alternatively, listen to the car radio – preferably a 'talking' programme which holds your attention. If there is no available distraction, try solving sums in your head, or giving a silent commentary on the road state ahead – anything, in fact, to keep your mind off your stomach. The more you think about it, the worse it feels: the effect works both ways.

Finally in this general context of 'knowing about the problem', it is worth pointing out that for astronauts in either weightless or rotating spacecraft, knowledge about the unusual force environment and its sensory effects is vital to their well-being and safety. They need to know, for instance, that moving their heads out of the plane of rotation in artificial gravity, or in any direction in weightlessness (where the movement has an angular component), will create bizarre inputs to their vestibular receptors which are likely to result in disorientation and space sickness. This knowledge is particularly important during the initial, pre-adapted stages of the mission. An understanding of the mechanics of the stimulus will enable them to move their heads in such a way as to minimize the disturbing effects of the unusual stimulus. Recent experiments in a rotating room, for instance, have shown that the unpleasant effects of a head movement in artificial gravity are minimal if it is followed within four seconds by an equal and opposite head motion. This second motion cancels out the effects of the first by bringing the cupula back to its neutral position.

It is also important that astronauts should know the way in which their symptoms of space sickness are likely to develop. To this end, a simple rating scale of subjective well-being has been developed, running from zero – 'I feel fine' to ten – 'I feel awful, just like I'm about to be sick'. Research at Pensacola[3] has shown that most people know the subjective route from 'feeling fine' to 'feeling nauseated' extremely well, and can track its time course meaningfully using the intervening ratings (one to nine). It has been found, for example, that adaptation activities can proceed quite satisfactorily up to a well-being rating of three; beyond that the 'avalanche effect' develops, and any attempt at further adapting head movements is useless. Knowing this, and knowing the route from zero to ten, astronauts can pace their activities during the early pre-adapted stages of a flight so that when they feel themselves to be at a well-being state of three, they can keep their heads still until the sensations subside. At this stage along the route symptoms spontaneously disappear in a matter of seconds once the effective stimulus has been removed. But at later stages the disturbances may last for several hours after the causative stimulus has ceased. It is obviously important to avoid reaching this more advanced state of sickness.

Adaptation

Man can adapt to practically anything that fails to kill him outright. It is this innate ability to adjust to new circumstances that guarantees him his place in the sun. What concerns us here is how we can capitalize on this natural flexibility to overcome the problems created by the unnatural state of passive motion and by the alien environments through which we are transported.

The process of evolution has dealt us a very mixed hand. Although we are equipped with outdated motion detectors (at least with respect to man-made modes of locomotion) and a limited capacity for processing information, we are also endowed with enormous powers of self-modification through which we can minimize the ill effects of these design limitations. One of the jobs of the psychologist in this field is to study these self-correcting mechanisms and discover how they function so that they might be exploited to their best advantage.

Like 'fatigue', the term 'adaptation' is one that psychologists use to describe a number of quite separate processes. The one thing they have in common is that they all entail some kind of *internal adjustment* to the outside world. In this book the term 'adaptation' has been used to describe two quite different phenomena, and we have also discussed a third process – the acquisition of skill – which although not named as such could meaningfully be regarded as a form of adaptation. Let us now examine these three separate adaptive processes which we can label: *sensory adaptation, perceptual adaptation,* and *skill adaptation.*

Sensory adaptation is the process, described in Chapter 4, which is responsible for our erroneous impressions of speed after travelling at a steady rate on a motorway. In this case the phenomenon works against us to create a transport problem; but this is only one example of a very widespread process. A similar diminution in sensation occurs in all our senses (except perhaps the otoliths) whenever we are exposed to a constant stimulus for any length of time.

It is sensory adaptation that makes us unaware of the pressure of our clothes, or the steady ticking of a clock in the same room. It also allows us to tolerate the din of the pneumatic drill in the street outside or the bath water which was almost too hot to bear at the first touch. But it is a two-edged business. While it blunts our awareness of a steady-state stimulus, at the same time it sensitizes us to the absence of this stimulus, or any change in its intensity. This is one of its important biological functions: to alert us to change.

When the elevated railway was removed from the streets of Manhattan, New Yorkers who had grown accustomed to the rattling of trains past their bedroom windows protested because the silence kept them awake. Similarly, people who live close to busy airports often find it difficult to sleep when the aircraft are grounded through bad weather (or a strike). A recent newspaper item (*Guardian*, 24 September 1970) told of an estate agent who had been asked by an elderly couple to find them a house 'on a main road because the noise of traffic is essential'. Their previous home was beside a busy trunk road where the thunder of lorries and cars had become so much a way of life that they would miss it in a quiet neighbourhood.

These after-effects of sensory adaptation are even more pronounced when the stimulus to which we have become adapted has an opposite – as blue has yellow, concave has convex, motion in one direction has motion in the opposite direction, and so on. As we saw in Chapter 4, the cessation of the adapted stimulus will often provoke an illusory perception of the opposite stimulus quality. When we have grown accustomed to very hot water, tepid water feels cold by comparison. When we have been watching a striped drum turning in one direction, the sight of a stationary drum will create a compelling sensation of apparent motion in the opposite direction. If we look at a grey colour after starting at blue, it will appear yellow; and a pale yellow will appear even more intensely yellow. These are all examples of the principle that Dr J. J. Gibson called 'adaptation with negative after-effect' (see Chapter 4).

The need for sensory adaptation arises from the fact that the

H

central nervous system can only handle so much information at any given time. An unchanging stimulus conveys little of importance. If we continued to respond to it at the same neural level as we did initially, we would be making an uneconomic use of our limited information-handling capacity. Consequently, the brain automatically arranges for an unchanging sensory input to become attenuated or 'filtered out' as it reaches the receptor. In neural terms, this means that the rate of firing in the pathways which carry this unchanging message to the brain gradually declines until it levels out at a rate which, in an unadapted person (i.e. one who is meeting the stimulus for the first time), would signify a less intense physical stimulus. For example, after travelling for some time at a steady 70 mph, the rate of firing from the image-retina receptors is the same as it would be if we had just attained a speed of, say, 50 mph. In this particular instance, of course, the adaptation process is inappropriate for the circumstances because we need to gauge our cruising speed accurately when we are in control of a vehicle. But this is a problem of our own making. In our natural environment this adaptation process serves us well in conserving our limited mental capacity for more important signals, namely the detection of change and novelty. It is, after all, the leaping rather than the sleeping tiger which demands our instant attention.

Sensory adaptation, however, is a relatively primitive mechanism which is shared in some degree by the lowliest of animals. For our present purposes we are more interested in the remedial properties of *perceptual adaptation* which, although it bears a superficial resemblance to sensory adaptation, is a fundamentally different process. Perceptual adaptation is the phenomenon, discussed at some length in Chapters 1 and 2, which is responsible for the gradual disappearance of motion sickness and other disturbances when people remain for some time in the same condition of *sensory rearrangement*.

For sensory adaptation to occur, all that is required is the presence of a steady-state stimulus to *one* kind of sense organ. But for perceptual adaptation to occur, we need to disrupt the delicate harmony that normally exists between the *many* senses concerned with detecting motion and maintaining bodily orientation, that is, between the eyes and the various 'inertial' receptors – the vestibular system and the non-vestibular proprioceptors (i.e. kinaesthesis). In Chapter 1 we saw that this condition of 'rearrangement' could be achieved in many different ways – by wearing an optical device which inverts the retinal image, thus turning the visual world upside-down; by head movements in weightlessness and rotation that uncouple the inputs from the canals and the otoliths; by watching Cinerama or operating a fixed-base vehicle simulator with a moving visual display; by riding in a vehicle which restricts the passengers' view of the outside world; and many other ways besides. The one thing that is common to all of these situations is that the motion information signalled by one of the motion detectors (and sometimes more than one) is different from that signalled by the rest – whereas under natural conditions they would all be signalling the same message. This, then, is what is meant by sensory rearrangement.

The end-result of perceptual adaptation is normal perception. Its progress is marked by the gradual disappearance of the various disturbances (motion sickness, perceptual illusions and the like) which characterized the initial phase of sensory rearrangement. Unlike sensory adaptation, there is no reduction in the overall intensity of the sensory inputs. What happens is that after a certain time spent interacting with the rearranged conditions, people respond to this atypical environment in almost exactly the same way as they would to their natural or typical circumstances. In a rotating room, for example, head movements which initially provoked nausea and illusions of apparent motion eventually feel the same as those produced by the same head movements in a stationary environment. This is in sharp contrast to the effects of sensory adaptation where the end-result is a diminished subjective response to a particular kind of constant stimulus. This effect could be described as moving towards a *neutralization* of the sensory experience. But in perceptual adaptation, the effect is one of moving towards the *normalization* of perception.

To explain the occurrence of perceptual adaptation, we need to assume the presence of two neural components within the brain (see Figure 6). First, a neural storage unit that retains important facts conveyed by the previous stimulus inputs from the various spatial receptors – its quality, intensity, direction and so on. We can assume that this information is retained in the form of stimulus 'traces'. The second component is a comparator unit which matches the current sensory inputs (i.e. the information coming through the senses at that instant) with traces of preceding inputs retrieved from the storage unit. When the incoming information and the stored information are different – as, for example, when we step aboard a rotating device and move the head out of the plane of rotation – the comparator notes the discrepancy and, as a result, generates a mismatch signal which sets in train the symptoms of motion sickness and other related disturbances.

The events just described are assumed to occur during the initial stages of sensory rearrangement. But what happens after we have remained in this environment for some time? The theory argues that the storage unit gradually fills up with traces of the rearranged stimulus, and when this updating process reaches a certain point, the comparator is more likely to select new (i.e. rearranged) rather than old traces for matching with the prevailing rearranged sensory input. During this updating process the strength of the mismatch signal gradually declines and with it the severity of the disturbances which it causes. When only new traces are retrieved by the comparator, the stored information and that currently being communicated by the spatial senses will be the same, and no mismatch signal will be generated. At this point the process of perceptual adaptation is said to be complete for that particular set of rearranged conditions.

Thus, in a rotating room, or on a ship, or in weightlessness, continued interaction with the unusual conditions gradually modifies the traveller's spatial memory store until the rearranged sensory inputs become more familiar than the inputs from the previously typical environment. In short, the traveller becomes a changed animal: one that is specifically adjusted to rotation, or ship motion, or zero gravity, rather than to the normal terrestrial environment. And we can see this most clearly when he attempts to return to his natural surroundings.

Once an individual has become fully adapted to a particular set of rearranged spatial inputs, a change in those conditions, even one that restores him to his natural state, will cause a recurrence of the disturbances that marked the initial stages of rearrangement. For example, when the rotating room stops spinning, and the occupant continues to move his head in the way that achieved adaptation to the turning motion, he is likely to become nauseated and experience illusions of apparent motion in the *opposite direction* to those he felt during the initial stages of rotation. The same kind of thing happens after a person has become adapted to inverting lenses and then removes them; or when he steps off an ocean liner after a long voyage; or after any period of adaptation to an atypical or rearranged environment.

The penalty for being able to adjust so successfully to unusual spatial conditions is that, having done so, the orientation centres of the brain have to relearn the typical arrangement of position and motion signals when the individual returns to his natural environment. This is because the contents of the storage unit, having been reconstituted to suit the atypical conditions, are now at variance with the sensory information from the normal surroundings. Consequently the mismatch signal is again generated, producing symptoms of motion sickness and other disturbances – which, if they have a directional sign, will be opposite to those experienced in the initial stages of rearrangement. However, since the informational characteristics of the natural situation are very familiar – or, in psychological terms, are 'overlearned' – the re-adaptation process is likely to be relatively rapid. But initially at least, these after-effects can be as severe as the disturbances suffered during the early exposure to the atypical environment.

As we saw in Chapter 1, this kind of theoretical argument helps us to understand many of the puzzling features of motion sickness. For instance, it explains why symptoms can occur at the cessation of a disturbing motion as well as at its onset. It also explains why riding in a vehicle simulator can produce sickness in the absence of any real vestibular stimulation – simply because it *is* absent. And it also tells us why it is that experienced vehicle operators are more affected by this rearrangement than naïve ones – because the skilled drivers and pilots have had the opportunity to build up expectations of how the visual and inertial inputs are combined in actual vehicle motion. But, more importantly, it gives us some idea of what must be done to prevent these disturbances: namely, establish traces of the appropriate rearranged inputs within the neural store so that its contents are no longer incompatible with the information coming from the spatial senses. This is Nature's own preventive. Can we accelerate the process?

Most of the work aimed at answering this question has been directed towards preventing motion sickness in the rotating spacecraft of the not-too-distant future. I described some of these techniques in Chapter 2. Unlike weightlessness, it is possible to simulate the disturbing properties of artificial gravity by employing a rotating device like the Pensacola Slow Rotation Room. This being the case, it becomes feasible to think of *pre-adapting* future astronauts to this particular form of sensory rearrangement *before* they actually encounter it under operational conditions in space. In other words, at sometime before their mission, astronauts can be put through an adaptation schedule – like those discussed in Chapter 2 – where they are exposed to graded levels of the sick-making stimulus which are of sufficient strength to allow the appropriate traces to be formed within the neural store, but which are not strong enough to produce actual symptoms. The rationale behind this is that when they eventually meet the same kind of disturbing stimulus in the rotating spacecraft, the presence of the pre-formed stimulus traces will accelerate the process of adaptation and thus minimize the likelihood of severe disorders occurring during the initial period of maladaptation. Although these preventive measures have yet to be tested in practice, there is considerable research evidence to indicate that they will constitute the most effective form of protection against space sickness, primarily because they rely upon the body's own adjustment mechanisms and not upon drugs or any other external agency.

In our present stage of knowledge the most effective form of adaptation schedule for preventing motion sickness in rotating spacecraft seems to be something like that depicted in Figure 25. The schedule consists of four blocks of head movements, two in the clockwise direction and two in the counterclockwise direction. Each block consists of six velocity steps up to a terminal speed of 6 rpm – which is likely to be close to the spin-rate of the rotating spacecraft. At each of these velocity steps, the astronaut carries out a series of prescribed ninety-degree head movements in each of four quadrants: front, back, left and right. It will be noticed from Figure 25 that, as the speed increases, the astronaut spends more time (and executes more head motions) at each step. This takes account of the fact that although the physical speed increment remains constant at 1 rpm, the subjective response evoked by this increment increases as the absolute velocity rises. Thus more head motions are needed to achieve adaptation after a step from 5 to 6 rpm than after an equal-sized jump from, say, 1 to 2 rpm.

Another point to be noticed is that the first two blocks of head motions are carried out with the eyes closed or covered, while the last two are executed with internal visual reference. The latter means that the astronaut has his eyes open but can only see the interior of the rotating device, which is stationary with respect to him: this is the kind of situation that is likely to be encountered in the real spacecraft. Recent experiments have shown that people can adapt to 6 rpm with internal visual reference very much more quickly if they first adapt to 6 rpm with their eyes closed. Not only that, a combination of 'vision-absent' with 'internal visual reference' is far less likely to cause sickness *en route* than starting the unadapted individual off in conditions of internal visual reference.

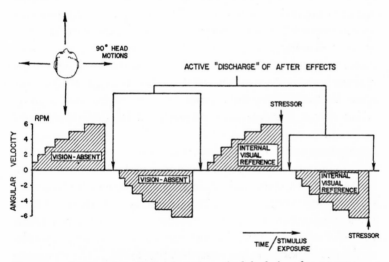

Figure 25 Suggested preflight adaptation schedule designed to prevent space sickness among astronauts on future rotating spacecraft. See text for explanation.

At the end of each block of step-increments, the astronaut is brought back to stationary and asked to execute the same head movements as he did while rotating. The purpose of this is to discharge the after-effects built up during the perrotational adaptation. Now we said earlier that these after-effects will be in the opposite direction to those experienced during the preceding rotation. This means that these after-effects will be identical to the effects produced by rotating in the opposite direction. There is experimental evidence to show that if people are asked to adapt to one direction of rotation, and then spun in the opposite direction, they will adapt far more rapidly to the second direction of rotation if they have had a chance actively to discharge the after-effects from the first. These after-effects serve to give the person a 'start' in the opposite direction of rotation, which always (in the schedule described previously) follows the preceding direction.

A few words are needed to explain the term 'stressor'. As the end of the schedule is approached, it is necessary to know how much protection against motion sickness the astronaut has acquired. One way of assessing this is to put him through an extremely stressful series of movements that, in an unadapted person, would be sure to produce symptoms. These movements are also designed to be in excess of those required during normal space operations, so that if the astronaut can get through them without ill effects, he is unlikely to be too disturbed when he meets the 'real thing' in space flight. If these 'stressor tests' show that the astronaut has not acquired sufficient protection to overcome his basic susceptibility, more step-increment blocks can be added to the schedule until he finally meets the 'stressor test' criterion.

One important question that still remains to be answered is: how long does the adaptation acquired by such a schedule last? Some recent experimental findings give us a clue.[4] In this study eight healthy young men received eight step-increment adaptational sessions in alternate directions of rotation over a total period of twenty-four weeks. The first four sessions corresponded to the adaptation schedule described previously, and each session was separated by an interval of one week. Then followed an interval of six weeks in which they received no further rotation, after which came two further sessions again separated by a week. Then there was a twelve-week interval without rotation followed by the two final rotational sessions separated again by one week. Figure 26 gives an indication of the average amount of motion sickness suffered on each session. Two measures were used: the

Well-Being Scale ranging from zero (I feel fine) to ten (I feel awful, just like I'm about to be sick); and a Symptom Score based on the number and the degree of signs and symptoms exhibited by the subjects. In both cases, the higher the score, the worse the subjects felt. From Figure 26 it can be seen that both indices of motion sickness diminished rapidly over the first four sessions. But the encouraging fact is that there appeared to be very little loss of protection after either the six- or the twelve-week interval without further rotation. In other words, the protection conferred by the first four sessions (and 'topped up' by the subsequent sessions) remained intact for a period exceeding five months. This suggests that the adaptation schedule outlined earlier may well prove to be a viable means of preventing motion sickness in rotating spacecraft, since the protection it bestows appears to be retained over relatively long periods of time.

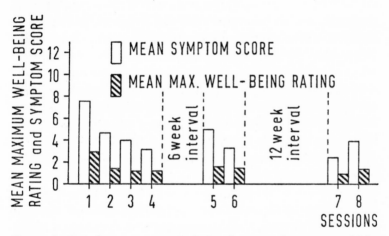

Figure 26   Data from a recent study designed to assess the extent to which protection against motion sickness is retained over time. For both the Symptom Score and the Well-Being ratings, a high value indicates the presence of severe sickness.

Unfortunately, a similar method of prevention is not really practicable against the more mundane forms of travel sickness experienced in cars and ships. It can only be used to its best advantage when there are relatively few people to protect – like astronauts – and the time and facilities necessary to put them through these elaborate and costly procedures. At the present, therefore, only space sickness and perhaps air sickness (in selected groups like military aircrew) can be effectively prevented by this method. However, ordinary sufferers from motion sickness should take heart from the fact that every trip they take in a vehicle acts to some extent like an adaptation schedule in that it lessens their chances of future sickness in the same vehicle. Each exposure to the sick-making stimulus consolidates the appropriate traces within the spatial memory store so that the next time the same motion is met these traces will be retrieved.

Finally, let us turn to the third kind of adaptation mentioned at the beginning of the chapter: *skill adaptation*. This is the most important of all the adjustment mechanisms because it comes into play irrespective of the vehicle, or the environment through which it travels. It is this process which enables the experienced pilot or driver to organize the vast amount of information reaching his senses in such a way that it can be effectively handled by his single-channel, limited-capacity, mental computer. Only through the successful acquisition of skill adaptation can the man meet the demands of the modern vehicle. And the fact that it is normally achieved testifies to the enormous plasticity of the human brain.

It was pointed out in Chapter 5 that skill depends primarily upon the reorganization of the incoming information. A mass of unrelated 'bits' of information is packaged into a few meaningful 'chunks' so that it can be readily processed by the limited-capacity computer. The key to this packaging process is the appreciation of redundancy, or knowing which of the myriad signals reaching our senses can be safely disregarded as it tells us nothing new or important about the task. Once this has been achieved, we begin to have time to spare. Time to anticipate what lies ahead, and time to adjust our actions so that they acquire that smooth, polished look which is the distinguishing feature of truly skilled performance.

All the overt characteristics of skilled performance – good timing, economy of effort, smoothness of action, the absence of haste, automatization – hinge upon an effective restructuring of the information reaching the senses. The proper execution of a skill depends above all on making the correct use of external cues and signs. At one time it was thought that skills were of the same basic nature as habits, only more complicated. But a skill, even a very simple one, is quite different from habit. Unlike habits, which once initiated tend to proceed without external control (like undressing, where one action serves as the stimulus for the next in a relatively fixed sequence), skills depend for their successful execution upon a continuous appreciation of one's own actions and the actions of the vehicle: that is, upon internal and external feedback. As soon as this feedback exceeds the mental computer's capacity to process it effectively, either because there is too much of it, or because the 'information package' begins to disintegrate as it does with increasing fatigue or stress, the quality of the skill gradually declines until it breaks up into a series of disjointed responses to apparently unconnected signals. When this happens, the skilled man behaves like a novice: he has consciously to attend to what he is doing, and to work very much harder than when he was at peak efficiency in order to maintain a semblance of adequate performance.

The acquisition of skill allows us to adjust to the unnatural demands of vehicle control, and in particular to the greatly increased quantity and rate of flow of information, as compared to that encountered in self-propelled locomotion. But skill is extremely fragile. Unfortunately, few people realize just how delicate it is. Many car drivers, for instance, assume that driving skill is something which, once acquired, never disappears. But this is not true at all. Complex skills like those involved in handling a car need constant practice to maintain their integrity. Their keen 'edge' can be blunted by even a few days of inactivity. In practical terms, this means that the man who only drives at week-ends is less skilled than the man who uses his car every day. It is not so much that the 'week-end driver' forgets how to change gear or to steer, or that he forgets the rules of the road. The degradation of his skill is far more subtle than that, and hence more dangerous. What suffers is his ability to process the incoming information effectively. To use the packaging analogy, this means that, during the week without driving, his information 'packages' become a little frayed at the edges. He uses up more of his spare mental capacity than he would if he were in practice, and in consequence he is less likely to act effectively when the demands of the task are suddenly increased as in an emergency. The fragility of skill has long been appreciated by aviators. To retain his flying licence, the pilot must show evidence that he is in current flying practice. Perhaps a similar demand could be made upon drivers.

Throughout this book, I have emphasized two basic limitations that constitute 'evolution barriers' when we attempt to transport ourselves in a vehicle. First, there is the fact that our position and motion senses are so constructed that they only function accurately and in harmony when we move in the way that Nature intended – on our own two feet. Second, the human brain ceases to function effectively when the information reaching it from the outside world either exceeds or falls below certain built-in limits, and vehicles frequently carry us into situations where the incoming informational load falls outside this optimum range.

In this final chapter I have discussed two forms of adaptation, perceptual adaptation and skill adaptation, which, if properly understood and exploited, can overcome many of the psychological problems created by stepping outside these locomotory evolution barriers. Of course, we could solve all of these problems by reverting back to our natural self-propelled mode of locomotion, but this idyllic state of affairs will probably not return until we have entirely exhausted the earth's dwindling reserves of fuel and much else besides. In the meantime technology will continue feeding on itself, and much as we may wish it, we cannot – for the time being, at least – halt its ever-accelerating rate of progress. Under these circumstances the best that the psychologist can do is to study man's remarkable powers of adaptation, and to use this knowledge to minimize the 'capability gap' between ourselves and whatever technologists create to transport us in the future.

Afterword

But when a great invention like that of railways brings us not only immense advantage but also some concurrent mischief, there are plenty of people who will confine their attention to the latter and are keener at carping than at appreciating merit.

In case I should have appeared too much like one of these carping critics, placing too much emphasis on the 'concurrent mischief' rather than the 'immense advantage' of vehicular motion, let me try to redress the balance by giving the final word to Professor E.

Foxwell, from whose essay, 'Express Trains – An Apology' (1884), the above quotation was taken.[5] Professor Foxwell was enthusiastically and unashamedly in favour of express trains in particular and of rapid vehicular motion in general. 'Everybody is in love with motion,' he wrote, 'all living souls are under its spell.' His essay sets forth a number of psychological benefits that stem directly from high-speed travel, and some of these are listed below. I do not apologize for using quotations so freely, since only Professor Foxwell's own words can properly convey the passionate flavour of his argument.

The first benefit is that 'new energy is induced by quick loco-motion'. 'High speed,' he argues, 'enables men to do more work and do it better, to come across a wider choice of facts and form surer decisions for dealing with them.' He sums up his point with the following analogy: 'Express trains are to a country what long thighs are to an individual, but long thighs and intelligence are said to be related; and thus the profusion of English expresses is a happy sign, for it is the growth of intelligence that gives the world half its buoyancy.'

The second bonus of high-speed travel is that 'much pain is mitigated', particularly in the young. 'Nowadays the softest girl has her cruellest parting soothed by the winged words that reach her next day through the post . . .' 'The penny post has spread sunshine across the world, but the penny post is only a corollary of express trains, and, comforting as a certainty of letters is, the arrival of warm flesh and blood throws them quite into the shade. Expresses consummate the post.'

The third benefit anticipates McCluhan's notion of the 'global village': express trains, Foxwell asserts, widen our horizons. 'For express trains are through-currents of life, which arouse localism from its habits of aloofness, and stir up a disposition for contact, for intelligent "society".' These 'through-currents of life' bring social change:

Vulgarity, snobbishness, and parochial servility are dissolving into a thoughtful regard for the circumstances that inclose human affairs. We can see signs of this change all around us – in our books, our servants, our furniture, and nowhere more than in the eyes of children and the dress they wear. Along with this new simplicity may also be seen a new hope, which is coming on quietly like a sturdy child. Hope arrives in the train of new conditions and a fresh breeze began to blow over the world when the railway was opened from Stockton to Darlington; for that extra-parochial enterprise ushered in extra-parochial reward.

Finally, there are the therapeutic benefits of high-speed travel. The motion of express trains is like that of the sea, 'unconsciously touching the senses all day long. Like the touch of a lover, it breeds a quiet superb certainty of power; things *can* be done, and a new effort arises to set about considering *how*.' New hope, fresh energy, a desire for endeavour, all of these and more come to us in the express train. Professor Foxwell sums it all up as follows:

So that standing on the platform of our great inland stations we watch a salutary stir in the ebb and flow of restless men; we see men under the treatment of Motion and know there is a chance for them. Over every great railway station – as over a hospital, or indeed at any other scene of engineering operations – the flag of Hope waves bright in the air, while under the roof by day and night our befriending expresses move in and out on their errands of health. In the absence of angels to come and stir our modern pool of Bethesda, we turn a warm welcome to these nineteenth-century substitutes, who condescend not once now and then to break the gloom, but are always with us at work every hour spreading good spirits and encouragement across the land. What the sea does once a year to freshen individual lives the railways are doing every day for the national life, in a manner less picturesque but not less effective.

Clearly there is a great deal more to the complex relationship between men and vehicles than could ever be expressed in the mechanistic jargon of the contemporary psychologist. The man component of the man-machine system, for all the common features he shares with the machine, has a disconcerting tendency to reassert his humanity in the most unpredictable ways. Consider, for example, this recent newspaper report:

Police disarmed a man who peppered thousands of pounds worth of cars with bullets in a London garage yesterday . . . Police said several cars were badly damaged. 'The man had some sort of grievance – we are trying to ascertain what it was.'[6]

References

Introduction: Travel and the Evolution Barriers

1 A. Toffler, *Future Shock* (New York, Random House, 1970).

2 J. M. Smith, *The Theory of Evolution* (Harmondsworth, Penguin Books, 1958).

Chapter 1 Motion Sickness

1 J. T. Reason and A. Graybiel, *Aerospace Medicine*, 41 (1970), 166.

2 Hippocrates, *Aphorisms*, IV, sec. xiv.

3 H. J. Rubin, *Journal of Aviation Medicine*, 13 (1942), 272.

4 The experimental evidence for this is discussed by K. E. Money in *Physiological Reviews*, 50 (1970), 1. Those who would like more information about research on motion sickness are advised to begin with this excellent and comprehensive review article.

5 Readers who wish to know more about the structure and function of the vestibular system should begin by consulting the following texts: I. P. Howard and W. B. Templeton, *Human Spatial Orientation* (New York, Wiley, 1966); and T. D. M. Roberts, *Neurophysiology of Postural Mechanisms* (New York, Plenum, 1967). (Non-technical readers should not be put off by this title: the chapters dealing with the vestibular system are clearly and simply written.)

6 The 'overstimulation of the otolith' theory was stated most forcefully by G. De Wit in *Acta Oto-Laryngologica*, Supplement 108 (1956). A more recent assertion of this point of view was made by L. B. W. Jongkees in the *Third Symposium on the Role of the Vestibular Organs in Space Exploration* (Washington DC, National Aeronautics and Space Administration (1967), p. 311.

7 F. H. Quix, *Monographies Oto-Rhino-Laryngol. Intern.*, 8 (1922), 828.

8 B. Clark and J. D. Stewart, *Aerospace Medicine*, 33 (1962), 1426.

9 See D. Tyler and P. Bard, *Physiological Reviews*, 29 (1949), 311.

10 For a straightforward explanation of the rather complex mechanics of the Coriolis vestibular reaction, see F. E. Guedry and E. K. Montague, *Aerospace Medicine*, 32 (1961), 487. An alternative way of analysing this canal stimulus is given by Howard and Templeton, op. cit.

11 The likely origins of visually-induced motion sickness were first considered by C. A. Claremont in *Psyche*, 11 (1931), 86. Later experimental work on this problem, particularly as it occurs in vehicle simulators, is cited in note 12.

12 J. W. Miller and J. E. Goodson, *Aerospace Medicine*, 31 (1960), 204. See also G. V. Barrett and C. L. Thornton, *Journal of Applied Psychology*, 52 (1968), 304. In a recent study it was found that susceptibility to motion sickness in a car simulator was positively and significantly related to the degree of driver-experience, and, to a lesser extent, to the degree of passenger experience. This is in line with observations made in aircraft simulators – J. T. Reason and E. Diaz, *Flying Personnel Committee Report No. 1310* (London: Ministry of Defence (Air)).

13 G. M. Stratton, *Psychological Review*, 4 (1897), 341, was the first to experiment with rearranged vision. In recent years, this has become a major area of research in experimental psychology – see Howard and Templeton, op. cit., or W. Epstein, *Varieties of Perceptual Learning* (New York, McGraw Hill, 1967).

14 H. A. Witkin, *Psychological Monographs*, 63 (1949), 1.

15 R. W. Wood, *Psychological Review*, 2 (1895), 277.

16 These counter-arguments are stated most concisely by G. R. Wendt in the *Journal of Aviation Medicine*, 19 (1948), 24.

17 A fuller discussion of the notion of 'receptivity' is given in J. T. Reason, *New Society*, 15, no. 395 (1970).

18 The most recent evidence suggests that of these two factors, adaptability and receptivity, the former exerts a far greater influence on susceptibility than the latter. However, among *slow adapters* only, receptivity is positively and significantly related to motion sickness susceptibility. See J. T. Reason and A. Graybiel, *AGARD Conference Preprint No. 109* (NATO, Neuilly-sur Seine, 1972).

19 Those interested in a more detailed evaluation of motion sickness drugs should consult J. J. Brand and W. L. M. Perry, *Pharmacological Review*, 18 (1966), 895. Also see C. D. Wood, in *Fourth Symposium on the Role of the Vestibular Organs in Space Exploration* (Pensacola, Fla. Naval Aerospace Medical Institute, 1968).

Chapter 2   Space Sickness

1 Charles A. Berry, in a paper given to the Fifth Symposium of the Role of the Vestibular Organs in Space Exploration at the Naval Aerospace Medical Institute (Pensacola, Fla., August 1970).

2 R. Schweickart, personal communication.

3 G. L. Komendantov and V. I. Kopanev, in *Problems of Space Biology* (ed. N. M. Sisakyan and V. I. Yazdovskiy), vol. II (Moscow, 1962).

4 Charles A. Berry, *Aerospace Medicine*, 40 (1969), 793.

5 R. R. Gilruth, *Spaceflight*, 11 (1969), 260.

6 For a clear exposition of how these Coriolis forces will act upon an astronaut in a rotating spacecraft, see Howard and Templeton, op. cit.

Chapter 3   Deceptions in the Air: Pilot Disorientation

1 J. B. Nuttall and W. G. Sanford, in *Medical Aspects of Flight Safety* (ed. E. Evrard, P. Bergeret and P. van Wulfften Pathe), (New York, Pergamon, 1959).

2 A. J. Benson, in *Textbook of Aviation Medicine* (ed. A. Gillies), (Oxford, Pergamon, 1965).

3 K. K. Gillingham, *A Primer of Vestibular Function, Spatial Orientation and Motion Sickness* (Review 4–66, Brooks Air Force Base, Texas, USAF School of Aerospace Medicine, 1966).

4 W. C. Hixson, J. I. Niven and E. Spezia, *Naval Aerospace Medical Research Laboratory Reports No's 1108 and 1109* (Pensacola, Fla., Naval Aerospace Medical Research Laboratory, 1970).

5 These actual episodes of disorientation were reported in B. Clark and A. Graybiel, *Vertigo as a cause of pilot error in jet aircraft* (Report No. 44, US Naval School of Aviation Medicine, Pensacola, Fla., 1956).

6 B. Clark and M. A. Nicholson, *Aviator's vertigo: a cause of pilot error in Naval Aviation students* (Research Report NM 001 059.01.37, US Naval School of Aviation Medicine, Pensacola, Fla., 1953).

7 B. Clark and A. Graybiel, *Disorientation: A cause of pilot error* (Research Report No. NM 001 110 100.39, Pensacola, Fla. US Naval School of Aviation Medicine, 1955).

8 Ibid.

9 Ibid.

10 B. Clark, M. A. Nicholson and A. Graybiel, *'Fascination'*: *a cause of pilot error* (Research Report No. NM 001 059.01.35, US Naval School of Aviation Medicine, Pensacola, Fla., 1953).

Chapter 4 Deceptions on the Ground: The 'Mental Speedometer'

1 For a fuller account of motion perspective, and of its importance for the vehicle operator, see J. J. Gibson, *The Perception of the Visual World* (Boston, Houghton Mifflin, 1950), Chapter 7.

2 See D. H. Hubel, *Scientific American*, 168 (November 1963); also H. B. Barlow and R. M. Hill, *Nature*, 200 (1963), 1,345.

3 G. G. Denton, *Road Research Laboratory Report No.* LN/861 (Crowthorne, Road Research Laboratory, 1966).

4 G. G. Denton, *Road Research Laboratory Report No.* LR/97 (Crowthorne, Road Research Laboratory, 1967).

5 G. G. Denton, *Ergonomics*, 9 (1966), 203.

6 F. Schmidt and J. Tiffin, *Journal of Applied Psychology*, 53 (1969), 5.

7 For a more comprehensive account of the history and the factors affecting the perception of this illusion of apparent motion, see H. C. Holland, *The Spiral After-Effect* (Oxford, Pergamon Press, 1965).

8 J. J. Gibson, *Psychological Review*, 44 (1937), 222.

9 H. B. Barlow and R. M. Hill, op. cit.

10 A. G. Goldstein, *Journal of Experimental Psychology*, 54 (1957), 457.

Chapter 5 The Limited Channel

1 R. L. Moore, *Journal of the Institution of Highway Engineers* (August 1969).

2 K. Oatley, *Brain Mechanisms and Mind* (London, Thames & Hudson, 1972), p. 10.

3 See E. G. Boring, *History of Experimental Psychology* (New York, Appleton-Century-Crofts, 1950).

4 For a review of the evidence for the 'single channel' hypothesis, see A. T. Welford, *Fundamentals of Skill* (London, Methuen, 1968); also D. E. Broadbent, *Decision and Stress* (London, Academic Press, 1971).

5 This conception of the car driver owes much to the ideas of Dr E. C.

Poulton. See *Psychology at Work* (ed. P. Warr), (Harmondsworth, Penguin Books, 1971); and *International Road Safety and Traffic Review*, 14 (1966), 2.

6 For a very readable account of the importance of knowledge of results in the acquisition of a skill, see J. Annett, *Feedback and Human Behaviour* (Harmondsworth, Penguin Books, 1969). See also D. H. Holding, in *Skills* (ed. D. Legge), (Harmondsworth, Penguin Books, 1970).

7 R. W. Cummings, *Australian Road Research*, 1 (1964), 4 – cited by R. L. Moore, op. cit.

8 R. W. Lawson, *Nature*, 161 (1948), 4,083.

9 G. C. Drew, *Quarterly Journal of Experimental Psychology*, 3 (1951), 73.

10 See R. L. Moore, op. cit.

11 See T. Rockwell, in *Human Factors in Highway Traffic Safety Research* (ed. T. W. Forbes), (London, J. Wiley, 1972).

12 See T. Rockwell, op. cit.

13 A. F. Sanders, in *The Selective Process in the Functional Visual Field* (Soesterberg, Netherlands, Institute of Perception, 1963).

14 I. D. Brown and E. C. Poulton, *Ergonomics*, 4 (1961), 35.

15 See R. L. Moore, op. cit.

16 A. Crawford, *Ergonomics*, 6 (1963), 153.

17 J. Cohen, E. J. Dearnaley and C. E. M. Hansel, *British Medical Journal* vol. 1 (1958), 1,438.

18 J. Cohen, *Behaviour in Uncertainty* (London, Allen & Unwin, 1964), p. 71.

19 A. Crawford, *Ergonomics*, 5 (1962), 513.

20 See R. L. Moore, op. cit.

21 The hierarchical analysis of skilled behaviour in the language of computer programming owes much to the ideas expressed by G. A. Miller, E. Galanter and K. Pribram in their very influential book, *Plans and the Structure of Behaviour* (New York, Rinehart & Winston, 1960). For subsequent developments, see P. M. Fitts and M. I. Posner, *Human Performance* (Belmont, Calif., Brooks Cole, 1967); J. Annett, *Feedback and Human Behaviour*, op. cit.; J. Annett, in *British Medical Bulletin* (Cognitive Psychology) 27 (1971), 266; D. M. Robb, *The Dynamics of Motor Skill Acquisition* (New York, Prentice Hall, 1972); J. P. Guilford, *Journal of General Psychology*, 86 (1972), 279; T. Shallice, *Psychological Review*, 79 (1972), 383.

22 V. S. Ellingstadt, R. E. Hagen and K. A. Kimball, *An Investigation of the Acquisition of Driving Skill* (Technical Report No. 11, Vermillion, S. Dakota, Department of Psychology, University of South Dakota, 1970).

Chapter 6 Overload and Underload

1 J. M. Rolfe, *Psychology and Aviation Medicine* (Farnborough, RAF Institute of Aviation Medicine, 1962).

2 Ibid.

3 J. M. Munden, *Road Research Laboratory Report No. 24* (Crowthorne, Road Research Laboratory, 1966).

4 See J. M. Munden, *Road Research Laboratory Report No. LR 88* (1967).

5 J. Walker, *Road Research Laboratory Note No. 3929* (1961).

6 See R. L. Moore, op. cit.

7 See E. C. Poulton, *International Road Safety and Traffic Review*, 14 (1966), 2.

8 R. L. Moore, op. cit.

9 J. G. Miller, in *Psychophysiological Aspects of Space Flight* (ed. B. E. Flaherty), (Columbia University Press, 1961).

10 See R. L. Moore, op. cit.

11 For a comprehensive survey of the research literature on vigilance, see D. R. Davies and G. S. Tune, *Human Vigilance Performance* (London, Staples Press, 1970).

12 D. R. Davis, *Ergonomics*, 2: 24 (1958). See also *Ergonomics*, 9 (1966), 211.

13 Cited in *Drive*, no. 15 (Autumn 1970), p. 72.

14 D. W. J. Corcoran, quoted by Davies and Tune, op. cit., p. 213.

15 See D. R. Davies, *Science Journal*, 6 (August 1970), 26.

16 For more detailed information regarding the effects of sensory deprivation, the reader should consult P. Solomon *et al.* (eds), *Sensory Deprivation* (Cambridge, Mass., Harvard University Press, 1961), J. A. Vernon, *Inside the Black Room* (Harmondsworth, Penguin Books, 1966); and J. P. Zubek (ed.), *Sensory Deprivation: Fifteen Years of Research* (New York, Appleton-Century-Crofts, 1969).

17 See J. Cohen and B. Preston, *Causes and Prevention of Road Accidents* (London, Faber, 1968), p. 55.

18 B. Clark and A. Graybiel, *The Break-Off Phenomenon* (Project NM 001 110 100, Pensacola, Fla., US Naval School of Aviation Medicine, 1956).

19 W. Bridgeman and J. Hazard, *The Lonely Sky* (New York, Holt, 1955).

20 A. M. Hastin Bennett, 'Sensory Deprivation in Aviation', in P. Solomon *et al.* (eds), op. cit.

21 J. P. Zubek (ed), op. cit.

22 J. Slocum, *Sailing Alone Around The World* (London, Pan Books, 1950; first published 1900), pp. 42–3.

Chapter 7   Fatigue and Stress

1 D. R. Davis, *Pilot Error* (London, HMSO, 1948).

2 A. T. Welford, R. A. Brown and J. E. Gabb, *British Journal of Psychology*, 40 (1950), 195.

3 Sir Frederic C. Bartlett, *Proceedings of the Royal Society*, Series B, 131 (1943), 247. Also in D. Legge (ed.), *Skill* (Harmondsworth, Penguin Books, 1970).

4 R. S. Schwab, in *Symposium on Fatigue* (ed. W. T. Floyd and A. T. Welford), (London, H. K. Lewis, 1953), p. 143.

5 K. F. Jackson, *Pilot Performance* (Flying Personnel Research Committee Report No. 907, London, Air Ministry, 1956).

6 D. Beaty, *The Human Factor* (London, Secker & Warburg, 1969).

7 D. M. Denison and M. A. Ledwith, *Aerospace Medicine*, 37 (1966), 1010.

8 H. Strughold, *Your Body Clock* (London, Angus & Robertson, 1971).

9 K. E. Klein, H. Brüner, H. Holtmann, H. Rehme, J. Stolze, W. D. Steinhoff and H. M. Wegmann, *Aerospace Medicine*, 41 (1970), 125.

10 S. Aschoff, *Science*, 148 (1965), 1,427. See also *Aerospace Medicine*, 40 (1969), 844.

11 R. A. McFarland, *Human Factors in Air Transportation* (New York, McGraw Hill, 1953).

12 See R. A. McFarland, op. cit.

13 A. Crawford, *Ergonomics*, 4 (1961), 143.

14 N. W. Heimstra, *Ergonomics*, 13 (1970), 209.

15 I. D. Brown and E. C. Poulton, *Ergonomics*, 4 (1961), 35.

16 I. D. Brown, *Ergonomics*, 8 (1965), 467.

17 A. G. Bills, *American Journal of Psychology*, 43 (1931), 230.

18 See H. J. Eysenck, *Fact and Fiction in Psychology* (Harmondsworth, Penguin Books, 1965).

Chapter 8   Style, Personality and Accidents

1 The original report by Major Greenwood and Miss Hilda Woods is extremely difficult to obtain. However, it has been reprinted almost in its entirety in W. Haddon, E. A. Suchmann and D. Klein, *Accident Research* (New York, Harper, 1964), p. 389.

2 Cited in Haddon *et al.*, op. cit., p. 397.

3 Cited in Haddon *et al.*, op. cit., p. 410.

4 See M. S. Viteles, *Industrial Psychology* (New York, Norton, 1932). This work is also discussed by J. Tiffin and E. J. McCormick, *Industrial Psychology* (London, Allen & Unwin, 1961).

5 A. G. Arbous and J. E. Kerrich, *Industrial Medicine and Surgery*, 22 (1953), 141. Also reprinted in Haddon *et al.*, op. cit., p. 418.

6 For a recent defence of the notion of accident proneness, see the very readable book by Lynette Shaw and Herbert Sichel, *Accident Proneness* (Oxford, Pergamon, 1971).

7 D. R. Davis, *Journal of Neurology, Neurosurgery and Psychiatry*, 9 (1946), 119. See also *Pilot error – some laboratory experiments* (London, HMSO, 1948).

8 H. J. Eysenck, *The Dynamics of Anxiety and Hysteria* (London, Routledge & Kegan Paul, 1957). A review of the studies on inert-overactive responders, together with diagrams of the apparatus, can be found on pp. 135–45 of this book.

9 P. H. Venables, *British Journal of Psychology*, 46 (1955), 101.

10 P. H. Venables, *Journal of Applied Psychology*, 40 (1956), 21.

11 S. W. Quenault, *Road Research Laboratory Reports Nos* LR *70*, LR *146*, *and* LR *212* (1967–8). This work is also summarized in an article by Anthony Curtis in *Motor*, no. 3,520, 3 December 1969.

Chapter 9   Reconciling Man and Vehicle

1 I. D. Brown, *New Scientist*, vol. 48, no. 731 (December 1970).

2 A. J. Benson, in *Textbook of Aviation Physiology* (ed. A. Gillies), (Oxford, Pergamon, 1965).

3 J. T. Reason and A. Graybiel, *Aerospace Medicine*, 41 (1970), 166.

4 J. T. Reason and A. Graybiel, *AGARD Conference Preprint No. 109*, op. cit.

5 E. Foxwell, *English Express Trains: Two Papers* (London, Stanford, 1884).

6 *Guardian*, 28 October 1972.

Index